Contemporary Issues in Leisure Sciences

Celebrating the 40th anniversary of the journal of *Leisure Sciences*, this book focuses on where leisure sciences (as a field) started and what the future might hold for both. The foremost scholars in our field dialogue, debate, critique, and reflect on leisure studies' progress and future. Authors consider and write about the key issues and controversies of the field, developments we should be celebrating, and directions of study we should be pursing. Scholars also consider research gaps that exist in leisure research, issues we should be thinking about, and where we are now in relation to where previous projections expected. Topics in this book include race, ethnicity, immigration, and leisure; sex research; critical leisure studies; leisure and social isolation; radical leisure; and post-qualitative ontology.

The chapters in this book were originally published as a special issue of *Leisure Sciences*.

Diana C. Parry is a feminist scholar who engages in research that advocates that the personal is political while focusing on women's health and leisure. Parry intentionally uses her research and service to advance a social justice agenda by advocating for a holistic understanding and conceptualization of health for women.

Corey W. Johnson is a feminist, qualitative researcher, and scholar who focuses on power relations between dominant and non-dominant populations. Johnson uses his research alongside teaching, and service, engaging in advocacy, activism, civic-engagement, service-learning, and community partnerships, to create change and unique learning opportunities for individuals and institutions.

Contemporary Issues in Leisure Sciences

Edited by
Diana C. Parry and Corey W. Johnson

LONDON AND NEW YORK

First published 2018
by Routledge
2 Park Square, Milton Park, Abingdon, Oxon, OX14 4RN, UK

and by Routledge
711 Third Avenue, New York, NY 10017, USA

Routledge is an imprint of the Taylor & Francis Group, an informa business

© 2018 Taylor and Francis

All rights reserved. No part of this book may be reprinted or reproduced or utilised in any form or by any electronic, mechanical, or other means, now known or hereafter invented, including photocopying and recording, or in any information storage or retrieval system, without permission in writing from the publishers.

Trademark notice: Product or corporate names may be trademarks or registered trademarks, and are used only for identification and explanation without intent to infringe.

British Library Cataloguing in Publication Data
A catalogue record for this book is available from the British Library

ISBN 13: 978-0-8153-4748-4

Typeset in Minion Pro
by diacriTech, Chennai

Publisher's Note
The publisher accepts responsibility for any inconsistencies that may have arisen during the conversion of this book from journal articles to book chapters, namely the possible inclusion of journal terminology.

Disclaimer
Every effort has been made to contact copyright holders for their permission to reprint material in this book. The publishers would be grateful to hear from any copyright holder who is not here acknowledged and will undertake to rectify any errors or omissions in future editions of this book.

Contents

Citation Information		vii
Notes on Contributors		ix
Editors' Note		xi

Introduction to the Special Issue Looking Back, Looking Forward: 40 Years of Leisure Sciences
Corey W. Johnson, Diana C. Parry, and Faith-Anne Wagler — 1

1 "Risky" Leisure Research on Sex and Violence: Innovation, Impact, and Impediments
Liza Berdychevsky — 9

2 Are We Ready for "Radical Leisure"?
B. Dana Kivel — 19

3 All the Lonely People: Social Isolation and the Promise and Pitfalls of Leisure
Troy D. Glover — 25

4 The Serious Leisure Perspective and the Experience of Leisure
A. J. Veal — 36

5 Leisure Sciences and the Humanities
Paul Heintzman — 55

6 Research on Race, Ethnicity, Immigration, and Leisure: Have We Missed the Boat?
Monika Stodolska — 62

7 The Case of the 12-Year-Old Boy: Or, The Silence of and Relevance to Leisure Research
Rasul A. Mowatt — 73

CONTENTS

8 Evocative Words and Ethical Crafting: Poetic Representation in
Leisure Research 90
Sandra Sjollema and Felice Yuen

9 Questions for Postqualitative Inquiry: Conversations to Come 107
Brian E. Kumm and Lisbeth A. Berbary

10 The Time Machine: Leisure Science (Fiction) and Futurology 121
Brett D. Lashua

Index 131

Citation Information

The chapters in this book were originally published in *Leisure Sciences*, volume 40, issues 1–2 (2018). When citing this material, please use the original page numbering for each article, as follows:

Introduction
Introduction to the Special Issue Looking Back, Looking Forward: 40 Years of Leisure Sciences
Corey W. Johnson, Diana C. Parry, and Faith-Anne Wagler
Leisure Sciences, volume 40, issues 1–2 (2018) pp. 1–8

Chapter 1
"Risky" Leisure Research on Sex and Violence: Innovation, Impact, and Impediments
Liza Berdychevsky
Leisure Sciences, volume 40, issues 1–2 (2018) pp. 9–18

Chapter 2
Are We Ready for "Radical Leisure"?
B. Dana Kivel
Leisure Sciences, volume 40, issues 1–2 (2018) pp. 19–24

Chapter 3
All the Lonely People: Social Isolation and the Promise and Pitfalls of Leisure
Troy D. Glover
Leisure Sciences, volume 40, issues 1–2 (2018) pp. 25–35

Chapter 4
The Serious Leisure Perspective and the Experience of Leisure
A. J. Veal
Leisure Sciences, volume 39, issue 3 (2017) pp. 205–223

Chapter 5
Leisure Sciences *and the Humanities*
Paul Heintzman
Leisure Sciences, volume 40, issues 1–2 (2018) pp. 36–42

CITATION INFORMATION

Chapter 6
Research on Race, Ethnicity, Immigration, and Leisure: Have We Missed the Boat?
Monika Stodolska
Leisure Sciences, volume 40, issues 1–2 (2018) pp. 43–53

Chapter 7
The Case of the 12-Year-Old Boy: Or, The Silence of and Relevance to Leisure Research
Rasul A. Mowatt
Leisure Sciences, volume 40, issues 1–2 (2018) pp. 54–70

Chapter 8
Evocative Words and Ethical Crafting: Poetic Representation in Leisure Research
Sandra Sjollema and Felice Yuen
Leisure Sciences, volume 39, issue 2 (2017) pp. 109–125

Chapter 9
Questions for Postqualitative Inquiry: Conversations to Come
Brian E. Kumm and Lisbeth A. Berbary
Leisure Sciences, volume 40, issues 1–2 (2018) pp. 71–84

Chapter 10
The Time Machine: *Leisure Science (Fiction) and Futurology*
Brett D. Lashua
Leisure Sciences, volume 40, issues 1–2 (2018) pp. 85–94

For any permission-related enquiries please visit:
http://www.tandfonline.com/page/help/permissions

Notes on Contributors

Lisbeth A. Berbary is Assistant Professor at the University of Waterloo, Canada.

Liza Berdychevsky is Assistant Professor at the University of Illinois at Urbana-Champaign, USA.

Troy D. Glover is Professor and Department Chair at the University of Waterloo, Canada.

Paul Heintzman is Associate Professor at the University of Ottawa, Canada.

Corey W. Johnson is a Professor at the University of Waterloo.

B. Dana Kivel is Professor at the California State University, USA.

Brian E. Kumm is an Asistant Professor at the University of Wisconsin – La Crosse, USA.

Brett D. Lashua is a Reader in Leisure and Culture at Leeds Beckett University, Carnegie Faculty, UK.

Rasul A. Mowatt is Associate Professor and Chair at Indiana University, USA.

Diana C. Parry is a Professor at the University of Waterloo.

Sandra Sjollema is a poet, workshop facilitator, researcher, and the coordinator of L'Anneau Poétique, a community-based creative writing group in Côte-des-Neiges.

Monika Stodolska is a Professor at the University of Illinois at Urbana-Champaign, USA.

A. J. Veal is Adjunct Professor at the Business School, University of Technology Sydney, Australia.

Faith-Anne Wagler is a doctoral candidate, University of Waterloo, Canada.

Felice Yuen is Associate Professor at Concordia University, Canada.

Editors' Note

When we took over as Co-Editors of *Leisure Sciences* in January 2016, we quickly realized that the journal would celebrate the big 4-0 the very next year. We wondered if we could move quickly enough to put together a collection of manuscripts to chart new directions for the future of our field. We decided to try. In that spirit, we drafted a call for papers alerting authors to our aspirations and quick turnaround times. We received an overwhelming number of submissions and after working diligently with the authors, the best of the best were assembled and represent the 40th anniversary issue of *Leisure Sciences* (2018) volume 40; double issue 1/2. As we assessed the contributions and looked toward this book, we identified a few other manuscripts that had been published previously that would make meaningful contributions to a book on *Contemporary Issues in Leisure Sciences* and decided to include them here. We are quite excited and proud of this contribution to the literature and the body of knowledge. We hope that everyone from seasoned scholars to undergraduate students see it as a valuable map for where leisure sciences (or leisure studies) as a field has been and may be headed.

Happy Reading.

Corey W. Johnson and Diana C. Parry

Introduction to the Special Issue Looking Back, Looking Forward: 40 Years of Leisure Sciences

Corey W. Johnson, Diana C. Parry, and Faith-Anne Wagler

ABSTRACT
This special 40th anniversary issue focuses on where leisure sciences (as a field) and *Leisure Sciences* (as a journal) started and what the future might hold for both. As such, we have provided a space for dialogue, debate, critique, and reflection relating to leisure studies' progress and future. Authors were asked to consider and write about key issues and controversies of the field, developments we should be celebrating, and directions of study we should be pursing. The call for this special issue also asked scholars to consider research gaps that exist, issues we should be thinking about, and where we are now in relation to where previous projections expected. Reflection on the progress of *Leisure Sciences* over the past 40 years and its role in advancing the field of leisure research was also encouraged.

Introduction

This special 40th anniversary issue focuses on where leisure sciences (as a field) and *Leisure Sciences* (as a journal) started and what the future might hold for both. As such, we have provided a space for dialogue, debate, critique, and reflection relating to leisure studies' progress and future. Authors were asked to consider and write about key issues and controversies of the field, developments we should be celebrating, and directions of study we should be pursing. The call for this special issue also asked scholars to consider research gaps that exist, issues we *should* be thinking about, and where we are now in relation to where previous projections expected. Reflection on the progress of *Leisure Sciences* over the past 40 years and its role in advancing the field of leisure research was also encouraged.

In 1977, the first issue of *Leisure Sciences* published articles discussing privacy in the wilderness, parks and recreation service, mapping the beauty of forest landscapes, recreation management, the impact of aquatic resources on recreation behavior, and the history and future of tourism development. Forty years later, the most recent issue of *Leisure* Sciences includes articles about mothers with young children, personal character strengths and leisure, distance and the assessment of recreation access, park management, recreation and self-regulation skills in youth, and family leisure measurement. To celebrate the 40th anniversary of *Leisure Sciences*, it is important to consider ways the field has shifted or has not shifted over time while also considering our direction for the future.

Looking back

Since publication began in 1977, special issues of *Leisure Sciences* have focused on diverse topics, and these give a sense of how the content of this journal has changed over time. Special issues of *Leisure Sciences* include human dimensions in wildlife management (1985); leisure in the coastal zone (1986); behavioral modeling and recreation and tourism (1990); leisure constraints/constrained leisure (1991); relevance of leisure research (1995); recreation conflict research (1995); normative perspectives on outdoor recreation behavior (1996); disciplinary and transnational comparisons of leisure research and scholarship (1997); leisure and commodification (2001); understanding recreation and the environment within the context of culture (2002); leisure, stress, and coping (2003); leisure research, active lifestyles, and public health (2005); creative analytic practice (2007); analysis of multiple data sets in outdoor recreation research (2008); people and nature-based recreation (2010); research frameworks that further social justice (2014); family leisure (2016); popular leisure in a digital age (forthcoming, 2017); feminist physical and cultural studies (forthcoming, 2017); contemporary politics and leisure (forthcoming, 2017); posthumanist qualitative research in leisure studies (forthcoming, 2018); and this 40th anniversary contribution (2017).

In addition to special topics in *Leisure Sciences*, the *Journal of Leisure Research* published a millennial issue (2000) containing reflections on the past and future of leisure research. In this issue, several researchers articulated concerns that the field was becoming insular and isolated, risking becoming overspecialized and irrelevant (Godbey, 2000; Kelly, 2000; Shaw, 2000). Similarly, Samdahl and Kelly (1999) discussed how many citations within leisure journals were to our own journals, and not to contemporary leisure research in general. Other researchers called for the field of leisure studies to embrace its interdisciplinary roots and seek knowledge from diverse paradigms. Patterson (2000) believed that researchers needed to work more toward an understanding and use of the philosophy of science. At a similar time to this special issue, Dupuis (1999) raised a concern that qualitative researchers were too influenced by postpositivist frameworks that impacted data-collection and writing and that leisure studies needed to adopt reflexive methodologies. Seventeen years since this special issue was published, it is important to reflect on how leisure research has progressed and the places and spaces we would like leisure studies to move in the future. These considerations could lead to critical insights about ways we can adjust and advance our scholarship, research, and practice and perhaps ways we have already improved.

One method for reviewing the rich history of *Leisure Sciences* over the past 40 years is examining the calls for change that scholars have made within our publication. What follows is a selection of the research published within *Leisure Sciences* (the journal) that respond to a call to action of what the future of leisure sciences would hopefully hold.

Research for the "meaning" of leisure has long been a barometer to assess the prevailing winds of the field. Coalter (1997) compared and contrasted leisure sciences and leisure studies, and although concluding they have different "epistemological, methodological, and theoretical perspectives," he critiques both veins of study for failing to understand a "full picture" of leisure. In this article, Coalter concluded that leisure studies, with a sociological focus, and leisure sciences, with a socio-psychological focus, leave gaps in understanding of the situated nature of leisure meanings and "their relationship to wider sources of meaning and identity" (p. 265). Coalter therefore called for both fields (studies/sciences), and journals, to broaden their study of everyday experiences of leisure and consider whether there are fixed meanings of leisure as well as links between leisure meanings and personal meaning and identity. Within his article there is also a prediction that feminism will have an increasing presence within leisure sciences, and along with that would come a challenge to positivist research foundations and methods.

The filed has certainly had numerous "identity crisis," as we are situated in different cultures and often grew together out of different histories. In one example examining the roots of leisure research in Europe, Mommaas (1997) concluded that leisure research in the 1990s was at a crossroads due to its expanding topical foci. Mommaas felt that although the field was becoming fragmented, certain areas of study, for example, consumption, tourism, sports, and culture, were gaining popularity. Mommaas stated that leisure studies of the future would be challenged to "realign itself to these new areas of interest" and ended with a question of whether the field could come together under a collective understanding of leisure, or whether that was even desirable. In response to Mommaas, Stebbins (1997) discussed his belief that fragmentation is beneficial for the field of leisure studies and may actually move the field toward a more unified and distinct field of study, which would help bring greater understanding to specific experiences of leisure.

The insularity of leisure research has been a concern as well. In 1999, Valentine, Allison, and Schneider analyzed content in leading leisure science journals (Journal of Leisure Research, *Leisure Sciences*, and *Leisure Studies*) to determine the level of cross-national research being published. They concluded that despite the rise of globalization, there was little (1.5% of the articles they analyzed) cross-national research studies described. Based on this, the authors urged scholars to work toward more international perspectives. In line with this, Chick, the editor of *Leisure Sciences* in 2000, responded to Valentine et al.'s article with a call for leisure researchers to establish cross-cultural comparative research.

Questions of relevance have also troubled leisure scholars. Hemingway and Parr (2000) furthered a discussion around the relationship between leisure research and leisure practice. They elaborated on a discussion that had been prevalent in internal communications among leisure scholars about how leisure research can remain relevant and ensure it is useful and meeting the needs of recreation and leisure practitioners. Hemingway and Parr put forth the argument that research and practice are independent constructs and that a relationship between the two must be thoughtfully constructed. Similarly, Sylvester (1995) stated that to stay relevant in society, leisure studies must remain strongly linked to leisure practice and services. This tension between the connection of research and practice is complex, but in Sylvester's perspective also necessary.

What is the importance of questioning the ways research generates knowledge about leisure? As previously mentioned, Dupuis (1999) also proposed that leisure researchers remain relevant by adopting reflexive methodologies that step away from positivist roots and be more in line with theoretical orientations that leisure scholars professed to hold. Dupuis invited scholars and students to embrace their emotions and experiences within their research, and the research process, and to view these dimensions as crucial to "strong, rigorous qualitative research and good science" (p. 59).

Matters of equity have increasingly been brought to the attention of the field. In 2001, Aitchison examined the authorship of six leisure and tourism journals to explore the gendered nature of knowledge construction, legitimation, and reproduction. Aitchison reviewed the journals from 1982 through 1997 and concluded that for every four articles written by men, there was one article written by women. Furthermore, of the journals examined, men comprised 80% of the refereed authors. While the leisure journals fared better than management journals in women being represented as authors and on editorial boards, Aitchison aptly concluded that leisure journals still had a ways to go toward gender equality.

Another area proposed as a future direction for the field was forensics. Forensics, loosely meaning the law or legal system, is an area that Williams (2006), a self-professed forensic leisure scientist, called for future leisure scholars to explore. Williams noted there are a wealth of areas related to incarceration and crime that relate to leisure, and that studying the connection between the two areas will help the field branch out and avoid becoming insular. For example, Williams notes relationships of leisure to crime, correctional recreation, and leisure of those in forensic occupations (e.g., police officers). Williams also believes that bringing a leisure perspective to the study of forensics could illuminate "new ways of viewing and explaining crime and crime-free living" (p. 94). It is Williams's hope that a "symbiotic" relationship can be formed between leisure research and forensics and that "critical new knowledge be generated and applied to important social problems" (p. 94).

Taken together, this review of past areas of research and calls for future directions demonstrates where we have come from as a field and also where we still may go. By re-examining the calls to action (research) that past scholars made, we can situate our past with our present and future.

Looking forward: Our thoughts on where will leisure research go

Before identifying where we believe leisure research will go, we also want to acknowledge the strides leisure research has already made. One area that we have seen progress in is research related to identity markers. Certainly from the start of *Leisure Sciences* there is increased understanding of how the experience of leisure is intersectional with identify markers. Initially race and gender were the focus but now, there is plethora of identity markers that we know influence leisure. As this research continues to progress, we believe those will continue to be defined and redefined with the influence on leisure explored.

Having a diverse and interesting history, it is important to consider where we, the current editors of *Leisure Sciences*, see the field progressing. First, there are places we would like to see the field continue to go. Leisure research has always benefited from an influx of theoretical issues taken up in other fields and applied in a leisure context. We believe it will continue to benefit our field and journal to constantly examine what emerges elsewhere and how it might apply to our research. This constant openness is a strength of our field and an important part of who we are. We also believe that we, as a field and journal, need to continue to push theoretical, methodological, and representational issues, which will change the way leisure research is conducted and represented. By continually striving to understand and articulate our philosophical research stance, our research purpose, approach, and findings can better align and make for new and interesting discoveries about leisure and research.

Upon reflecting on our field and journal, it is also clear to us that while our field has certainly evolved in many ways, there are places we believe the field *should* go. Substantively, it would be exciting to see more research that explores new or emergent areas. For example, while there is some research that explores the darker side of leisure (e.g., D.J. William's research on forensic leisure), additional research about pornography, sexuality, and the influence of technology such as geosocial networking applications (GSNAs) would align the focus of leisure research with current social issues and reflect our changing society.

As social justice researchers ourselves, we would also like to see a furthered focus on social justice. This would be reflected by leisure scholars who want to use the process and products of research to change the world, and who position themselves as working *with*, not *for*, a community of study. In this way, the process and product of research are also inextricably linked. We also believe another important advancement in our field would be more interdisciplinary (not multidisciplinary) work that produces more international partnerships. By this, we mean that our work will truly cross the boundaries of disciplines and not simply *apply* various perspectives; our work would merge perspectives *across* fields, and locations, to form new research and understandings.

As a field, we must also acknowledge the tension of research/practice links that continue to unfold, for example, the recent conflict in the United States between the National Recreation and Parks Association (NRPA), of which leisure research has been represented, and the journals they "own" (*Journal of Leisure Research* and *Schole*). This is just one example where we can see tensions that exist between leisure research and recreation/leisure practice with implications for the larger field. With this being a recent development, we see that change is happening and the future remains uncertain as we watch the action materialize Based on this, we predict that new relationships between the two will emerge as researchers adopt a social justice lens. This will result in no formal separation between research and practice.

This issue

Focusing their analysis on past and present research and trends, scholars from within and outside of the leisure studies field discuss key issues in the field and how they see leisure studies and *Leisure Sciences* engaging with relevant conversations in the future. While some authors in this special issue situate their work where the field of leisure studies has been, other scholars reflect on where we could and *should* be heading as a field. Overall, many suggestions for the diversification and improvement of the study of leisure are offered.

To start, Liza Berdychevsky, in her article "'Risky' leisure research on sex and violence: Innovation, impact, and impediments," develops a history of the prevalence and focus of sex and violence research in the leisure field and urges researchers to continue asking new questions and pushing leisure research in "riskier" areas. Leisure acts as a unique dual space where sexually risky and violent behaviors can be motivated and/or practiced, but also where recreation programs promote the prevention and discussion of sexually risky practices. Despite this, leisure scholars can be impeded in their study of these topics by various challenges, for example, identification of the topic as taboo. Berdychevsky suggests that more leisure research focused on sex, violence, health, and wellbeing will help form connections between leisure and other areas such as public health and criminal justice, moving the field away from the risk of "siloization."

Thinking critically about what the future of leisure and leisure research could look like, B. Dana Kivel's "Are we ready for 'radical leisure'?" examines the role that leisure researchers have and should have in resisting the hegemony of work. Beyond researching leisure phenomenon, Kivel suggests leisure scholars should promote the importance of leisure and advocate for less work and more leisure. This process also necessitates an examination of personal work and leisure balance and how the leisure field, and leisure journals, can play a role in resisting a culture that centralizes work and deprioritizes leisure. Linking past views of leisure to current interpretations of leisure, Brett Lashua in "The time machine: Leisure science (fiction) and futurology" details how past research/views on the future have impacted current leisure views while also exploring what current leisure scholars are predicting the future of leisure will look like. After an analysis of past future work, Lashua examines current trends, for example, Universal Basic Income, to discuss what the future of leisure and leisure research may look like. This article also discusses how *Leisure Sciences* (the journal) can act as a tool for past reflection and future predictions and projections.

In his article "All the lonely people: Social isolation and the promise and pitfalls of leisure," Troy Glover identifies social isolation as a critical social issue not being addressed by the leisure studies field. Recognizing the benefits of social connection and pervasiveness of social isolation, Glover urges the field to consider additional research and recognition of social isolation as a problem in order to centralize and attempt to address this complex and growing social problem. Highlighting the (limited) relevant leisure research on social capital, Glover emphasizes the potential contributions leisure has to reducing social isolation, but also its potential role in contributing to superficial ties and furthering social isolation. Through his analysis of relevant literature and discussion of the growing problem, Glover encourages the leisure field, and journal, to attend to the growing need for understanding of the role leisure can, and does, play in creating and reducing social isolation.

Paul Heintzman guides us through the role that humanities research has played in the publication history of *Leisure Sciences* in his article "Leisure sciences and the humanities." He concludes through an empirical examination of the work published by the journal that although the editorial policies and instructions to authors have encouraged humanities contributions, these works have not been frequently published. Heintzman asserts that in order to meet the goals of a journal seeking "philosophical and policy treatises …" and "an interdisciplinary diversity of topics," a re-focus is required to purposefully include these elements. He encourages a push beyond the inclusion of humanities research exclusive to special issues, in order to make the next 40 years of *Leisure Sciences* even stronger than the first 40.

Next, Monika Stodolska's article "Research on race, ethnicity, immigration, and leisure: Have we missed the boat?" recalls how research in these key areas has developed and also questions whether leisure scholars' current direction and scholarship is relevant. Based on her review of leisure research on race, ethnicity, and immigration in the past 40 years, Stodolska notes major areas of research that have evolved and some potential future areas of study. Stodolska also examines current political discourse in North America to ascertain whether the current direction of research in this subfield is appropriate or needs to change directions.

Moving to past silences and a social justice imperative, Rasul Mowatt writes a manifesto entitled "The case of the 12-year-old boy: Or, the silence of & relevance to leisure research," which highlights the absence of leisure research critiquing the structural and systematic racism present in leisure. Through his exploration of the Tamir Rice case, Mowatt articulates the importance of leisure, race, social justice, and quality of life scholars recognizing and reflecting in their work that for some, leisure settings have the same potential to be life-threatening as beneficial spaces. Through an analysis based on racial threat theory and the color-blind racial ideology, Mowatt also calls for accountability in the leisure field in working towards awareness of the problem of racial inequity in leisure and focusing on improvement.

Lastly, Brian Kumm and Lisbeth Berbary's article entitled "Questions for post-qualitative inquiry: Conversations-to-come" identifies alternative ways of thinking about leisure research from a postqualitative stance. Despite the leisure field having a diversity of methodological approaches and relatively quickly embracing qualitative research, Kumm and Berbary identify that much work is based in humanist onto-epistemologies and theories which retain positivist roots. Based on this, the authors encourage leisure scholars to consider opening up space for alternative forms of inquiry and methodological approach and explores how post-qualitative inquiry provides the opportunity to do so.

Overall, this special issue contains diverse ideas from leisure scholars about our history as a field, where we are currently, and where we could and should go in the future. Taken together, we see the field progressing in interesting ways and urge leisure researchers and scholars to continue going to new places, asking new questions, and being thoughtful about the way we conduct research. We encourage leisure scholars to find your passion, and make it happen. Let the field reflect what you think is important, and by this we can drive change and push boundaries. Stay committed to the field and the journal as an outlet for your work. Remember that diversity of thought and research is welcome. Above all, look forward while still looking back.

Our gratitude

As we celebrate this important milestone, we would also like to thank all those who have served the journal over the past 40 years including all the "behind-the-scenes" professional publishing staff at Taylor-Francis, thousands of reviewers, and hundreds of associate editors. Finally, the task of editing a journal with the size, scope, and influence of *Leisure Sciences* is no easy task, and we are grateful to do so in this current moment with a huge debt owed to those who have done so before us. They include:

1977–1982/83 Volumes 1–5
Carlton S. Van Doren Rabel J. Burdge (co-founding editors)
1983/84 Volume 6
Carlton S. Van Doren Donald R. Field
1985–1988 Volumes 7–10
Robert B. Ditton Donald R. Field
1989–1990 Volumes 11–12
Robert B. Ditton
1991 Volume 13
Robert B. Ditton Thomas L. Goodale
1992–1993 Volumes 14–15
Thomas L. Goodale
1994–1998 Volumes 16–20
Daniel R. Williams
1999–2001 Volumes 21–23
Garry Chick
2002–2008/9 Volumes 24–31
Karla Henderson M. Deborah Bialeschki
2009/10 Volume 32
Karla Henderson
2010/11–2012 Volumes 33–34
Patricia A. Stokowski Walter F. Kuentzel
2013–2015 Volumes 35–37
Gerard Kyle
2016–2018 Volumes 38–40
Corey W. Johnson Diana C. Parry
Happy Anniversary!

References

Chick, G. (2000). Editorial: Opportunities for cross-cultural comparative research on leisure. *Leisure Sciences*, 22, 79–91.
Coalter, F. (1997). Leisure sciences and leisure studies: Different concept, same crisis? *Leisure Sciences*, 19, 255–268.
Dupuis, S. L. (1999). Naked truths: Towards a reflexive methodology in leisure research. *Leisure Sciences*, 21, 43–64.
Godbey, G. (2000). The future of leisure studies. *Journal of Leisure Research*, 32(1), 37–41.

Hemingway, J. (1999). Critique and emancipation: Towards a critical theory of leisure. In T. L. Burton & E. L. Jackson (Eds.), *Leisure: Prospects for the twenty-first century* (pp. 487–506). State College, PA: Venture.

Hemingway, J. L., & Parr, M. G. W. (2000). Leisure research and leisure practice: Three perspectives on constructing the research-practice relation. *Leisure Sciences, 22,* 139–162.

Kelly, J. R. (2000). The "real world" and the irrelevance of theory-based research. *Journal of Leisure Research, 32*(1), 74–78.

Mommaas, H. (1997). European leisure studies at the crossroads? A history of leisure research in Europe. *Leisure Sciences, 19,* 241–254.

Patterson, M. E. (2000). Philosophy of science and leisure research. *Journal of Leisure Research, 32*(1), 106–110.

Samdahl, D. M., & Kelly, J. J. (1999). Speaking only to ourselves? Citation analysis of *Journal of Leisure Research* and *Leisure Sciences. Journal of Leisure Research, 31*(2), 171–180.

Shaw, S. M. (2000). If our research is relevant, why is nobody listening? *Journal of Leisure Research, 32*(1), 147–151.

Stebbins, R. A. (1997). Meaning, fragmentation, and exploration: Bête noire of leisure science. *Leisure Sciences, 19,* 281–284.

Sylvester, C. (1995). Relevance and rationality in leisure studies: A plea for good reason. *Leisure Sciences, 17,* 125–131.

Williams, D. J. (2006). Forensic leisure science: A new frontier for leisure scholars. *Leisure Sciences, 28,* 91–95.

"Risky" Leisure Research on Sex and Violence: Innovation, Impact, and Impediments

Liza Berdychevsky

ABSTRACT
Controversial topics of sex and violence and their impacts on health and wellbeing have been virtually ignored in leisure scholarship. Leisure provides both risk and protective factors. Some leisure contexts offer opportunities for self-expression and experimentation and motivate involvement in sexually risky and violent behaviors. Conversely, recreation programs can serve as prevention and intervention tools for addressing risky practices. Several impediments complicate the investigation of these issues, including (1) perception of sex and violence as taboo topics, (2) methodological challenges, (3) fragmentation of knowledge on these matters caused by the silo mentality in leisure and tourism literature, and (4) placement of sex and violence in the category of "risky" research that is challenging to publish. Studying the links among leisure, sex, violence, health, and wellbeing connects leisure scholarship to public health and criminal justice. This could advance leisure studies and help overcome marginalization and isolation from other disciplines.

Introduction

Leisure sciences, both as a field and as a journal title, came a long way since their inception, which is demonstrated in the vast body of knowledge on various important leisure-related topics. However, some controversial issues have been consistently ignored by leisure researchers, reflecting some lingering problematic gaps in leisure scholarship. Such topics include the potential links among leisure, sex, and violence and, ultimately, their impacts on health and wellbeing as well as a sense of self. The notable exceptions are a few studies and two special issues on leisure and sexuality in *Leisure Studies* entitled "Sexy Spaces" (Caudwell & Browne, 2011a) and violent, criminal, and delinquent leisure behaviors in *Leisure/Loisir* entitled "Deviant Leisure" (Stebbins, Rojek, & Sullivan, 2006). These investigations demonstrated that these contentious topics should be vigorously pursued to enhance our understanding of sex and violence in leisure contexts and to advance the field of leisure.

Leisure is fundamental to understanding contemporary issues associated with both sexuality and violence, and many sexual and violent behaviors should be considered as leisure. While instrumental or forced sex cannot be construed as leisure (at least, not for all parties involved), sexual activity that is freely chosen, pleasurable, and performed for its own sake fits most definitions of leisure (Godbey, 2008; Meaney & Rye, 2007). Indeed, sex for recreational purposes is typically a self-contained activity with intrinsic sensual, diverting, and relational meanings. In the late modern societies, sex has acquired a status of recreational activity related to the sense of self, freedom, and happiness (Attwood & Smith, 2013). Sex, being one of the examples of sensory stimulation, can be construed as a type of casual leisure (Stebbins, 2001). Alternatively, some sexual lifestyles (e.g., "swinging lifestyle") can be understood as hobbyist subcultures and forms of serious leisure (Worthington, 2005). Likewise, many violent behaviors possess leisurely qualities (at least for the perpetrators) and fit in the realm of deviant leisure, which includes transgressive behaviors that violate criminal and noncriminal moral norms (Stebbins, 1996). This is a vital area of study since "deviant leisure is increasing in our society" (Sullivan & LeDrew, 2007, p. 125) and claims "there is an essential transgressive element in leisure culture per se (Rojek, 1999, p. 86)."

Hence, the dearth of research on sex and violence in leisure studies is not caused by the lack of fit of these topics under the umbrella of leisure behaviors, and the lost opportunities can be costly. Thus, the purpose of this conceptual article is twofold: first, to present the current embryonic state of knowledge in leisure scholarship on the matters of sex and violence and their links to health and wellbeing, with the focus on the potential for innovation and impact in pursuing these topics, and second, to discuss the impediments to investigating sex and violence and the lost opportunities for leisure sciences due to avoiding "risky" research topics.

Innovation and impact of "risky" leisure research

The relationships among leisure, sex, and violence are complex and worthy of academic attention. Various leisurely characteristics (e.g., freedom and exploration, or boredom) can motivate people's involvement in sexually risky and violent behaviors. The multiplicity of leisure contexts (e.g., everyday leisure, tourism environments, sporting events) should also be explored in relation to these behaviors since different leisure contexts exert various influences on people's comportment, encouraging conformity to social norms, or conversely, authentic uncensored expression, transgression, resistance, and inversion of everyday rules.

Sexual leisure

Sex and the sexual, in all their diversity, are much neglected yet essential components of many leisure experiences (Carr & Poria, 2010), while the vast potential for innovative conceptual insights and practical implications remains untapped. Many leisure contexts serve as low-surveillance playgrounds for sexual exploration, and leisurely characteristics offer both risk and protective factors. For instance, some natural recreational areas are used for "dogging" (i.e., voyeuristic and exhibitionistic sexual practices) that, if left unregulated, contributes to the social and environmental decline of these recreational areas by attracting anti-social behaviors, prostitution, substance use, and crime (Byrne, 2006). Additionally, the lack of available adequate community leisure and recreation resources results in an understimulating environment and leisure boredom, whereas bored and unsupervised youth become prone to substance use, sexual risk taking, sexually aggressive attitudes, and sexual victimization (Miller et al., 2014; Weybright, Caldwell, Ram, Smith, & Wegner, 2015).

Conversely, leisure travel experiences typically characterized by anything but boredom can also be conducive to sexual risk taking since they are often perceived as counter-normative settings offering liberating anonymous environments and appropriate mood for sexual experimentation and transgressions (Apostolopoulos, Sönmez, & Yu, 2002; Berdychevsky, 2016; Berdychevsky & Gibson, 2015b). In turn, sexual risk taking in tourism can lead to various physical, sexual health, emotional, mental, and socio-cultural consequences affecting health and wellbeing (Berdychevsky & Gibson, 2015a). Also, the darker side of sexual behavior in tourism is captured by the phenomenon of sex tourism (this term is not easily defined but generally refers to sexual encounters involving any kind of financial transaction) that becomes particularly heinous when it involves child prostitution and human trafficking for sexual exploitation (Jeffreys, 1999; Ryan & Hall, 2001). The latter concerns are also haunting the organizers of mega and major sporting events (e.g., Olympic Games, FIFA World Cup) because such mass gatherings of visitors are believed to attract the issues of prostitution, child sexual exploitation, and sex trafficking (Brackenridge, Rhind, & Palmer-Felgate, 2015; Hayes, 2010).

It is important to keep in mind, however, that not all cases of commercial sex work are uniformly problematic (Attwood & Smith, 2013). For instance, indiscriminate fusing of heinous child sex trafficking with voluntary adult prostitution ignores the substantial variation in sex work, vilifies all the manifestations of commercial sexual exchange, and leads to the victimization of sex workers (Thomas, 2015; Weitzer, 2013). While the cases of prostitution wherein workers are coerced, threatened, or trafficked should be condemned and criminalized, sex work that is freely chosen and performed under safe and fair working conditions is often perceived as acceptable and was even legalized in some countries, including the Netherlands, Germany, and New Zealand.

Furthermore, the studies presented above reflect a tendency to focus on problematic sexual behaviors in leisure contexts, but this does not represent the complexity of sex and the sexual in leisure experiences. Leisure spaces can serve as important playgrounds where sexual and gendered identities can be negotiated, contested, inverted, and transformed. For example, women's attendance at commercial strip shows as leisure venues can be a source of resistance to sexual double standards, where women can be "sexual scrutinizers," which some find pleasurable and empowering (Pilcher, 2011). Moreover, even in more common striptease leisure settings where males are clients and females are service providers, various service characteristics (e.g., who initiates the striptease or whether touching is forbidden or circumscribed) both reproduce and challenge the simplistic gender-based dichotomy of domination and subordination (Ryan & Martin, 2001).

Additionally, women's consumption of erotic and pornographic materials in their leisure can both liberate and constrain their sexuality, which has implications for health and wellbeing (Parry & Light, 2014). Women's leisure experiences in nightclubs also allow them to (re)negotiate feminine ideals and public displays of sexuality (Kovac & Trussell, 2015). In addition, women's employment of erotic capital in roller derby allows them to leverage their sexuality for personal gain (to attract fans) and to embrace their sexual agency (Parry, 2016). Finally, women's sexual behavior during their tourist experiences often offers opportunities for self-exploration, empowerment, transformation, and inversions of sexual roles (Berdychevsky, 2016; Berdychevsky, Gibson, & Poria, 2015).

Investigating sex in/as leisure adds a psycho-socio-cultural perspective to understanding sexuality, which complements a more commonly adopted bio-medical approach. For instance, sex as leisure experience can help people cope with depression by offering distraction, preserving a sense of normalcy, providing positive emotions, and facilitating connection and emotional closeness; although, sex can also be constrained by depression and antidepressants (Berdychevsky, Nimrod, Kleiber, & Gibson, 2013). Sex as leisure also plays multiple roles across the life course. In young adulthood, leisurely sexual experimentation supports various developmental tasks and fulfills the needs for excitement and sensation seeking (Berdychevsky, 2016). In older adulthood, sex as leisure can serve adaptive purposes and help resist ageist asexual stereotypes. Moreover, preserving and/or reinventing sexual activity as leisure may promote physical, psychological, and social wellbeing in later life (Berdychevsky & Nimrod, 2017).

Exploring the links between leisure and sexual behavior also have implications for prevention and intervention programs addressing risky sexual behaviors, early sexual debut, and spread of the sexually transmitted infections (Berdychevsky, 2017; Miller et al., 2014). For instance, HealthWise South Africa is a school-based program aiming to reduce sexual risk taking and substance use by focusing on the positive use of free time and addressing leisure boredom (Caldwell et al., 2008). Another example is the Illinois Caucus for Adolescent Health that implements performance-based sexual health education using leisure repertoire of movement, music, humor, and other theatrical devices to help youth learn, enjoy, role-play, and express themselves.

The roles of leisure should not be overlooked in sexuality education for older people as well (Berdychevsky & Nimrod, 2015), since humor, role-playing, self-expressive exercises, and connection with others can mitigate seniors' discomfort associated with discussing sex and contribute to both sexual enhancement programs (aiming to maintain and improve sex life in later life) and prevention programs (focusing on mitigating risks and preventing sexually transmitted infections). Such programs for seniors should also comprehend sex as a meaningful leisure activity in older adulthood to help them resist ageist societal stereotypes portraying them as asexual, which is detrimental to their health and wellbeing (Berdychevsky & Nimrod, 2015; 2017). Lastly, leisurely characteristics of tourist experiences, which often account for the situational disinhibition effect on sexual behavior (Eiser & Ford, 1995), should be considered by sexual health practitioners targeting people in such contexts (Berdychevsky, 2017). Therefore, the impact of clarifying the links between leisure and sexuality should not be underestimated.

Violent and deviant leisure

Various forms of violence as leisure have recently drawn some scholarly attention in the niche of deviant leisure, but the "leisure" component in deviant leisure is still severely understudied (Williams, 2017). In this sense, violence fits under the category of mephitic leisure that includes the acts intended to harm the others or the self (Rojek, 2000). Violence manifests itself in leisure in various forms. For example, vicarious consumption of violence as deviant leisure is ubiquitous in Western culture, considering the demand for video games, movies, TV, music, and print media that disseminate (and often glorify) representations of violence, torture, murder, and dismemberment (Franklin-Reible, 2006; Delamere & Shaw, 2006).

Violence is also present in some recreation spaces as gangs often occupy these spaces in disadvantaged neighborhoods and gang members use their leisure to mark an imprint upon the territories they control with physical violence, sexual violence, intimidation, racketeering, graffiti, and drug use and distribution (Rojek, 1999; Stodolska, Berdychevsky, & Shinew, 2017; Stodolska, Acevedo, & Shinew, 2009). Hence, gang members' leisure pursuits restrict leisure experiences of other residents in the community because people's violence and crime perceptions in the neighborhood prevent them from visiting parks and other outdoor recreation spaces that require crossing gang territories (Stodolska, Shinew, Acevedo, & Roman, 2013).

Also, a study of federally sentenced people's perceptions of leisure revealed that leisure for them was often equated with addictions, loss of control, chaos, and crime (Yuen, Arai, & Fortune, 2012). Likewise, the roles of leisure were analyzed in relation to repeated domestic violence and sexual assault, suggesting that different leisure patterns accompany various stages in offending and fuel the cycle of violence (Williams & Walker, 2006). Even serial murder was investigated as a form of deviant leisure, analyzing the roles of leisure across the stages of fantasizing, planning, carrying out, and reliving/reminiscing about the acts (Gunn & Cassie, 2006; Williams, 2017), although the idea that a person may kill for leisure is detestable to many people (Rojek, 2000).

It is also important to consider the forms of violence in/as leisure where the "victim" is a consenting recipient of violent actions. For instance, consensual sadomasochistic activities and BDSM (Bondage and Discipline, Sadism and Masochism) culture were investigated as leisure practices and a lifestyle (Franklin-Reible, 2006; Williams, 2009). It was found that BDSM meets many leisure criteria, including a sense of personal freedom, pleasure, relaxation, adventure, self-expression, and positive emotions (Williams, Prior, Alvarado, Thomas, & Christensen, 2016). BDSM as a lifestyle was also construed as serious leisure because it involves substantial learning curve and perseverance, financial expenditures, social network, socio-psychological benefits, unique ethos, and personal identification (Newmahr, 2010). Despite the element of violence frequently involved in BDSM and its social construction as deviant, it seems to offer participants a feeling of affiliation, increased self-confidence, enhanced skills, deepened intimacy, and a sense of empowerment (Franklin-Reible, 2006). Likewise, a study of the underground subculture of human vampires suggested that self-identified vampires are often misunderstood because the term vampire has been applied to various forms of violent crime (including necrosadism, necrophilia, and cannibalism), while indeed "vampire lifestyles seem to be creative, expressive forms of serious leisure" (Williams, 2009, p. 210).

Most of the studies discussed in this section have adopted the deviant leisure perspective. Perhaps the closest equivalent of this term in tourism literature is "dark tourism," which refers to "production and consumption of taboo topics such as death and the (re)presentation of the dead" in leisure travel experience (Stone & Sharpley, 2013, pp. 55–56). Attractions visited during such leisure travel experiences vary (e.g., concentration camps, disaster sites), but the common motivation is a fascination with violence and death. Indeed, violence is related to tourism in various complex ways as "some of the very forces that motivate tourism contain the seed of criminality" (Ryan, 1993, p. 181). Tourists can be deliberate or incidental victims of violent crime, and they are easy targets due to being relaxed, off guard, leisure-oriented, self-indulgent, and outside of their familiarity zones and safety networks. Likewise, the phenomena of sex tourism (if a sex worker is forced) and human trafficking to serve tourists and visitors at sporting events, discussed in the previous section, should also be construed as forms of violence.

The impact of understanding the links between violence and leisure is notable because leisure and recreation programs can serve as prevention, intervention, and rehabilitation tools to address people's engagement in violent practices and lifestyles. For example, Cure Violence (nongovernmental training, teaching, and research organization focused on a health approach to violence prevention) branch in Chicago employs a range of recreation and sport activities to entice gang members to participate in intervention counseling and to expose them to prosocial alternatives to the gang lifestyle. New Life Centers of Chicagoland also offer at-risk youth a variety of educational and leisure activities (including Sports Outreach Leagues and art therapy) that take them off the streets and provide with safe spaces and positive developmental tasks.

Additionally, studying and restructuring violent offenders' leisure patterns might shed new insights on criminal behaviors and motivations, prevent crime, reduce the risk of continued violence, and/or help solve the cases more efficiently (Williams, 2006; 2017; Williams &

Walker, 2006). Furthermore, leisure and correctional recreation can help incarcerated offenders cope with the prison environment and facilitate their rehabilitation upon transitioning out of prisons to increase their independence, self-reliance, and chances for successful community re-entry (Williams, 2006; Yuen, Arai, & Fortune, 2012). Indeed, it was found that leisure functioning (specifically, intrinsic motivation and perception of freedom in leisure) is strongly related to offender rehabilitation (Link & Williams, 2017).

Impediments to "risky" leisure research and lost opportunities

The previous two sections on sexual and/or violent leisure showcase that tapping into the potential of the innovative research questions exploring sex and violence in leisure contexts should be alluring. Leisure literature, however, demonstrates that this is not the case, and it leads to the question of why so little attention is paid to these meaningful research topics in leisure scholarship. At least partially, this can be explained by the following arguments.

First, sex and violence are socially construed as the taboo topics and are often perceived as unworthy of the dignified academic discourse. Sex has hardly ever been a topic for a rational and open discussion in general and in leisure scholarship in particular (Berdychevsky, Nimrod, Kleiber, & Gibson, 2013; Carr, 2016; Carr & Poria, 2010). Typically, sex in leisure scholarship is researched adopting a moralistic approach aiming to solve some problem (e.g., sexual risk taking, sexual double standards and inequality, sex tourism), as if sex as a positive leisure experience related to health and wellbeing is below the dignity of the sophisticated academic attention. Indeed, in the Western sex-saturated society, such a stance on studying sex is simply hypocritical.

Also, the relationship between leisure and violence has been typically framed from the vintage point of the deviant leisure perspective, with a prominent focus on crime (Williams, 2006; Williams & Walker, 2006). While this strategy is often justifiable, it is frequently narrow and limiting the efforts of understanding complex behaviors. The label "deviant" in itself might serve as a deterrent for leisure researchers to investigate violence. Although, various alternative names have been offered, such as dark, marginal, or transgressive leisure and purple or taboo recreation (Franklin-Reible, 2006; Sullivan & LeDrew, 2007), their connotations and emotional baggage are also far from enticing (e.g., choosing to study a marginal niche in a field that is often marginalized is not particularly motivating). In general, understanding various forms of violence as leisure clashes with the traditional view of leisure as related to the common good, which leaves little, if any, room for considering violent behaviors as leisure (Franklin-Reible, 2006; Sullivan & LeDrew, 2007; Williams, 2017).

Perhaps, there is fear that investigating sex and violence in/as leisure may undermine the academic credibility of leisure sciences, and there is also a mistaken belief that studying these topics should be left to medical practitioners and criminologists (Godbey, 2008; Gunn & Caissie, 2006; Rojek, 1999; Sullivan & LeDrew, 2007). These tendencies hinder the progress in clarifying the meaningful links among leisure, sex, and violence. Hence, to understand the complexity of the roles of sex and violence in leisure experiences researchers need to stop "being inhibited by a moral straightjacket" (Carr & Poria, 2010, p. 3). This is important because dismissing leisure research that does not necessarily fit the stereotype of "inherently good/appropriate" threatens the legitimacy of leisure sciences as a field (Franklin-Reible, 2006).

The second reason for the dearth of research on sexual and violent behaviors in/as leisure is the fact that such studies are complicated by numerous methodological challenges. Social desirability and reactivity effects are particularly pressing when studying sex and/or violence as people are reluctant to disclose, or tend to under- or over-report such behaviors depending on the circumstances and their personal profiles. Also, with such sensitive topics, research participants' concerns about anonymity and confidentiality become acute. Likewise, faulty memory and a tendency to suppress traumatic experiences or socially condemned behaviors are particularly important concerns affecting the trustworthiness of the data and interpretations when studying sex and/or violence. Additionally, the differences between the psychological and socio-demographic profiles of the responders and nonresponders in such studies are meaningful and often preclude generalizations. These issues require "religious" adherence to the ethical research standards and often invite increased scrutiny by the institutional review boards that many researchers prefer to avoid.

The third complication is caused by the lack of dialogue between the sibling leisure and tourism fields. While some studies on sex and/or violence are scattered throughout leisure and tourism journals, effective cross-pollination and accumulation of the knowledge base on these topics is prevented by the fragmentation caused by the silo mentality in leisure and tourism literature. While the diversity of specializations can contribute to pluralism and the accumulation of specialty-specific knowledge, increased segmentation and a lack of communication and collaboration between leisure and tourism scholars also lead to the detrimental fragmentation of knowledge and a crisis of collective identity and intellectual mission (Henderson, 2010).

The fourth impediment is related to the definitional issues that complicate the investigation of sex and violence in leisure contexts. Similar to the concepts of leisure and tourism, there are no universally accepted definitions of sex and violence. Definitions of sex range from traditional narrow definitions focusing on penile-vaginal intercourse to broad(er) approaches including any activities with sexual overtone with or without penetration (Oppermann, 1999). A survey of people's perceptions of behaviors that constitute "having sex" revealed no universal consensus, which has implications for both research and clinical practice (Sanders et al., 2010). Likewise, violence does not lend itself well to a simple definition because it can be self-directed, interpersonal, and collective, including physical, sexual, and psychological manifestations, as well as deprivation and neglect (World Health Organization, 2002). Although this plurality is not necessarily a weakness as it can be construed as a testament to the complexity of these phenomena, it might still inhibit the accumulation of relevant knowledge and comparisons across studies.

Finally, these sensitive and challenging topics do not lend themselves well to the publishing canons that encourage recycling established ideas with some incremental extensions at the expense of innovation. Namely, these topics do not fit well into the realm of "safe" mainstream research but are rather in the category of "risky" research that is more challenging to get published. Graduate students and junior faculty are often advised to refrain from "risky" research, or at least postpone it until after promotion and tenure, which is "a weapon to get conformity" (Johnson, 2009, p. 487).

Conclusions

Leisure researchers have been wondering for decades, "if our research is relevant, why is nobody listening?" (Shaw, 2000, p. 147). These concerns remain relevant today as leisure sciences are perceived to be in crisis that we could overcome by embracing change and keeping our research relevant to the broader social issues and trends, articulating our collective identity and overcoming the silo mentality among the sibling fields, celebrating the contributions of leisure research, and forming inter/multi/transdisciplinary collaborations (Henderson, 2010).

Conducting "risky" research and partnering with relevant disciplines is an opportunity to showcase the importance of leisure scholarship and its contribution to the understanding of the pressing social needs and public health issues. Investigating the links among leisure, sex, and violence and their impacts on health and wellbeing connects leisure scholarship to the fields of sexuality, public health, social work, and criminal justice. Such connections are important in light of the pertinent concerns that leisure as a field has been struggling to overcome marginalization and isolation, or even ghettoization, from other disciplines to gain recognition and proper funding (Caudwell & Browne, 2011b; Henderson, 2010).

Shying away from "risky" research of the pressing social issues in leisure contexts, such as violence or sex-related matters, means "choosing to avoid conflict and complexity in order to gain irrelevant safety" (Kelly, 1990, p. 374). Surely, remaining on the safe terrain might be an easier and seemingly reasonable choice, but it is not conducive to the progress of the leisure field. To put it in the words of Bernard Shaw, "The reasonable man adapts himself to the world; the unreasonable one persists in trying to adapt the world to himself. Therefore, all progress depends on the unreasonable man (Shaw, 1903/1922, p. 238)."

References

Apostolopoulos, Y., Sönmez, S., & Yu, C. H. (2002). HIV-risk behaviors of American spring break vacationers: A case of situational disinhibition? *International Journal of STD & AIDS, 13*(11), 733–743.

Attwood, F., & Smith, C. (2013). Leisure sex: More sex! Better sex! Sex is fucking brilliant! Sex, sex, sex, SEX. In T. Blackshaw (Ed.), *Routledge handbook of leisure studies* (pp. 325–342). London, England: Routledge.

Berdychevsky, L. (2016). Antecedents of young women's sexual risk taking in tourist experiences. *Journal of Sex Research, 53*(8), 927–941.

Berdychevsky, L. (2017). Sexual health education for young tourists. *Tourism Management, 62*, 189–195.

Berdychevsky, L., & Gibson, H. J. (2015a). Phenomenology of young women's sexual risk-taking in tourism. *Tourism Management, 46*, 299–310.

Berdychevsky, L., & Gibson, H. J. (2015b). Sex and risk in young women's tourist experiences: Context, likelihood, and consequences. *Tourism Management, 51*, 78–90.

Berdychevsky, L., Gibson, H. J., & Poria, Y. (2015). Inversions of sexual roles in women's tourist experiences: Mind, body, and language in sexual behavior. *Leisure Studies, 34*(5), 513–528.

Berdychevsky, L., & Nimrod, G. (2015). "Let's talk about sex": Discussions in seniors' online communities. *Journal of Leisure Research, 47*(4), 467–484.

Berdychevsky, L., & Nimrod, G. (2017). Sex as leisure in later life: A netnographic approach. *Leisure Sciences, 39*(3), 224–243.

Berdychevsky, L., Nimrod, G., Kleiber, D. A., & Gibson, H. J. (2013). Sex as leisure in the shadow of depression. *Journal of Leisure Research, 45*(1), 47–73.

Brackenridge, C. H., Rhind, D., & Palmer-Felgate, S. (2015). Locating and mitigating risks to children associated with major sporting events. *Journal of Policy Research in Tourism, Leisure and Events, 7*(3), 237–250.

Byrne, R. (2006). Beyond lovers' lane—the rise of illicit sexual leisure in countryside recreational space. *Leisure/Loisir, 30*(1), 73–85.

Caldwell, L. L., Younker, A. S., Wegner, L., Patrick, M. E., Vergnani, T., Smith, E. A., & Flisher, A. J. (2008). Understanding leisure-related program effects by using process data in the HealthWise South Africa project. *Journal of Park and Recreation Administration, 26*(2), 146–162.

Carr, N. (2016). Sex in tourism: Reflections and potential future research directions. *Tourism Recreation Research, 41*(2), 188–198.

Carr, N., & Poria, Y. (Eds.). (2010). *Sex and the sexual during people's leisure and tourism experiences*. Newcastle upon Tyne, England: Cambridge Scholars Publishing.

Caudwell, J., & Browne, K. (2011a). Special issue: Sexy spaces. *Leisure Studies, 30*(2), 117–265.
Caudwell, J., & Browne, K. (2011b). Sexy spaces: Geography and leisure intersectionalities. *Leisure Studies, 30*(2), 117–122.
Delamere, F. M., & Shaw, S. M. (2006). Playing with violence: Gamers' social construction of violent video game play as tolerable violence. *Leisure/Loisir, 30*(1), 7–25.
Eiser, J. R., & Ford, N. (1995). Sexual relationships on holiday: A case of situational disinhibition? *Journal of Social and Personal Relationships, 12*(3), 323–339.
Franklin-Reible, H. (2006). Deviant leisure: Uncovering the "goods" in transgressive behavior. *Leisure/Loisir, 30*(1), 55–71.
Godbey, G. (2008). *Leisure in your life: New perspectives*. State College, PA: Venture Publishing.
Gunn, L., & Caissie, L. T. (2006). Serial murder as an act of deviant leisure. *Leisure/Loisir, 30*(1), 27–53.
Hayes, V. (2010). Human trafficking for sexual exploitation at world sporting events. *Chicago-Kent Law Review, 85*(3), 1105–1145.
Henderson, K. A. (2010). Leisure studies in the 21st century: The sky is falling? *Leisure Sciences, 32*(4), 391–400.
Jeffreys, S. (1999). Globalizing sexual exploitation: Sex tourism and the traffic in women. *Leisure Studies, 18*(3), 179–196.
Johnson, C. W. (2009). Writing ourselves at risk: Using self-narrative in working for social justice. *Leisure Sciences, 31*(5), 483–489.
Kovac, L. D., & Trussell, D. E. (2015). "Classy and never trashy": Young women's experiences of nightclubs and the construction of gender and sexuality. *Leisure Sciences, 37*(3), 195–209.
Link, A. J., & Williams, D. J. (2017). Leisure functioning and offender rehabilitation: A correlational exploration into factors affecting successful reentry. *International Journal of Offender Therapy and Comparative Criminology, 61*(2), 150–170.
Meaney, G. J., & Rye, B. J. (2007). Sex, sexuality, and leisure. In R. McCarville & K. MacKay (Eds.), *Leisure for Canadians* (pp. 131–138). State College, PA: Venture Publishing.
Miller, J. A., Caldwell, L. L., Weybright, E. H., Smith, E. A., Vergnani, T., & Wegner, L. (2014). Was Bob Seger right? Relation between boredom in leisure and [risky[sex. *Leisure Sciences, 36*(1), 52–67.
Newmahr, S. (2010). Rethinking kink: Sadomasochism as serious leisure. *Qualitative Sociology, 33*, 313–331.
Oppermann, M. (1999). Sex tourism. *Annals of Tourism Research, 26*(2), 251–266.
Parry, D. C. (2016). "Skankalicious": Erotic capital in women's flat track roller derby. *Leisure Sciences, 38*(4), 295–314.
Parry, D. C., & Light, T. P. (2014). Fifty shades of complexity: Exploring technologically mediated leisure and women's sexuality. *Journal of Leisure Research, 46*(1), 38–57.
Pilcher, K. E. M. (2011). A "sexy space" for women? Heterosexual women's experiences of a male strip show venue. *Leisure Studies, 30*(2), 217–235.
Rojek, C. (1999). Deviant leisure: The dark side of free-time activity. In E. L. Jackson & T. L. Burton (Eds.), *Leisure studies: Prospects for the twenty-first century* (pp. 81–95). State College, PA: Venture Publishing.
Rojek, C. (2000). *Leisure and culture*. New York, NY: Palgrave.
Ryan, C. (1993). Crime, violence, terrorism and tourism: An accidental or intrinsic relationship. *Tourism Management, 14*(3), 173–183.
Ryan, C., & Hall, C. M. (2001). *Sex tourism: Marginal people and liminalities*. London, England: Routledge.
Ryan, C., & Martin, A. (2001). Tourists and strippers: Liminal theater. *Annals of Tourism Research, 28*(1), 140–163.
Sanders, S. A., Hill, B. J., Yarber, W. L., Graham, C. A., Crosby, R. A., & Milhausen, R. R. (2010). Misclassification bias: Diversity in conceptualizations about having "had sex." *Sexual Health, 7*(1), 31–34.
Shaw, B. (1903/1922). *Man and superman: A comedy and a philosophy*. New York, NY: Brentano's.
Shaw, S. (2000). If our research is relevant, why is nobody listening? *Journal of Leisure Research, 32*(1), 147–151.
Stebbins, R. A. (1996). *Tolerable differences: Living with deviance*. Toronto, Canada: McGraw-Hill Ryerson.
Stebbins, R. A. (2001). The costs and benefits of hedonism: Some consequences of taking casual leisure seriously. *Leisure Studies, 20*(4), 305–309.

Stebbins, R. A., Rojek, C., & Sullivan, A. M. (2006). Special issue: Deviant leisure. *Leisure/Loisir, 30*(1), 3–305.

Stodolska, M., Acevedo, J. C., & Shinew, K. J. (2009). Gangs of Chicago: Perceptions of crime and its effect on the recreation behavior of Latino residents in urban communities. *Leisure Sciences, 31*(5), 466–482.

Stodolska, M., Berdychevsky, L., & Shinew, K. J. (2017). Gangs and deviant leisure. *Leisure Sciences.* doi:http://dx.doi.org/10.1080/01490400.2017.1329040

Stodolska, M., Shinew, K. J., Acevedo, J. C., & Roman, C. G. (2013). "I was born in the hood": Fear of crime, outdoor recreation and physical activity among Mexican-American urban adolescents. *Leisure Sciences, 35*(1), 1–15.

Stone, P. R., & Sharpley, R. (2013). Deviance, dark tourism and "dark leisure": Towards a (re)configuration of morality and the taboo in secular society. In S. Elkington & S. Gammon (Eds.), *Contemporary perspectives in leisure: Meanings, motives and lifelong learning* (pp. 54–64). London, England: Routledge.

Sullivan, A. M., & LeDrew, D. (2007). Exploring leisure's boundaries. In R. McCarville & K. MacKay (Eds.), *Leisure for Canadians.* State College, PA: Venture Publishing.

Thomas, J. N. (2015). Responding to academic critiques of sex work: Practical suggestions from a sex-positive perspective. *Journal of Positive Sexuality, 1,* 16–20.

Weitzer, R. (2013). Sex trafficking and the sex industry: The need for evidence-based theory and legislation. *101*(4), 1337–1369.

Weybright, E. H., Caldwell, L. L., Ram, N., Smith, E. A., & Wegner, L. (2015). Boredom prone or nothing to do? Distinguishing between state and trait leisure boredom and its association with substance use in South African adolescents. *Leisure Sciences, 37*(4), 311–331.

Williams, D. J. (2006). Forensic leisure science: A new frontier for leisure scholars. *Leisure Sciences, 28*(1), 91–95.

Williams, D. J. (2009). Deviant leisure: Rethinking "the good, the bad, and the ugly". *Leisure Sciences, 31*(2), 207–213.

Williams, D. J. (2017). Entering the minds of serial murderers: The application of forensic leisure science to homicide research. *Leisure Sciences, 39*(4), 376–383.

Williams, D. J., Prior, E. E., Alvarado, T., Thomas, J. N., & Christensen, M. C. (2016). Is bondage and discipline, dominance and submission, and sadomasochism recreational leisure? A descriptive exploratory investigation. *Journal of Sexual Medicine, 13,* 1091–1094.

Williams, D. J., & Walker, G. J. (2006). Leisure, deviant leisure, and crime: "Caution: Objects may be closer than they appear." *Leisure/Loisir, 30*(1), 193–218.

World Health Organization. (2002). *World report on violence and health.* Retrieved from http://www.who.int/violence_injury_prevention/violence/world_report/en/summary_en.pdf?ua=1

Worthington, B. (2005). Sex and shunting: Contrasting aspects of serious leisure within the tourism industry. *Tourist Studies, 5*(3), 225–246.

Yuen, F., Arai, S., & Fortune, D. (2012). Community (dis)connection through leisure for women in prison. *Leisure Sciences, 34*(4), 281–297.

Are We Ready for "Radical Leisure"?

B. Dana Kivel

ABSTRACT
For that past 40 years, hundreds of articles have been published in the major journals that examine leisure, recreation, and parks in North America, for example, the *Journal of Leisure Research, Leisure Sciences*, and *Journal of Recreation and Park Administration*. Yet, we are no closer to influencing policy, shifting public opinion, or persuading ourselves and each other that the idea of leisure is something that we should value, embrace, and fight for in terms of a shorter work week and, for that matter, a shorter work life. What is our professional commitment to promoting leisure, advocating for shorter work weeks and for mandatory vacation time? This article explores issues related to leisure, resistance and the hegemony of work.

"Let us be lazy in everything, except in loving and drinking, except in being lazy."—Lessing (Marszalek, 2011, p. 23).

In the summer of July 2010, I was finishing my fifth year as department chair and was feeling pretty burned out—the largest economic recession in history since the depression had led me to have to lay off virtually all of our contingent faculty; promises of pay increases in our union contract were rescinded; understandably, morale on campus and in our department was rock bottom; and I had just overseen a process of implementing furloughs for all faculty and staff that resulted in an overall 10% pay decrease for everyone. It was summer and it was hot, and I was in desperate need of two things: peace and quiet and cooler temperatures. I decided to head for the mountains of Santa Cruz, California, to a place called "Vajrapani Retreat Center" for a 10-day silent retreat. Prior to registering for this event, I had done some meditation and had been part of a group of people who had spent months preparing to participate in a week-long, fasting retreat on Mount Shasta—camping by yourself at a particular location but in proximity to 50 others doing the same thing. Vajrapani, it turned out, was different.

I went there not knowing anyone and not knowing what exactly a 10-day silent retreat would involve. Looking back on this experience, I realize that the website, most likely, was intentionally vague. Once I got settled in, had dinner and spoke with a few people, I started to relax about it and thought, "hey, this is going to be great—good food, a little conversation here and there with interesting people from all over the world in a beautiful setting in the Santa Cruz mountains." Then, we had a little talk after dinner. Really, it was our four teachers doing the talking. They explained what the process was: up at 5:00 a.m. and the first sitting meditation would begin at 5:30. The days would rotate between sitting and walking meditation from

5:30 a.m. until 9:00 p.m., with an hour for a work meditation—working in the kitchen, cleaning the meditation hall, etc.—and an additional hour break in the middle of the day. In addition, the teachers gave dharma talks in the evening—talks that focused on different aspects of meditation and Buddhism, the five aversions, the eightfold path to enlightenment, Sukkha (joy) and Dukkha (suffering), and other aspects of self-actualization that I would never attain, so early on, I stopped taking notes. My anticipated level of enjoyment of the 10 days was starting to diminish. Then came time for the commitment process—as a group, all 45 of us (closer to 39 or 40 by the end of the 10 days) made a verbal commitment to abstain from using alcohol and drugs (unless prescriptions), sexual behavior, taking things that did not belong to us (there were no locks on the doors and no place to store valuables in our rooms), and finally, no talking … to anyone … at all … for 10 days. When you are sitting at your campsite on Mount Shasta by yourself, it is easy to not talk to anyone, but when you are living in a community with people, the idea of not talking was a challenge. I was warned that the first 36 hours were the hardest. They call this period of time letting go of the monkey mind—the nonstop chatter and conversations in your head, things like examining why you are at the retreat, how stupid silent retreats are and chastising yourself for not fully knowing that a 10-day silent retreat meant there would be no talking or contact with people apart from sitting next to or in front of or behind them in the meditation hall. There was also no direct eye contact. The first few days proved to be too difficult for some people who left. In fact, however, we could do some talking and connecting with people. Our four teachers set aside time to meet with new people to check in with them about how things were going and to answer questions about the retreat process. This meant you could engage in speaking two to four minutes every few days or you could write notes to the teachers, but not to other students.

Once the 36 hours went by and then the 48 and then the 72 on up until the end, it did, in fact, get easier to engage in sitting and walking meditation and to actively quiet my mind. It was an amazing process to witness—seeing my mind go from monkey to not quite zen mind, but pretty close. At one point, I was having a hard time and one of my teachers, a tatted 35-year-old white man who had spent time in prison but who later became a teacher, author, and leader of a movement called "dharma punx," shared with me a mantra that has been a good friend and guide for me the past seven years. He said, "when you are struggling to quiet your mind, say this phrase: "nowhere to go; nothing to do; no one to be." I repeat this mantra to myself when I'm having a hard time going to sleep or when I need to ground myself before a meeting or a potentially difficult conversation. And, in saying this phrase, I also realized two things: one, you cannot think two different or disparate things at once, which is a great thing to know and to learn (one idea or thought at a time); and this mantra, which echoes the Aristotelian notion of leisure—freedom from the necessity of being obligated—should be the essence of what leisure is as we move well into this 21st century.

For the past 40 years, hundreds of articles have been published in the major journals that examine leisure, recreation, and parks in North America – the *Journal of Leisure Research, Leisure Sciences* and *Journal of Recreation and Park Administration*. Yet, despite research and conceptualizations around these topics, we are no closer to influencing policy, shifting public opinion, or persuading ourselves and each other that the idea of leisure is something that we should value, embrace, and fight for in terms of a shorter work week and, for that matter, a shorter work life. As we contemplate the next 40 years of *Leisure Sciences*, it seems the perfect moment to not only reflect on what we have learned but also what we think in terms of generativity—what will be the legacy of this journal for the next several generations of readers? How relevant will our field be, especially if, in 2057, people are still working 40+ hours a week with no paid vacations and those with paid vacations do not fully use them?

The early 20th century was synonymous with the struggles of the labor movement and the 40-hour work week, codified at the end of the 1930s, continues to be standard throughout the United States. Almost 20 years into this century, that labor movement, hard fought with many victories, has largely been diminished or has been coopted by the rise of neoliberalism. Swidler (2016) wrote: "The organized labor movement of the moment, fighting rearguard actions against neoliberalism, appears unable to mount a … cultural critique of work" (pp. 32–33). I am not sure which is worse—our failure as a society to embrace a collective understanding of and appreciation for leisure or our inability and/or unwillingness to offer a collective critique of work while also not doing more to agitate for shorter work weeks and mandatory vacation time. In fact, not only do we not embrace leisure, but we do not, as Swidler suggests, know how to "resist" work. She cites the professoriate to make her case. She argued:

> … academic professionals, notorious for their own ever-rising standards of work hours and productivity, have failed to appreciate the importance of work resistance, not merely as a weapon of class rebellion, but as an essential element of sustainability for the planet. (Swidler, 2016, p. 32)

We may speak about and engage in many leisure and leisure pursuits—we're not total hypocrites, but we are also serious workaholics. The job never ends: when you're not teaching, you are preparing to teach or grading or researching the next article or preparing files for tenure and promotion or reviewing a manuscript or preparing presentations for conferences or reading articles about the need to do all these things. As I was starting my career, I was told, "if you don't have something in the hopper, you better be worried." The implication was always be thinking, writing, teaching or doing something, going somewhere, or becoming someone relative to work.

If we are too busy reading, researching, or writing about leisure to enjoy and/or benefit from it, what does that say about us? In her essay "Radical Leisure," Swidler made the argument there should be more of an alignment between organized labor and those fighting to shorten the work week. Among the fighters, she referenced Juliet Schor, "Take Back Our Time" and "Voluntary Simplicity" networks, and the historian Benjamin Hunnicutt who, she described, " … has devoted much of his career to describing labor's fight for shorter hours in the United States" (p. 29). Apart from Professor Hunnicutt, no one else from our field is mentioned. In some ways, we are so focused on doing research about what leisure is and isn't and about who does and doesn't have it and about what gets in the way of people doing it or how it does or doesn't influence how people see themselves, their relationships with others and the world, that we seem to have forgotten that there is a critical relationship between the construct of work and the construct of leisure.

What is our commitment to promoting leisure, critiquing work, advocating for shorter work weeks and for mandatory vacation time and, perhaps even more importantly, why aren't we, collectively as a field, resisting work? This essay explores some of these questions.

When we write about leisure without also acknowledging, analyzing, and/or challenging the construct of work as the central organizing principle of our lives, then we are unwittingly contributing to the hegemony of work. Marszalek (2011) argued that " … a core belief system of capitalism—that a job satisfies our basic social needs—exposes the ideology of scarcity and sacrifice that supports capitalism's discipline of production" (p. 10). Reid, Golden, and Katerberg (2010) argued that "until now, leisure has been seen as an add-on to the main focus of life which has devoted itself to production and consumptions. Given those ideas may have outlived their usefulness and penultimate place in human affairs, there is a need for society to construct an alternative raison d'etre" (pp. 83–84).

For the past few decades, we have seen several shifts in the nature of work—the lessening of opportunities for employment and the nature of employment. We have also seen tremendous growth among contingent workers, especially adjunct faculty on college campuses. Some refer to these individuals as the " … 'precariat'—those who submit to precarious employment" (Marszalek, 2011, p. 15) while others refer to them as members of the "gig" economy—those who do not want traditional 9–5 jobs but rather seek out opportunities to be contract workers (Hampton, 2016). Being a contractual worker can easily lead to job insecurity and exploitation, but " … some workers are seeking opportunities for empowerment in collaboration and cooperative ownership" (Hampton, p. 17).

Through our research, we know, both implicitly and explicitly, that leisure is as important and sometimes even more important than work; that it enhances the quality of people's lives; that people value their leisure; and that it influences virtually every aspect of our lives. Yet, perhaps our laser-sharp focus on doing research to justify the importance of leisure in our society without simultaneously and collectively challenging the underlying economic structure of capitalism and the institution of work may have far-reaching implications for the long-term impact of our research. An imbalance has been created since the social historians, the socialists, anarchists, and labor movement organizers and activists have continued to challenge the meaning, value, and construct of work in our society while we have focused almost exclusively on shoring up the leisure side of the equation. Critiques and analyses of work have been made primarily through examining social class (e.g., Hutchison, 1988; Shinew, Floyd, McGuire, & Noe, 1995); identity (e.g., Kleiber, 1999) and issues of constraints (e.g., Crawford, Jackson, & Godbey, 1991; Henderson & Ainsworth, 2000; Raymore, Godbey, & Crawford, 1994; Scott & Jackson, 1996; Scott & Munson, 1994). These studies have been critically important in terms of recognizing inequitable issues of access to leisure and the ways in which individuals who have been constrained have also developed strategies for negotiating these different constraints.

In contrast to these studies, which focused on individuals or groups, Clarke and Critcher (1985) in the "Devil Makes Work" examined leisure within a larger institutional framework relative to labor; and Rose and Dustin (2009) took an institutional approach to their critique of neoliberalism's impact on higher education programs in our field. Within this critique, they made explicit the connection between work and leisure. They asserted that "a common critique from leisure studies is that Calvinism and a Protestant work ethic have led people to value work, materialism, consumption, and capitalism over classical notions of leisure" (p. 39). Although Rose and Dustin argue this may be a common critique, it has not been a sustained critique that has manifested throughout the bulk of our research and scholarship.

We know that leisure is subordinate to work for the vast majority of people in the United States. Unemployment is still high, especially in factory towns of all sizes, and once thriving farm communities have been swallowed up by international agribusiness. Also, contingent labor is precarious and potentially exploitative. Knowing all this, how should we begin to frame our analyses and discussions of leisure vis-à-vis the construct of work? What exactly and precisely is our role—to educate, advocate, agitate, and/or collaborate with each other, with unions, with policy makers? Who is and should be challenging the role and meaning of work in society and how can we "resist work"?

In my experience of this field, rarely, if at all, have we collectively as The Academy of Leisure Sciences (TALS), formerly known as Society of Park and Recreation Educators (SPRE), made pronouncements about public policy issues. Historically, I think we have deferred to NRPA as the public policy and advocacy mouthpiece of our field. This has to shift. I am hopeful that we will find our collective footing so that as a unified field we might speak out on labor-related issues since there is a connection between the beneficial outcomes that we seek in terms of leisure and the ways in which we situate and position the role of work and labor in our society. Indeed, while we have made some strides shifting from identity-based research (e.g., Kivel, 2000; 2005) toward more structural analyses (e.g., Arai & Kivel, 2009; McDonald, 2009; Mowatt, 2009; Mowatt, French, & Malebranche, 2013) and have incorporated analyses around resistance (Shaw, 2001; Johnson & Samdahl, 2005; Rose & Dustin, 2010; and Theriault, 2014), and intersectionality (e.g., Henderson & Gibson, 2013), we have not focused our efforts on the relationship among leisure and unemployment, underemployment, and institutionalized oppressions.

A recent example illustrates the problem. At the end of 2016, Dr. John DeGraaf, president of the "Take Back Your Time" organization in Seattle, sent a note to the TALS network informing us that, after 15 years, he would be stepping down and hoped the organization would continue. A few people in the field wrote responses thanking Dr. DeGraaf for his important work and dedication to education and advocacy. There were four or five individual responses on the network, but no collective response of thanks or collective response to say we would pick up the mantle. Personally, I thought to myself, "this is going to be a huge loss if the organization does not continue," but I didn't step up, nor did I encourage others to do so. I still wonder why I didn't step up since I know we have to constantly work toward challenging and resisting the hegemony of work.

I include myself in here when I say: I don't think we can complain that the public doesn't take our work seriously if we, ourselves, cannot be moved to take action to support a cause that fundamentally influences all aspects of the research and scholarship that we do. Individually, we have a tremendous impact on the communities in which we live, but collectively, I'm not sure how powerful our voice is or has been. I think there is not only a gap between theory and practice in the field, but a gap in terms of our desire for our work to be of public value and relevance and our willingness to advocate for it. Swidler's notion of "radical leisure" will not miraculously appear, nor will a manifesto outlining the steps for collective action around work resistance.

As we move toward the next 40 years, if we want this journal to be not only a vehicle for education and research but also a transformative platform for social change vis-à-vis the nature of leisure, then we must also, simultaneously, include critical analyses of the nature and structure of work. Indeed, if we want the right to be lazy and if we want to embrace Aristotelian leisure and have nowhere to go, nothing to do, and no one to be, then we will need to speak about, write about, and make space for discussion and dissent about the hegemony of work. Yes, we will have to work toward resisting work and, more than that, we will need to become allies and activists with those fighting for change in the communities in which we live and work.

References

Arai, S., & Kivel, B. D. (2009). Critical race theory and social justice perspectives on whiteness, difference(s) and (anti)racism: A fourth wave of race research in leisure studies. *Journal of Leisure Research, 41*(4), 459–472.

Clarke, C., & Critcher, J. (1985). *The devil makes work: Leisure in capitalist Britain*. Urbana, IL: University of Illinois Press.

Crawford, D. W., Jackson, E. L., & Godbey, G. (1991). A hierarchical model of leisure constraints. *Leisure Sciences, 13*(4), 309–320.

Hampton, P. (2016, Fall). Welcome to the gig economy. *YES! Magazine, 79*, 17–22.

Henderson, K. A., & Ainsworth, B. E. (2000). Enablers and constraints to walking for older African American and American Indian women: The cultural activity participation study. *Research Quarterly for Exercise and Sport, 71*(4), 313–321.

Henderson, K. A., & Gibson, H. J. (2013). An integrative review of women, gender, and leisure: Increasing complexities. *Journal of Leisure Research, 45*(2), 115–135.

Hutchison, R. (1988). A critique of race, ethnicity and social class in recent leisure-recreation research. *Journal of Leisure Research, 20*(1), 10–30.

Johnson, C. W., & Samdahl, D. M. (2005). The night they took over: Misogyny in a country-western gay bar. *Leisure Sciences, 27*(4) 331–348.

Kivel, B. D. (2000). Leisure, experience and difference: What difference does difference make? *Journal of Leisure Research, 32*(1), 79–81.

Kivel, B. D. (2005). Examining racism, power and white hegemony in Stodolska's conditioned attitude model of individual discriminatory behavior. *Leisure Sciences, 27*(1), 21–27.

Kleiber, D. (1999). *Leisure experience and human development: A dialectical approach*. New York, NY: Basic Books.

Marszalek, B. (2011). *The right to be lazy: Essays by Paul Lafargue*. Oakland, CA: AK Press.

McDonald, M. G. (2009). Dialogues on whiteness, leisure and (anti)racism. *Journal of Leisure Research, 41*(1), 5–21.

Mowatt, R. A. (2009). Notes from a leisure son: Expanding the meaning of whiteness in leisure. *Journal of Leisure Research, 41*(4), 511–528.

Mowatt, R. A., French, B. H., & Malebranche, D. A. (2013). Black/female/body hypervisibility and invisibility: A black feminist augmentation of feminist leisure research. *Journal of Leisure Research, 45*(5), 644–660.

Raymore, L., Godbey, G., & Crawford, D. (1994). Self-esteem, gender, and socioeconomic status: Their relation to perceptions of constraint on leisure among adolescents. *Journal of Leisure Research, 26*(2), 99–118.

Reid, D. G., Golden, L., & Katerberg, L. (2010). Removing the scar: Social solidarity and leisure policy. In S. M. Arai, H. Mair, & D. G. Reid (Eds.), *Decentering work: Critical perspectives on leisure, social policy, and human development*. Alberta, Canada: University of Calgary Press.

Rose, J., & Dustin, D. (2009). The neoliberal assault on the public university: The case of recreation, park, and leisure research. *Leisure Sciences, 31*(4) 397–402.

Scott, D., & Jackson, E. L. (1996). Factors that limit and strategies that might encourage people's use of public parks. *Journal of Park and Recreation Administration, 14*(1), 1–11.

Scott, D., & Munson, W. (1994). Perceived constraints to park usage among individuals with low incomes. *Journal of Park and Recreation Administration, 12*, 79–96.

Shaw, S. M. (2001). Conceptualizing resistance: Women's leisure as political practice. *Journal of Leisure Research, 33*(2), 186–201.

Shinew, K. J., Floyd, M. F., McGuire, F. A., & Noe, P. (1995). Gender, race and subjective social class and their association with leisure preferences. *Leisure Sciences, 17*(2), 75–89.

Swidler, E. (2016). Radical leisure. *Monthly Review: An Independent Socialist Magazine, 68*(2), 26–34.

Theriault, D. (2014). Organized leisure experiences of LGBTQ youth: Resistance and oppression. *Journal of Leisure Research, 46*(4), 448–461.

All the Lonely People: Social Isolation and the Promise and Pitfalls of Leisure

Troy D. Glover

ABSTRACT
Maintaining meaningful social connections boosts health in amazing ways. Even so, social isolation pervades disturbingly in contemporary society. Because of its harmful consequences, social isolation represents one of the most serious social problems of our time, ironically in an age when connecting with others seems easy. Nevertheless, leisure studies remains quiet on this matter. If our field aims to enhance its social relevance, I argue it needs to focus more attention on the issue of social isolation. With this in mind, the purpose of this contribution to the 40th anniversary issue of *Leisure Sciences* is to position social isolation as an important topic in our field and to offer directions for future research. To these ends, this manuscript looks back at what we know about leisure and its implications for social isolation and looks forward to relevant questions aimed at driving the next generation of impactful leisure research.

Whether unattached or in a committed relationship, with or without children, North Americans struggle to maintain fulfilling and meaningful social connections in their lives, particularly as they age (Holt-Lunstad, Smith, Baker, Harris, & Stephenson, 2015). Yet doing so is crucial to our wellbeing, for meaningful social ties and the support they provide boost our health in important ways. Indeed, an impressive body of evidence shows that social support and feeling connected helps people maintain a healthy body mass index, manage blood sugars, enhance cancer survival, reduce cardiovascular mortality, alleviate depression, decrease posttraumatic stress disorder, and improve overall mental health (Martino, Pegg, & Frates, 2015). The benefits of social contact are so extraordinary that Hallowell (1999, p. 3) endorsed the idea of prescribing social connections to patients to improve their wellbeing: "just as we need vitamin C each day, we also need a dose of the human moment—positive contact with other people."

Despite the benefits of social contact, however, social isolation pervades troublingly in contemporary society. More Canadians than ever live alone (Statistics Canada, 2012), and almost one-quarter describe themselves as lonely (Sinha, 2014). In the United States, 40% of Americans indicate they are lonely, a figure that has doubled in 30 years (Wilson & Moulton, 2010). Living alone, having few social ties, and having scarce social contact are all indicators of social isolation (Holt-Lunstad et al., 2015). By social isolation, I mean " … a lack of personal relationships with family, friends, and acquaintances on which people can fall back in case of need" (Machielse, 2015, p. 339).

Sadly, a lack of meaningful social connections results in a host of detrimental health outcomes. Abundant evidence now demonstrates individuals who are socially isolated are at risk for premature mortality (Cacioppo & Patrick, 2008). Amazingly, the detrimental consequences of social isolation compares with well-established risk factors for mortality, including lack of access to health care, poor environmental quality, lack of immunization, injury and violence, obesity, poor mental health, risky sexual behavior, sedentary activity, smoking, and substance abuse (Holt-Lunstad et al., 2015). All told, social isolation represents one of the most pressing social problems of our time, ironically in an age when connecting with others seems so easy. Even so, leisure studies remains quiet on this matter.

A review of the contents of *Leisure Sciences* reveals social isolation has garnered astonishingly little attention relative to other topics. Topical areas in which social isolation has been cited (to a greater or lesser extent) include motherhood (Trussell, 2015; Trussell & Shaw, 2009; Valtchanov, Parry, Glover, & Mulcahy, 2016), aging (Dattilo et al., 2015; Fortune & McKeown, 2016; Lyons & Dionigi, 2007; Yarnal, Chick, & Kerstetter, 2008), inner city youth (Wilson Outley & Floyd, 2002), the immigrant experience (Stodolska, 2005), women in prison (Yuen, Arai, & Fortune, 2012) and constraints (Jackson & Henderson, 1995). While this list may appear long, it represents only a small fraction of the contents of this journal. Relative to the present day concern for social isolation as a societal problem and the potential leisure holds in addressing feelings of loneliness, social isolation ought to be more visible as a major focus in our field. Research relevance means directing our attention to pressing social needs. Few needs are greater, I would argue, than the need for meaningful social contact.

With this in mind, the purpose of this contribution to the 40th anniversary issue of *Leisure Sciences* is to position social isolation as a relevant topic in our field and to offer directions for future research. To achieve this aim, I will discuss social isolation and its risk factors, the positive and negative roles leisure can play in addressing it as a social problem, and the changing nature of social isolation in North America and its implications for leisure research.

Social isolation and its risk factors

People tend to rely on those closest to themselves for support. Whether in need of help, information, a hug, or a sounding board to guide decision making, those from whom an individual can access assistance typically make up his or her core social network. The closer and stronger the connection developed, the broader the scope of support available and the greater the likelihood to receive assistance when needed (Hurlbert, Haines, & Beggs, 2000). Having access to such crucial sources of support has serious implications for our health wellbeing, for our social networks provide us with access to resources, companionship, emotional support, person-to-person contacts, social engagement, and social influence (Berkman & Glass, 2000). These forms of support are vital to our wellbeing. Nevertheless, McPherson, Smith-Lovin, and Brashears (2006) revealed the size of our confidant networks has declined over time, with a significant shift away from neighborhood and community ties to reliance on familial ties. Though the extent of the decline reported has been contested (see Fischer, 2009), social isolation still represents a growing health issue.

The difference between social isolation and loneliness requires explanation. Social isolation refers to " ... an objective situation, namely the actual absence of informal supportive relationships", whereas the loneliness describes " ... a subjective and negatively experienced discrepancy between the quality and quantity of existing relationships and a person's desires or standards with regard to relationships" (Machielse, 2015, p. 340). Loneliness, in other words, can be thought of as *subjective* social isolation. Even though (objective) social isolation can be accompanied by feelings of loneliness, not all socially isolated people feel lonely (e.g., people who have no friends, but feel a strong, imaginative connection to a celebrity). Likewise, those who feel lonely are not necessarily isolated (more on this below). Accordingly, social isolation and loneliness often correlate only weakly (Coyle & Dugan, 2012). Consider patients in a long-term care facility. They may have tremendous care and support from facility staff but still feel lonely. Similarly, despite being married with children, an individual can feel alienated from his or her spouse and family. Given these examples, loneliness is germane to our discussion because it recognizes people can be well connected, yet still *feel* isolated.

Several risk factors influence social isolation. Cognitive impairment, economic scarcity, living alone, poor health, psychological distress, and being widowed can all impair an individual's ability to build and maintain personal relationships (see Biordi & Nicholson, 2013). Moreover, specific life events, such as the death of a loved one, divorce/separation, job loss, or relocating to a new community, can reduce or suppress existing social networks (Meeuwesen, 2006a). Social skills can influence strategies used to address negative circumstances. Those with effective social skills tend to confront their problems actively and productively, while those with poor social skills tend to use passive coping strategies such as avoidance, emotional denial, and withdrawal behavior (Meeuwesen, 2006b). The latter often leads to a further withdrawal from society, which can fuel problems in other areas of life, such as addiction, debt, depression or neglected personal hygiene (McNeilly & Burke, 2002). To halt this negative trajectory, intervention is often necessary. Leisure represents one possibility.

Leisure: An antidote to social isolation?

Our field offers plenty of evidence to demonstrate the value of leisure for coping (Iwasaki & Schneider, 2003). Iwasaki and Mannell (2000) distinguished between leisure coping beliefs (i.e., drawing on leisure in times of stress) and leisure coping strategies (i.e., situation-specific coping behaviors and cognitions available through leisure). The latter, they theorized, includes leisure companionship, leisure palliative coping, and leisure mood enhancement. Adding to this literature, Kleiber, Hutchinson, and Williams (2002) surmised that leisure helps individuals adapt to negative life events by, among other things, restoring continuity with the past, serving as a vehicle for personal transformation, generating optimism about the future, and offering distraction. Leisure has the potential to serve as a catalyst to address social isolation.

Ultimately, people need a purpose to come together socially. Klinenberg (2001), for example, identified the loss of attractions that entice people out of their homes as one of the conditions that fostered social isolation among the Chicago residents who died from a short but devastating heat wave in 1995. Accordingly, social network researchers increasingly focus their attention on the role of physical space (Adams, Faust, & Lovasi, 2012), having recognized that solidarity and cooperation intensify through in-person interaction. Individuals located in close physical proximity are, not surprisingly, more likely to interact face-to-face and form connections. For this reason, Yuen and Johnson (2017, p. 295) encouraged leisure scholars to focus on third places, "public gathering places that contribute to the strength of community" as destinations for sociability. Leisure and its promise of conviviality often draw people together in physical space.

To recognize the importance of leisure in addressing negative life events, Glover and Parry (2008) argued leisure represents an important "sphere of sociability" in which people mix together, thereby inspiring the development of durable social networks. Even "episodes" of leisure that happen in work contexts (e.g., water cooler talk) play a crucial role in promoting conviviality and the possibility of forging social ties with others (Glover, Parry, & Shinew, 2005). In promoting sociability, leisure establishes itself as an attractive draw for most individuals and the starting point for social capital production.

The social capital produced as a byproduct of leisure-based social ties represents the (social) value of leisure. By social capital, I mean " ... the consequence of investment in and cultivation of social relationships allowing an individual access to resources that would otherwise be unavailable to him or her" (Glover, Shinew, & Parry, 2005, p. 87). Like other forms of capital, social capital is premised upon the notion that an investment (in social relations) will result in a return (some benefit or profit) to the individual. By building relationships, individuals accumulate the potential to draw on those relationships when needed to gain support. If social isolation is defined by a lack of personal relationships that provide access to important resources (Machielse, 2015), anything that facilitates the production of social capital ought to be perceived as a relevant solution to it. A growing body of literature within our field shows that leisure serves as an indispensable vehicle for the formation, maintenance, and sustainability of social ties and an important social lubricant for the production of social capital (Glover, 2016).

Leisure, relationship building, and social capital

Studies show leisure forges three types of relationship building from which social capital is produced as a byproduct, relationships known in the social capital literature as bonding, bridging, and linking. Bonding refers to "trusting and co-operative relations between members of a network who see themselves as being similar in terms of their shared social identity" (Szreter & Woolcock, 2004, p. 654). Routinely, researchers report how leisure draws together people who share a common identity. For example, sports bring together youth (Glover & Bates, 2006); social clubs establish a fellowship that provide access to social support (Son, Yarnal, & Kerstetter, 2010); and casual gatherings provide an emotional outlet for participants to express their feelings in a supportive environment (Broughton, Payne & Liechty, 2017). In each case, leisure enables strong ties to develop.

Leisure encourages the materialization of social connections among individuals who see themselves as different, too. *Bridging social capital* refers to "relations of respect and mutuality between people who know that they are not alike in some sociodemographic (or social identity) sense (differing by age, ethnic group, class, etc.)" (Szreter & Woolcock, 2004, p. 655). Bringing different people together is no simple task because most individuals relate best to people like themselves (McPherson, Smith-Lovin, & Cook, 2001) and will sometimes clash or withdraw if they encounter others with whom they have little, if anything, in common. Even so, leisure gives its participants permission to accept the moment, share the experience, and dispense with pre-existing social structures. Accordingly, the literature reveals leisure can bridge strangers (Glover & Filep, 2015), persons of differing abilities (Devine & Parr, 2008), racial and ethnic groups (Shinew, Glover, & Parry, 2004), among others.

Leisure also links people to other organizations/services that can assist them. Szreter and Woolcock (2004) defined linking social capital as "norms of respect and networks of trusting relationships between people who are interacting across explicit, formal or institutionalized power or authority gradients in society" (p. 655). Macnaughton (2014) described how Victoria Dreams, an organized "street soccer" program for marginalized people, assisted its participants in making links to other social services and avenues for civic engagement. Similarly, Colistra, Schmalz, and Glover (2017) found membership at a county-owned community center in the Southeastern United States made a substantial contribution to user's health and well-being by giving users access to information, resources, and services made available through partnerships and collaborations the community center had established with local organizations and institutions. In short, leisure and its provision enable individuals to forge relationships with others across institutionalized positions.

In the context of combating social isolation, relationship building, whether bonding, bridging or linking, matters because it has the potential to produce social capital and gives people access to resources they would otherwise be without. As Lin (2001) noted, social capital facilitates action. It does so, first, by enabling *expressive action* (i.e., "getting by"), otherwise known as emotional support. Leisure-based social ties assist individuals in coping with their life situations, whether dealing with infertility (see Glover & Parry, 2008) or the challenges of parenting young children (see Mulcahy, Parry, & Glover, 2010). Second, social capital facilitates *instrumental action* (i.e., "getting ahead") by giving individuals access to resources that help them advance their social position. Graham and Glover (2014), for instance, showed how visitors to dog parks share information related to pet-related care and services within the social circles they form. Third, social capital enables *collective action* (i.e., "acting together"), an effort by more than one person to improve their shared condition and achieve change through joint organization, mobilization, and negotiation. Glover (2003), for example, described how a group of neighbors targeted an abandoned lot to build a community garden to actively change the conditions of their neighborhood. Collective action in whatever form aims to advance group interests.

These potential outcomes mean any efforts to build relationships are crucial to addressing social isolation. Though leisure does not guarantee the formation of meaningful relationships, it provides a meaningful context in which to get together. Ultimately, the actual realization of social capital depends on those engaged in leisure themselves. Understanding what kind of leisure best facilitates the development healthy relationships remains an important area of future research in which leisure studies can contribute significantly to the study of social isolation.

The literature provides some hints with respect to the difference various kinds of leisure make in terms of the quality of social capital developed. Yuen and Glover (2005) distinguished between leisure that encourages people to *socialize* (i.e., interact casually) and *mobilize* (i.e., act collectively to achieve a common goal), noting the former facilitates bonding, while the latter facilitates bridging. Interestingly, they found that socializing stems from casual leisure, whereas mobilizing arises from project-based leisure. Their findings suggest the value orientation that positions serious leisure as superior to casual leisure is unfortunate (and unnecessary) because it fails to appreciate the fundamental role casual leisure plays in facilitating relationship building, maintenance, and sustainability and the production of social capital. Conceivably, serious leisure, with its emphasis on deep attention to a craft or immersion in a solitary activity, can isolate and keep its participants from engaging with others. The role of casual, project-based, and serious leisure in addressing or furthering social isolation warrants future attention in our literature.

Leisure is no panacea

Though social capital can be leveraged for positive actions, it can just as easily result in negative outcomes. In this spirit, Glover and Parry (2008) described *obstructive actions* taken by individuals, usually for fear of social sanctions, that affected their wellbeing negatively. Participants in their study of women who experienced infertility felt compelled to support their friends who had similarly struggled with infertility, but who had successfully gotten pregnant, by attending baby showers, even though their participation in such events was detrimental to their own well-being. Accordingly, Glover and Parry identified obstruction action to acknowledge the potential ill-effects of relationships and recognize peer pressure as a powerful form of social capital. Obstructive action represents a setback that keeps an individual from "getting by" or "getting ahead." Its inclusion as an outcome of social capital alerts us to the potential costs of social capital developed through our leisure-based social ties. Social capital, in short, has a dark side that can lead to further social isolation.

Clearly, leisure can facilitate poor relationships that can exacerbate a sense of isolation. Generally, the more individuals *bond* with social actors who share a similar social identity and *bridge* with others to diversify their social identities, the more social capital they have at their disposal (Putnam, 2000). Social capital does not necessarily facilitate positive outcomes/actions, however. While a strong support network is generally considered fundamental to coping with health-related issues, some relationships can be harmful. Halpern (2005) noted close relationships with abusive, depressed, or disturbed individuals have damaging effects on mental health, adding that support produces feelings of helplessness and resentment and even a greater sense of isolation when it shifts into dependence. Knowing someone is insufficient; the relationship must be supportive and positive to have beneficial impacts.

Moreover, receiving support from someone may not denote a positive relationship. An individual can receive support, but if being the recipient reflects an exchange relationship or brings with it a sense of indebtedness, such encounters may contribute to the person's loneliness (Cacioppo & Patrick, 2008). Access to considerable support from others may have nothing to do with genuine friendship. It may come at a cost or from someone other than the person with whom an individual desires to connect. Leisure researchers need to consider the quality of relationships formed through leisure and its implications for social isolation.

Leisure itself can be isolating. Passive coping strategies that incorporate solitary leisure pursuits, such as watching screens, listening to music, and spending time on a computer or mobile device can further isolate individuals by keeping them from engaging meaningfully with others (Toepoel, 2013). Putnam (2000) credited the erosion of social capital, in part, on the transformation of leisure and the wedge that technology drives between our individual interests and our collective interests. He cited the "privatization" and "individualization" our use of leisure time as disruptions to our ability to forge meaningful relationships.

Interestingly, though passive leisure can be isolating in an objective sense, those who engage in it may not necessarily *feel* lonely. Contemporary leisure forms like viewing blogs, web chat rooms, and Instagram posts offer insight into the lives of strangers and propagate new relations of presumed intimacy. Their format, Rojek (2016) explained, encourages exchanges that reward displays of personal disclosure and screen amity, exchanges that foster semi-detached, removed relationships. Connections under these circumstances are established largely in the minds of individuals without meaningful ties existing. Social capital in the form of influence can be generated by these imaginary connections. Attitudes about the environment or politics, for example, can be influenced by celebrities with whom fans imagine having a relationship (Rojek, 2017). Such "ghost ties" can create a wider sense of connection, surpassing an individual's immediate ties and narrow circle of friends. Rojek (2016) pointed out, we carry on our lives with familiar strangers, yet these individuals remain apparitions whom we never encounter and never get to know. As a result, Rojek argued people in this contemporary age live under the illusion of being connected. Leisure centered on the establishment of these superficial connections deserves more investigation in our field to determine their implications for social isolation.

Loss of community in the age of social media?

Social isolation is no new problem, but rather a phenomenon whose meaning has changed over time. Arguably, social isolation can be viewed as a by-product of modernity. In many respects, addressing social isolation drove the development of the recreation profession in North America. Originating in response to the alienating conditions of urbanization and the industrial revolution in the late 19th century, leisure was envisioned by social activists to enhance community building. Putnam's (2000) more recent observation that Americans are becoming more isolated, as evidenced by the steady decline in associational memberships, including bowling leagues and other recreational associations, drew attention to more contemporary culprits of disconnectedness such as television watching, suburban sprawl, generational changes, and pressures of time and money. Evidently, advances in communications technology represent the leading present-day offender.

Discussion so far in this paper (and in our literature) has privileged face-to-face interaction. Putnam (2000) favored face-to-face interactions in the formation of social capital. He figured connecting from a distance was more impersonal and less effective as a strategy to invest meaningfully in relationships. However, the ubiquity of communications technology in everyday life has made online connections, at the very least, complementary with "offline" connections. Parry, Glover, and Mulcahy (2013), in their exploration of a membership-based online social networking site for mothers of young children, showed how the site provided a portal for "friend-shopping" by helping users find new friends through access to profiles of members and facilitating face-to-face interactions. Face-to-face interactions combined with continued electronic correspondence to enable "friend-shipping," the building of successful friendships. These findings are similar to Cacioppo and Patrick's (2008) notion that social media can address loneliness by serving as a "way station" used to facilitate face-to-face meetings. Of course, they can also serve as a "destination" whereby those who feel lonely interact digitally with others in a non-authentic way to make themselves feel accepted, but the interactions do little to make them feel less lonely (Cacioppo & Patrick, 2008). When detached from face-to-face interactions, then, it appears online connections have the potential to be isolating. Indeed, while social media can counteract the impact of geography on facilitating social interactions, it can also take time away from other face-to-face activities.

Feeling socially isolated in an age of hyperconnectivity may seem counterintuitive. Social media/networking (SM/N) platforms, such as Snapchat, Instagram, and Facebook make it undeniably easier for people to connect socially with others, and yet North American society remains more socially disconnected than ever (McPherson et al., 2006). How can this be so? In their recent review of social isolation as a sociological construct, Parigi and Henson (2014) described how communications technology and (SM/N) make social relationships easy to establish and maintain, yet shift the meaning of social isolation from not having any friends to a process in which relationships are formed that hold little or conflicting meaning. The number of contexts and groups an individual can join has increased significantly, albeit while seemingly contributing to the overall fragmentation of society into echo chambers comprised largely of homogenous, weak ties (Parigi & Henson, 2014). Advances in communications technology and SM/N appear to enhance social connectivity at the expense of the depth of our relationships.

Expanding our number of social ties through SM/N, in particular, does not necessarily generate more meaningful connections, but rather appears to add to the cognitive and emotional costs of maintaining and sustaining those connections, to the point of creating a sense of isolation. While we may boast an impressive number of "friends" on Facebook, we may have no one important with whom to discuss matters of substance (Parigi & Henson, 2014). SM/N make it possible to connect with a seemingly boundless number of people online while remaining subjectively socially isolated.

Expanding our social connections creates a tension between our enhanced access to potential resources and social support and the costs of maintaining and sustaining those new connections. Each additional social connection we create adds a cost to maintain a new tie, especially if the tie is disconnected from our existing social circle(s). SM/N, it turns out, decreases the likelihood that our social circles intersect (Parigi & Henson, 2014). As a result, each new connection we make can diminish our quality of life as we find ourselves increasingly and virtually surrounded by people who are not meaningful friends. For these reasons, Parigi and Henson (2014) argued social isolation no longer refers to having no social connections, but rather having few, if any, *meaningful* connections. Leisure researchers interested in advancing research on social isolation ought to adapt their research to investigate this profound shift.

Admittedly, ties can shift from latent (established, inactive relationships) to embryonic (potential relationships in which exchange has yet to occur) to mobilized over time (Mariotti & Delbridge, 2012). The dynamic nature of ties necessitates the recognition that connections developed through leisure, whether on or offline, are not fixed and have the potential to change. Moreover, it requires longitudinal examinations of tie strength, a topic largely absent from our literature. Social network analyses, in particular, would be a welcome addition to leisure studies, for they would generate new insights within our field while also drawing interest from outside.

Conclusion

Leisure studies as a field and *Leisure Sciences* as our field's leading refereed journal would benefit tremendously from greater attention paid to the topic of social isolation. While sound research on social isolation does exist within our literature, the topic remains surprisingly underexamined. A more concentrated focus on social isolation would add to the relevance of our research and the impact of this journal.

Meaningful relationships with people on whom we can lean and from whom we can draw support contribute crucially to our well-being and flourishing, as scores of research findings outside of our field demonstrate. Even so, a growing epidemic of social isolation pervades, therein representing perhaps the most troubling public health risk of our time. The damaging health effects of disconnectedness, loneliness, and social isolation astonish. Comparable to obesity, smoking, and violence, a lack of meaningful social contact weakens and shortens our lives (Holt-Lunstad et al., 2015). The promise of leisure as (at least) part of the solution to this social problem stems from its ability to attract individuals to connect with others and form meaningful relationships that produce the social capital necessary to get by and get ahead in life.

Or does it? Isolating activities and superficial connections built within leisure, on and offline, reveal leisure to be part of the problem in contributing to social isolation. The new face of social isolation connected to communications technology and SM/N remains embarrassingly underexplored and ignored by our field, despite its connection to leisure behavior and its profound effects on society. Greater attention to these matters would position our field well in the future.

Leisure studies, with an expanded focus on the promise and pitfalls of leisure on social isolation, has a role in contributing to our understanding and efforts to address social isolation. What forms of leisure facilitate (un)healthy relationships? What role(s), if any, do casual, project-based, and serious leisure play in addressing or furthering social isolation? What is the quality of relationships formed through various forms of leisure? How does leisure further isolate individuals? What are the implications of face-to-face versus online forms of leisure connection? Are online leisure-based connections superficial? How do social ties, whether developed online or face-to-face, change over time? We have generated few answers to these questions in the last forty years. Going forward, we have an opportunity to produce meaningful knowledge to assist in addressing one of the most pressing social problems of our time. Let's connect the dots before our field isolates itself from this important topic.

References

Berkman, L. F., & Glass, T. (2000). Social integration, social networks, social support, and health. *Social Epidemiology, 1,* 137–173.

Biordi, D. L., & Nicholson, N. R. (2013). Social isolation. In I. M. Lubkin & P. D. Larsen (Eds.), Chronic illness: Impact and intervention (pp. 85–115). Sudbury, MA: Jones and Bartlett.

Broughton, K. A., Payne, L., & Liechty, T. (2017). An exploration of older men's social lives and well-being in the context of a coffee group. *Leisure Sciences, 39*(3), 261–276.

Cacioppo, J. T., & Patrick, W. (2008). *Loneliness: Human nature and the need for social connection.* New York, NY: W. W. Norton & Company.

Colistra, C., Schmalz, D., & Glover, T. D. (2017). The meaning of relationship building in the context of the community center and its implications. *Journal of Park and Recreation Administration, 35*(2), 37–50.

Coyle, C. E., & Dugan, E. (2012). Social isolation, loneliness and health among older adults. *Journal of Aging and Health, 24*(8), 1346–1363.

Dattilo, J., Lorek, A. E., Mogle, J., Sliwinski, M., Freed, S., Frysinger, M., & Schuckers, S. (2015). Perceptions of leisure by older adults who attend senior centers. *Leisure Sciences, 37*(4), 373–390.

Devine, M. A., & Parr, M. G. (2008). "Come on in, but not too far:" Social capital in an inclusive leisure setting. *Leisure Sciences, 30*(5), 391–408.

Faust, K., & Lovasi, G. S. (2012). Capturing context: Integrating spatial and social network analyses. *Social networks, 34*(1), 1–5.

Fischer, C. S. (2009). The 2004 GSS finding of shrunken social networks: An artifact?. *American Sociological Review, 74*(4), 657–669.

Fortune, D., & McKeown, J. (2016). Sharing the journey: Exploring a social leisure program for persons with dementia and their spouses. *Leisure Sciences, 38*(4), 373–387.

Glover, T. D. (2003). The story of the Queen Anne Memorial Garden: Resisting a dominant cultural narrative. *Journal of Leisure Research, 35*(2), 190–212.

Glover, T. D. (2016). Leveraging leisure-based community networks to access social capital. In G. Walker, D. Scott, & M. Stoldoska (Eds.), *Leisure matters: The state and future of leisure studies* (pp. 277–286). State College, PA: Venture.

Glover, T. D., & Bates, N. R. (2006). Recapturing a sense of neighbourhood since lost: Nostalgia and the formation of First String, a Community Team Inc. *Leisure Studies, 25*(3), 329–351.

Glover, T. D., & Filep, S. (2015). On kindness of strangers in tourism. *Annals of Tourism Research, 50,* 159–162.

Glover, T. D., & Parry, D. C. (2008). Friendships developed subsequent to a stressful life event: Links with leisure, social capital, and health. *Journal of Leisure Research, 40*(2), 208–230.

Glover, T. D., Parry, D. C., & Shinew, K. J. (2005). Building relationships, accessing resources: Mobilizing social capital in community garden contexts. *Journal of Leisure Research, 37*(4), 450–474.

Glover, T. D., Shinew, K. J., & Parry, D. C. (2005). Association, sociability, and civic culture: The democratic effect of community gardening. *Leisure Sciences, 27*(1), 75–92.

Graham, T., & Glover, T. D. (2014). On the fence: Dog parks in the (un)leashing of community and social capital. *Leisure Sciences, 36*(3), 217–234.

Hallowell, E. M. (1999). *Connect: 12 vital ties that open your heart, lengthen your life, and deepen your soul.* New York, NY: Simon and Schuster.

Halpern, D. (2005). *Social capital.* Cambridge, England: Polity Press.

Holt-Lunstad, J., Smith, T. B., Baker, M., Harris, T., & Stephenson, D. (2015). Loneliness and social isolation as risk factors for mortality. *Perspectives on Psychological Science, 10*(2), 227–237.

Hortulanus, R., Machielse, A., & Meeuwesen, L. (2006). *Social isolation in modern society.* New York, NY: Routledge.

Hurlbert, J. S., Haines, V. A., & Beggs, J. J. (2000). Core networks and tie activation: What kinds of routine networks allocate resources in nonroutine situations? *American Sociological Review, 65*(4), 598–618.

Iwasaki, Y., & Mannell, R. C. (2000). Hierarchical dimensions of leisure stress coping. *Leisure sciences, 22*(3), 163–181.

Iwasaki, Y., & Schneider, I. E. (2003). Leisure, stress, and coping: An evolving area of inquiry. *Leisure Sciences, 25*(2–3), 107–113.

Jackson, E. L., & Henderson, K. A. (1995). Gender-based analysis of leisure constraints. *Leisure Sciences, 17*(1), 31–51.

Kleiber, D. A., Hutchinson, S. L., & Williams, R. (2002). Leisure as a resource in transcending negative life events: Self-protection, self-restoration, and personal transformation. *Leisure Sciences, 24*(2), 219–235.

Klinenberg, E. (2001). Dying alone: The social production of urban isolation. *Ethnography, 2*(4), 501–531.

Lin, N. (2001). *Social capital: A theory of social structure and action.* Cambridge, MA: Cambridge University Press.

Lyons, K., & Dionigi, R. (2007). Transcending emotional community: A qualitative examination of older adults and masters' sports participation. *Leisure Sciences, 29*(4), 375–389.

Machielse, A. (2015). The heterogeneity of socially isolated older adults: A social isolation typology. *Journal of Gerontological Social Work, 58*(4), 338–356.

Macnaughton, J. (2014). *A goal for social inclusion* (Unpublished master's thesis). University of Victoria, Victoria, BC, Canada.

Mariotti, F., & Delbridge, R. (2012). Overcoming network overload and redundancy in interorganizational networks: The roles of potential and latent ties. *Organization Science, 23*(2), 511–528.

Martino, J., Pegg, J., & Frates, E. P. (2015). The connection prescription: Using the power of social interactions and the deep desire for connectedness to empower health and wellness. *American Journal of Lifestyle Medicine, XX*(X), 1–10.

McNeilly, D. P., & Burke, W. J. (2002). Disposable time and disposable income: Problem casino gambling behavior in older adults. *Journal of Clinical Geropsychology, 8,* 75–85.

McPherson, M., Smith-Lovin, L., & Brashears, M. E. (2006). Social isolation in America: Changes in core discussion networks over two decades. *American Sociological Review, 71*(3), 353–375.

McPherson, M., Smith-Lovin, L., & Cook, J. M. (2001). Birds of a feather: Homophily in social networks. *Annual Review of Sociology, 27*(1), 415–444.

Meeuwesen, L. (2006a). Personal competences and social isolation. In R. Hortulanus, A. Machielse, & L. Meeuwesen (Eds.), *Social isolation in modern society* (pp. 81–99). London, England: Routledge.

Meeuwesen, L. (2006b). A typology of social contacts. In R. Hortulanus, A. Machielse, & L. Meeuwesen (Eds.), *Social isolation in modern society* (pp. 37–59). London, England: Routledge.

Mulcahy, C. M., Parry, D. C., & Glover, T. D. (2010). Play-group politics: A critical social capital exploration of exclusion and conformity in mothers groups. *Leisure Studies, 29*(1), 3–27.

Parigi, P., & Henson, W. (2014). Social isolation in America. *Annual Review of Sociology, 40,* 153–171.

Parry, D. C., Glover, T. D., & Mulcahy, C. M. (2013). From "stroller-stalker" to "momancer" courting friends through a social networking site for mothers. *Journal of Leisure Research, 45*(1), 23–46.

Putnam, R. D. (2000). *Bowling alone: The collapse and revival of American community.* New York, NY: Simon & Schuster.

Rojek, C. (2016). *Presumed intimacy: Parasocial interaction in media, society and celebrity culture.* New York, NY: John Wiley & Sons.

Rojek, C. (2017). The case of Belle Gibson, social media, and what it means for understanding leisure under digital praxis. *Annals of Leisure Research,* 1–5. doi:10.1080/11745398.2017.1290142

Shinew, K. J., Glover, T. D., & Parry, D. C. (2004). Leisure spaces as potential sites for interracial interaction: Community gardens in a segregated urban area. *Journal of Leisure Research, 36*(3), 336–355.

Sinha, M. (2014). *Canadians' connections with family and friends*. Spotlight on Canadians, Ottawa, ON: Results from the General Social Survey. Retrieved from http://www.statcan.gc.ca/pub/89-652-x/89-652-x2014006-eng.htm

Son, J., Yarnal, C., & Kerstetter, D. (2010). Engendering social capital through a leisure club for middle-aged and older women: Implications for individual and community health and well-being. *Leisure Studies*, *29*(1), 67–83.

Statistics Canada. (2012). *Portrait of families and living arrangements in Canada: Families, households and marital status, 2011 Census of Population*. Ottawa, ON, Canada: Statistics Canada.

Stodolska, M. (2005). Implications of the conditioned attitude model of individual discriminatory behavior for discrimination in leisure settings. *Leisure Sciences*, *27*(1), 59–74.

Szreter, S., & Woolcock, M. (2004). Health by association? Social capital, social theory, and the political economy of public health. *International Journal of Epidemiology*, *33*(4), 650–667.

Toepoel, V. (2013). Ageing, leisure, and social connectedness: How could leisure help reduce social isolation of older people? *Social Indicators Research*, *113*(1), 355–372.

Trussell, D. E. (2015). Pinstripes and breast pumps: Navigating the tenure-motherhood-track. *Leisure Sciences*, *37*(2), 160–175.

Trussell, D. E., & Shaw, S. M. (2009). Changing family life in the rural context: Women's perspectives of family leisure on the farm. *Leisure Sciences*, *31*(5), 434–449.

Valtchanov, B. L., Parry, D. C., Glover, T. D., & Mulcahy, C. M. (2016). "A whole new world": Mothers' technologically mediated leisure. *Leisure Sciences*, *38*(1), 50–67.

Wilson, C., & Moulton, B. (2010). *Loneliness among older adults: A national survey of adults 45+*. Prepared by Knowledge Networks and Insight Policy Research. Washington, DC: American Association of Retired Persons.

Wilson Outley, C., & Floyd, M. F. (2002). The home they live in: Inner city children's views on the influence of parenting strategies on their leisure behavior. *Leisure Sciences*, *24*, 161–179.

Yarnal, C. M., Chick, G., & Kerstetter, D. L. (2008). "I did not have time to play growing up … so this is my play time. It's the best thing I have ever done for myself": What is play to older women? *Leisure Sciences*, *30*(3), 235–252.

Yuen, F., Arai, S., & Fortune, D. (2012). Community (dis)connection through leisure for women in prison. *Leisure Sciences*, *34*(4), 281–297.

Yuen, F., & Glover, T. D. (2005). Enabling social capital development: An examination of the festival of neighborhoods in Kitchener, Ontario. *Journal of Park and Recreation Administration*, *23* (4), 20–38.

Yuen, F., & Johnson, A. J. (2017). Leisure spaces, community, and third places. *Leisure Sciences*, *39* (3), 295–303.

The Serious Leisure Perspective and the Experience of Leisure

A. J. Veal

ABSTRACT

The serious leisure perspective (SLP), which divides leisure activities into three distinct forms (serious, casual, and project-based), has been developed by Robert Stebbins over the last 40 years. This article evaluates the perspective as theory and as a typology. The theory associated with the SLP concerning social worlds, identification, and optimal leisure lifestyles is found to be generally untested because It has been developed in relation to the serious leisure form only. The validity of the typology is questioned on the grounds that "seriousness" is a continuum, rather than discrete categories, and that most leisure activities can be engaged in with varying degrees of seriousness. It is proposed that the SLP be replaced by a more flexible, open research approach, the Leisure Experience Perspective, which consolidates features of the SLP and other research traditions and theoretical perspectives.

Introduction

The serious leisure perspective (SLP) is a typology of leisure activity developed and promulgated by Robert Stebbins as an ongoing project since 1974 (Stebbins, 2007, pp. 103–105). It has been documented in a series of definitive articles (Stebbins, 1982, 1997, 2005a) and a number of consolidating or stocktaking books which draw together and develop associated research and commentary by Stebbins and others (Stebbins, 1979, 1992, 2001, 2007; Elkington & Stebbins, 2014). A prodigious volume of empirical research using the perspective has been produced by Stebbins and numerous others over the years, such that it has become an influential presence in the field of leisure studies.[1] The basic feature of the SLP is that leisure activity as a whole is divided into three *forms*: serious, casual, and project-based. As shown in Figure 1, these are further divided into *types* and *subtypes*, giving a total of 29 subtypes (or 39 if volunteering is divided into subtypes in all three forms). Each of the leisure forms is characterized by a set of *distinguishing qualities, costs* and *rewards*, or *benefits* in the case of casual leisure. The types, subtypes, and activities within a leisure form therefore share a common set of distinguishing qualities, costs and rewards/benefits.

Using mostly qualitative methods, Stebbins and others have empirically confirmed associations between the indicated features and activity types/subtypes for serious leisure

---

[1] See www.seriousleisure.net/

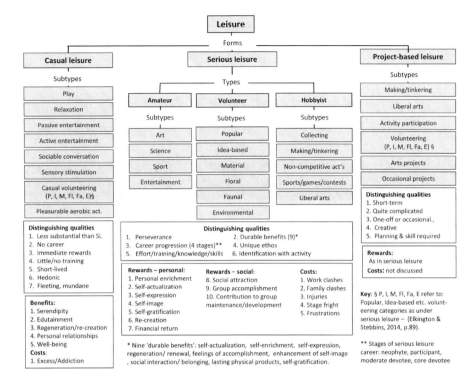

Figure 1. Serious leisure perspective: Summary.
Source: Based on Elkington & Stebbins, 2014, p. 15, with the addition of distinguishing qualities and rewards/costs, listing of project-based-occasional as a "subtype" rather than a "type" and omission of "devotee work."

activity. The same cannot be said for project-based and casual leisure activities, which have been subject to much less research, despite the latter accounting for an estimated 80% of all leisure activity (Stebbins, 2007, p. 134). Nevertheless, the claim is made that "so far as known at present, all leisure … can be classified according to one of the three forms and their several types and subtypes" (Elkington & Stebbins, 2014, p. 14). Furthermore, having been developed from a "grounded theory" process (Stebbins, 2007, p. 122), the SLP is also claimed to be an "established theory" (Elkington & Stebbins, p. 197) that "offers a classification and explanation of all leisure activities and experiences. And it accomplishes this by framing them in the social psychological, social, cultural and historical conditions in which each activity and accompanying experience take place" (Elkington & Stebbins, p. 14).

These are ambitious claims, but can they be substantiated? The analysis in this article raises considerable doubts about whether they can. First, it is argued that the theoretical constructs claimed to be underpinning the SLP as a whole are conceptually weak, with uneven empirical support. Second, it is argued that the discrete typology, which lies at the heart of the SLP, is logically unsound. It is concluded that attempts which have been made to present the SLP as an all-embracing framework for the study of leisure experiences are not helpful to the field and a looser, more eclectic approach to the study of leisure experiences would be more appropriate. The claimed theoretical credentials of the SLP are discussed first, followed by an examination of the typology itself and then some suggestions for development of the field.

The SLP as theory

Theory claims

Stebbins (2007, p. 53) claims that the SLP is a "truly integrated theoretic perspective", a "formal grounded theory" (Stebbins, 2007, p. 3), an "established theory" (Elkington & Stebbins, 2014, p. 197), and "a valid and useful explanation of human motivation, group formation, collective action, and the like" (Stebbins, 2007, p. 3). Its theoretical scope is said to range from the personal and psychological to the structural and socio-cultural (Stebbins, 2001, pp. 22–25). As one reviewer observed, Stebbins appears to be offering "a complete theory of leisure involvement" (Martin, 2008, p. 274).

While generally not as ambitious as Stebbins himself, others have also attributed significant theoretical qualities to the perspective. For example, Blackshaw (2010, p. 43) observes that serious leisure has taken leisure studies "in a new direction from other more conventional approaches which largely tend to focus their critical gaze on the dichotomy between work and leisure." Gillespie, Lefler, and Lerner (2002, p. 286) assert that the introduction of the SLP "heralded a conceptual shift in how leisure was studied." Worthington's (2006, p. 21) view is that, with the advent of serious leisure, "the very idea of 'leisure' was turned upside down," while, for Dilley and Scraton (2010, p. 125) it constituted a "significant theoretical development." Even commentators who suggest substantial change in the perspective endorse its theoretical status. Shen and Yarnal (2010, p. 165) refer to "serious leisure theory" and suggest that Stebbins has provided the "basis for the primary theoretical development in serious leisure." Gallant, Arai, and Smale (2013, p. 92) see serious leisure as a "theoretical development … uniquely formed within leisure studies" which "stands as one of the most significant concepts shaping leisure research over the last 30 years." Researchers who make use of the SLP in their empirical work often explicitly adopt it as a "theory" (e.g., Bartram, 2001, p. 5; Green & Jones, 2005, p. 166; Kane & Zink, 2004, p. 342; Shinew & Parry, 2005, p. 370; Heley & Jones, 2013, p. 277), a "theoretical framework" (e.g., Frew, 2006; Gravelle & Larocque, 2005, p. 46), or a "foundation" (Butler, 2010, p. iii).

A very different view of the SLP is that it is not theoretical at all but merely typological and descriptive. For example, a reviewer of one of Stebbins' books suggested that readers might find the SLP "overly taxonomic" in that "the delineations Stebbins makes between types of leisure careers are often descriptive, lacking in theoretical richness and depth" (Puddephatt, 2007, p. 1). Breeze (2013, p. 24) describes the SLP as "overly descriptive." Jones (2006, p. 57) argues that a reorientation of the perspective around the concept of social identity would make it possible "not only to *describe* serious leisure activity, but also to *explain* many aspects of serious leisure behavior" (emphasis added), implying that the SLP in its current form is only descriptive, not explanatory. Arguably still pertinent after more than 20 years is Hamilton-Smith's (1993, p. 12) observation that "perhaps Stebbins and others have devoted too much attention to the definition and description of serious leisure rather than its dynamics over time."

Theory is commonly distinguished from mere description on the basis of the criterion that it explains or offers understanding (Charmaz, 2006, pp. 125–128). Three groups of theoretical propositions can be identified in the SLP literature. The first group can be seen as complementary to the perspective and the second as intrinsic, while the third arises from critiques and can be seen as theory deficit. These are discussed in turn below.

Theory content: Complementary

The latest consolidating book includes a chapter on "The serious leisure perspective in the social sciences" which "explores the place of the SLP in, and its contribution to, social science theory" (Elkington & Stebbins, 2014, p. 39). It briefly discusses a number of topics, namely time; gender; the body; ethnicity; disability; inclusion, exclusion, and social class; social capital; consumption; quality of life; well-being; and nonprofit studies. Of these topics, only *well-being* arises in relation to intrinsic theory, and is discussed further below. Further linkages and applications are discussed in seven chapters devoted, respectively, to: tourism and events; consumption; arts, science and heritage administration; library and information science; therapeutic recreation; leisure education, life course and lifelong learning; and deviant leisure. These two sets of discussions explore a wide range of themes, some of which are central to leisure studies generally, but for the most part they remain external to the SLP (Stebbins, 2012b, p. 4), perhaps performing the function of "framing" the three SLP leisure forms as noted above. There is little sign of their impact on the parameters of the SLP, for example, in the form-specific lists of distinguishing qualities or costs/rewards.

A number of approaches to the study of the leisure experience, which can be seen as relevant to the SLP and as having theoretical as well as empirical ramifications, have been treated in a less systematic way in the SLP literature, where they tend to be ignored or considered as subsidiary to, or components of, the SLP or, at best, as complementary to it. They include the following.

- *Needs-based* research of Tinsley and colleagues (e.g., Tinsley & Eldredge, 1995) is based on the proposition that leisure experience satisfies needs, but it does not feature in the SLP literature.
- *Benefits-based* work by Driver and colleagues (e.g., Driver & Bruns, 1999; Driver, Tinsley, & Manfredo, 1991) merits only a brief mention in Stebbins (2007, p. 23).
- *Commitment* (Buchanan, 1985; Goff, Fick, & Oppliger, 1997; Mannell, 1993; Shamir, 1988; Tomlinson, 1993), is recognized by Stebbins (2007, p. 2) as an "important attitude" in serious leisure and as one of its "most profound consequences" (p. 71), but it is ignored in the latest consolidating book (Elkington & Stebbins, 2014).
- *Specialization* is founded on the work of Bryan (1977, 2008) and was developed over approximately the same time period as the SLP (see Cole & Scott, 1999; Scott & Shafer, 2001; Scott, 2012; Tsaur & Liang, 2008). However, it is viewed by Stebbins (2005b, 2012a; Elkington & Stebbins, 2014, p. 25) as just a version of his conception of a serious leisure career. It arises in the later discussion of the SLP as typology.
- *Constraints* research provides insights into the process of seeking access to leisure activity and has been shown to complement serious leisure concepts, both generally (Kennelly, Moyle, & Lamont, 2013; Lamont, Kennelly, & Wilson, 2012; Lyu & Oh, 2015; McQuarrie & Jackson, 1996) and in relation to women (Dilley & Scraton, 2010; Jackson & Henderson, 1995). However, while Stebbins (2007, p. 15; 2016a) admits that the construct is in some way associated with costs in the SLP, it is not mentioned in the latest consolidating book (Elkington & Stebbins, 2014).
- *Enduring involvement* has been extensively researched in relation to consumer behavior and applied to leisure experiences (Havitz & Dimanche, 1990; Jun, Kyle, & Vlachopoulos, 2012; Kyle & Chick, 2002; Lee & Scott, 2009; McIntyre, 1989) but had merited only a footnote in the SLP literature (Stebbins, 2007, p. 23, n. 5) until a recent discussion of "the seriousness dimension of involvement" (Stebbins, 2014, pp. 32–34).

These approaches are revisited in the concluding section of this article.

Theory content: Intrinsic

Three theoretical constructs identifiable in the SLP literature can be considered intrinsic to the perspective. Two of them arise from serious leisure distinguishing qualities, namely *social worlds* and *identification with the activity*; these are discussed below. The other four distinguishing qualities of serious leisure and those related to casual and project-based leisure are not presented in the SLP literature as having substantive theoretical dimensions. The third construct examined below, *motivation*, is related to the rewards system and can be seen as the core theoretical construct of the perspective.

The issue addressed here is the extent to which these theoretical constructs contribute to the SLP project by explaining the distinction among serious, casual, and project-based leisure forms and the extent to which they have been tested empirically. Three themes recur in this review: that SLP analysis is often focused more on description and classification than on theory development; that features presented in the SLP context as associated exclusively with the serious leisure form can often also be seen to be, to a greater or lesser extent, features of the casual leisure form; and that empirical testing of theoretical propositions is uneven, due particularly to the lack of comparative research on casual leisure.

Social worlds/tribes

The concept of *social worlds*, initially discussed in detail in Stebbins (2001, pp. 7–9) and based on the work of Unruh (1980), is incorporated into the SLP as a feature of the serious leisure distinguishing quality of a *unique ethos*. Serious leisure activities are said to be characterized by the existence of unique social worlds, while both serious and casual leisure are characterized by Maffesoli's (1996) related concept of modern *tribes* (Stebbins, 2007, p. 64). The similarity of the concept of social world to subculture is recognized by Stebbins (2001, p. 8), and he notes that it is therefore possible to "logically speak about ... social stratification in social worlds." However, rather than this leading to an opening up of the analysis to explore links with the rich cultural studies tradition in leisure studies and wider social systems of stratification, such as class, he steers his discussion inwards to consideration of the distinction between subcategories of serious leisure participants, namely *participants* and *devotees*. Furthermore, in Stebbins' (2007, p. 64) discussion of tribes, he develops his own three-fold typology arranged on a *complexity* continuum, with *social worlds* added at the most complex end, in a procrustean exercise to align the concepts of tribes and social worlds with SLP categories. Casual leisure, it seems, is associated only with tribes, while serious leisure is associated with both tribes and social worlds (Stebbins, 2007, p. 64). However, there is no evidence in the SLP literature of the distinctions between tribes and social worlds having been explored empirically. The concept of tribe is not mentioned in the latest consolidating book (Elkington & Stebbins, 2014), so the opportunity to engage with recently researched active dimensions of the behavior of modern tribes (e.g., Cova, Kuznets, & Shankar, 2007) is missed.

Identification

Serious leisure participants' *identification with the activity* is listed as the sixth distinguishing quality of serious leisure and "revolves around the preceding five" (Stebbins, 2007, p. 12). If serious leisure participants are found to be particularly motivated by the desire to create or confirm an identity, this would lend a potentially dynamic quality to the SLP in contrast to its relatively static, taxonomic qualities. Stebbins himself has written little on identification, and in the recent consolidating books it is defined only loosely, being summarized in less than ten lines (Stebbins, 2007, pp. 12–13; Elkington & Stebbins, 2014, p. 19). Furthermore, he makes no reference to the extensive theoretical literature on identity generally (e.g., Giddens, 1991) or as related to leisure activity (e.g., Glasser, 1973; Haggard & Williams, 1992). Nevertheless, qualitative empirical research (e.g., Anderson & Taylor, 2010; Baldwin & Norris, 1999; Gibson, Willming, & Holdnak, 2002; Jones, 2000) has confirmed the relationship with serious leisure activity. Jones (2006) has even argued, based on evidence from research on sport fans, that the SLP should be focused primarily on identification, but this suggestion has been ignored by Stebbins, despite apparent support for the idea in his own quantitative *structural model of serious leisure* (Heo, Lee, Kim, & Stebbins, 2012). It is claimed, in contrast, that identification is not associated with the casual leisure form since the latter is "too fleeting, mundane and commonplace to become the basis for a distinctive identity for most people" (Elkington & Stebbins, 2014, p. 19), but no specific empirical evidence is offered to support this assertion. However, the use of the word "most" introduces a note of ambivalence, and empirical studies such as those of Brown (2007) and Shen and Yarnal (2010) have indeed found that identification with an activity can be as important for casual participants as it is for serious participants. As with social worlds, therefore, identification has not been shown to be exclusively a distinguishing characteristic of the serious form of leisure.

Motivation

Theory concerning the individual's *motivation to participate* is arguably the most central to the SLP. It is, however, not linked with the distinguishing qualities of the leisure forms but with the rewards system. It has three components: the *profit hypothesis*, the *drive for rewards*, and the *pursuit of an optimal leisure lifestyle*.

The profit hypothesis states that the decision to initiate and continue participation in a serious leisure activity involves a balancing of the rewards experienced and costs incurred, with participation continuing as long as the former outweigh the latter (Elkington & Stebbins, 2014, p.19). This hypothesis did not arise from the grounded theory work associated with the SLP but from the starting point of Homans' (1974) general theory of social behavior (Stebbins, 1992, p. 93). As such, the process is also likely to apply to casual and project-based leisure and to work and virtually all human behavior. It is, for example, at the core of economic demand/consumption theory, with the term "utility" used in place of "rewards."

However, the primary aim of SLP empirical work has not been just to test the proposition that rewards exceed costs for participants, which would be somewhat trivial, but to identify and describe the particular rewards and costs involved for the different leisure forms. While considerable effort has been expended by Stebbins and others in compiling and confirming the relevant lists of rewards and costs, the result remains a basically descriptive exercise, as shown in the "typological map" in Figure 1. However, the concept of rewards gains theoretical significance in the SLP in light of a second proposition, that the goal of serious leisure participation is "the drive to experience the rewards of a given leisure activity" (Elkington & Stebbins, 2014, p. 20). Participation in serious leisure is therefore viewed as a form of goal-directed behavior. It might be expected, however, that this would also apply to the other two leisure forms. This is briefly indicated for project-based leisure (Elkington & Stebbins, p. 31) but only implied for casual leisure (Elkington & Stebbins, p. 28).

Given that many possible leisure activities are likely to offer the individual an excess of rewards over costs, the question arises as to the process by which individuals choose a set of activities from the array on offer. An explanation of this is offered in the third piece of the motivation theory, the search for an *optimal leisure lifestyle*. This involves the pursuit of one or more serious leisure activities, "complemented by judicious amounts of casual leisure or project-based leisure or both" (Stebbins, 1998; Elkington & Stebbins, 2014, p. 30). Serious leisure is seen as an essential ingredient of an optimal leisure lifestyle while casual and/or project-based leisure are complementary. If this were found to be the case, then serious leisure would clearly be a theoretically and practically significant concept and the major part of the theoretical work of the SLP would lie in the exploration of the optimal leisure lifestyle phenomenon. However, this task has been neglected, both empirically and conceptually, particularly because of the emphasis given to empirical exploration of the "distinguishing qualities," which play no part in the motivation theory.

The concept of an optimal leisure lifestyle takes us into the age-old philosophical debate on the role and nature of leisure in the "good life." This is notably exemplified by the Leisure Aristoteleans (Van Moorst, 1982), a source which has been acknowledged by Stebbins (1997, p. 117; 2007, p. 101). For a sociological approach to studying this issue, however, suitable social variables are required to serve as criteria for *optimality*. Three are mentioned by Stebbins, namely the realization of "human potential" and the enhancement of "quality of life and well-being" (Elkington & Stebbins, 2014, p. 30). Another variable used in this context is "life satisfaction" (Kim, Dattilo, & Heo, 2011; Mannell, 1993). Of these variables, only well-being is pursued in what follows since it is given most attention in the SLP literature.

Stebbins' treatment of the concept in the SLP schema is, however, inconsistent. For example, well-being is not identified as one of the specified rewards of serious leisure, but it *is* a benefit of casual leisure (Elkington & Stebbins, 2014, pp. 29–30). On the other hand, it is declared to be 'an *important by-product* of serious leisure' (Elkington & Stebbins, 2014, pp. 47–48, emphasis added) although, because of some of serious leisure's negative aspects, there is apparently no 'automatic link' between the two. Empirical testing is sparse. It was referred to in relation to optimal leisure lifestyle in an empirical study of serious sports participants (Stebbins, 2005c), in which it was found that casual leisure "contributed to overall well-being" as it was used by respondents to "optimally round out their use of free time" (Elkington & Stebbins, 2014, p. 30). In another study of members of hobbyist and voluntary groups (Stebbins, 2005d), well-being was invoked indirectly when respondents were deemed to be living optimal leisure lifestyles because they reported being "generally satisfied" with their present set of serious and casual leisure activities. However, the samples in these two studies included only people who were engaging in serious leisure activity, so the implied null hypothesis that an optimal leisure lifestyle is not achievable in the absence of serious leisure could not be tested. Parker, Hamilton-Smith, and Davidson (1993, p. 16), however, identified a number of subjects who did not engage in any serious leisure activity and raised, but did not answer, the question whether their leisure lives, and by inference their whole lives, should be evaluated as "deprived or inadequate in some way." Without reference to specific empirical evidence, Stebbins (2005c, p. 119) seems to be in no doubt about this when he declares that "many people seem to suffer from a spiritual malaise that their free time, filled exclusively with casual leisure as it is, is only minimally interesting, marginally exciting, if not boring." However, more than 30 years after the introduction of the leisure lifestyle idea, although not the precise terminology (Stebbins, 1982, p. 253), he has recently admitted that no one "has yet carried out a properly controlled study expressly designed to ascertain whether long-term involvement in a form of serious leisure actually leads to significant and enduring increases in feelings of well-being" (Elkington & Stebbins, 2014, p. 48). The question of the optimal leisure lifestyle therefore remains unfinished business for the SLP, despite its key significance for the framework. If the criterion for optimality is to be well-being, then this complex concept requires careful consideration (see, e.g., Diener, 2000; Heo, Lee, McCormick, & Pederson, 2010; OECD, 2013), but less than a page is devoted to its discussion in the latest consolidating book (Elkington & Stebbins, 2014, pp. 47–48).

The concept of "leisure lifestyle" merits some attention in its own right. A person's leisure lifestyle can be presumed to exist within a broader lifestyle. Lifestyle has been defined as "the distinctive pattern of personal and social behaviour characteristic of an individual or a group" (Veal, 1993, p. 247), with behavior including consumption activity; leisure; work (paid or unpaid); civic and religious activity; and activities involved in relationships with partners, family, relatives, friends, neighbors, and colleagues. Arguably, most people seek to optimize their *lifestyles*, with the leisure component being of varying significance. The optimality of the *leisure* component of lifestyle is likely to be contingent on the nature and relative importance of other domains of life, for example, work and family (Adler, 1996; Anderson, 2011; Lamont et al., 2012; Super, 1980). Mannell's (1993) exploration of the beneficial role of "high investment" (equivalent to serious) leisure activities in the lifestyles of retired people offers a baseline study, since his subjects have no paid work commitments and relatively minimal family responsibilities. For other age-groups, however, non-leisure domains of life could be so demanding that an optimal lifestyle might be one that does not include serious leisure. As Hutchinson and Kleiber (2005) establish, when people are feeling vulnerable or stressed it is often casual rather than serious leisure activity which is vital in enabling them to cope. It is also possible to imagine someone engaged in a range of activities, such as regular exercise activity, attendance at a range of cultural events, reading books, listening to a range of music, and socializing, which could reasonably be deemed to collectively constitute an optimal leisure lifestyle but which would not include any activity meeting the criteria for serious leisure. This could apply to people during certain phases of their lives and to some during the whole of their lives. It follows that a lack of serious leisure in a person's life need *not* necessarily result in a "spiritual malaise."

Intrinsic theory: Conclusions

A consistent feature of these intrinsic theoretical offerings of the SLP is that, having generally been developed almost exclusively in the context of empirical research on single serious leisure activities, their treatment in relation to leisure as a whole, which the SLP is claimed to encompass, is deficient, in both theoretical and empirical terms. The thesis of the SLP involves the proposition that social world/tribal experiences, identification with an activity, and contributing essential features of an optimal leisure lifestyle are exclusive qualities of a defined list of serious leisure activity subtypes, whereas they are potentially features of all leisure activities to a greater or lesser extent. Such a proposition can be advanced in relation to numerous other theoretical/analytical constructs used in leisure studies, such as those mentioned in the discussion of complementary theory above, namely: needs; benefits; commitment; specialization; constraints; and involvement. Any leisure activity experience can be assessed in terms of the salience of such constructs. This analysis leads to the conclusion that the presence or absence of "seriousness" is not necessarily the key organizing feature of leisure activity and experience as claimed in the SLP. Leisure is multidimensional and seriousness, with its specified list of supporting qualities/costs/rewards, is just one dimension. This proposition is further explored in the examination of the SLP as typology below and in the conclusions.

Theory deficit

Given Stebbins' (2001, pp. 22–25) claim that the SLP encompasses structural and sociocultural theory, a rare example of critical commentary in the leisure studies literature should be considered. This is the observation by Rojek (2000, p. 19), supported by Blackshaw (2010,

p. 43), that the SLP provides "no basis for regarding leisure as a lever for social change." Here social change refers primarily to relationships at the macro-societal level. This claim could have been partially countered in the early days of the serious leisure project when its central *raison d'être* was that serious leisure could play a role in response to, if not as a lever for, social change in the form of the widely anticipated work-time-reduced future (Stebbins, 1982, pp. 251–254; 1992, pp. 1–3). The pursuit of serious leisure was proposed as "the remedy to help solve the social problem of meaningless empty leisure" (Stebbins, 1992, p. 126); it was seen as being poised to solve a looming societal problem. The theme persisted into the 1990s and beyond in the context of an anticipated "leisure age" (Stebbins, 1998, p. 129) or "job-reduced future" (Stebbins, 2001, p. 147) based on the more dystopian postwork ideas of Rifkin (1995) and Aronowitz and DiFazio (1994). However, in recent SLP writings, in an era of longer working hours, "time-squeeze," and work-life balance problems for some and growing job-insecurity for others, the role of serious leisure, if any, in this changing social context is not addressed.

Social change is also a concern of Kuentzel (2012) in his comparison of serious leisure and recreation specialization. One of his arguments is that serious leisure is incapable of dealing with social change because of its structural-functional nature, in contrast to recreation specialization which can "accommodate critical theories of leisure behavior" (p. 376). In fact, both recreation specialization and the SLP are potentially multiparadigmatic. However, while Stebbins (1992, p. 133) distances the SLP from the "macro-sociological claims of the Marxists," downplays the significance of class issues (Elkington & Stebbins, 2014, pp. 44–45), and believes that "serious leisure can contribute significantly to communal and even societal integration" (Stebbins, 2001, p. 152), the perspective is not *necessarily* intrinsically conservative. For example, Blackshaw and Crabbe (2004, p. 51) see serious leisure as being a particularly suitable categorization for some forms of "leisure and styles of engagement that have otherwise been seen as 'unproductive' or 'deviant,'" such as certain youth subcultures. Furthermore, inasmuch as the SLP is typically focussed on group activity, Rojek (1999, p. 87), while not using the terminology of serious leisure, has noted that historically in Britain, "art clubs, choir groups, drama groups, Bible and poetry classes and rambling associations all functioned as conduits for the exchange and development of disaffected and oppositional values."

Kuentzel's brief comments have another dimension that should be highlighted. Basically, he views the SLP as a closed and static system, in contrast to the open and dynamic nature of recreation specialization. As suggested by the comment quoted earlier from Hamilton-Smith (1993, p. 12) and Breeze's (2013) frustrations with the SLP in regard to the changing environment of roller-derby, it is possibly the overconcern with typology-related description and the definitional tasks of the SLP which has resulted in a neglect of the issue of societal change and changes in the nature and social status of activities. More broadly, while Stebbins (2001, p. 24) has claimed that history is part of the SLP and has recognized that application of the SLP to the contrasting and changing conditions and cultures of developing countries is a challenge (Elkington & Stebbins, 2014, pp. 203–205), historical and broader cultural traditions, do not feature in its key parameters.

The SLP as typology

Our main concern is with the nature and validity of the discrete three-form leisure activity typology at the heart of the SLP. Stebbins himself sowed seeds of doubt about this format in his first definitive paper on serious leisure published more than 30 years ago, when he stated:

seriousness and casualness ... are merely poles of a complicated dimension along which individuals may be ranked by their degrees of involvement in a particular activity. Hence, a more sophisticated, research-informed construct will likely abandon eventually this primitive categorical terminology for terminology conveying continuousness. (Stebbins, 1982, p. 255)

Stebbins repeated this observation in 1992 (p. 6), but while the idea of a continuum of leisure experiences associated with the same activity was being pursued within other research frameworks, such as specialization (e.g., Kuentzel & Heberlein, 1997) and involvement (Havitz & Dimanche, 1997), it was not followed up in serious leisure for some decades. Shen and Yarnal (2010) identified a number of serious leisure studies which had failed to confirm the dichotomous (serious/casual) nature of the phenomenon, or the exclusive identification of individual activities with specific SLP forms. It was found that single leisure activities could engender a mixture of casual and serious experiences of varying intensity. In a study of participation in a single genre of dance, Brown (2007) found that some participants fitted into the casual category and some into the serious category, some fell between the two, and distinctive subgroups were found among both casual and serious participants. Studying a range of activities, Parker et al. (1971) introduced a *partly serious* category, while Sieghaler and O'Dell (2003) divided serious golf participants into four groups, including a *social* group whose participation patterns seemed decidedly casual in nature.

Shen and Yarnal's (2010) own quantitative empirical study of members of a social club reported a range of 'serious' and 'casual' experiences. They therefore concluded that, rather than classifying an *activity* into a serious/casual *dichotomy*, their own and others' serious leisure studies were actually locating *experiences* on a serious/casual *continuum*. Other serious leisure studies have supported these findings, with participants in the same activity being found to be enjoying a mix of serious and casual experiences. These have included sport fans (Jones, 2000; Gibson et al., 2002), participants in athletic events (Derom & Taks, 2011), gun collectors and skydivers (Anderson & Taylor, 2010), and bridge players (Scott & Godbey, 1992). Such studies can be said to have contributed to the grounded theory-based evolution of the SPL, but they are ignored in the latest consolidating book (Elkington & Stebbins, 2014): of the studies mentioned in this and the previous paragraph, only that of Sieghaler and O'Dell (2003) is referenced and then only in relation to subdivision of the serious leisure form into career-related categories.

On reflection, however, establishing that one leisure activity can be experienced in different ways by different participants at the same time and by the same person at different times, does not require the prism of the SLP and its prescribed program of detailed empirical study. The simple proposition is expressed in Stebbins' own comment: "The dabbling of a child on the piano (casual leisure) may lead to a serious leisure goal of becoming an amateur musician (serious leisure) on the instrument" (Elkington & Stebbins, 2014, p. 4). He might also have added that if the child were to embark on a program of tuition to achieve a certain level of competency at piano playing, this would be a project-based leisure exercise that could enable the child to continue to play the piano as a casual or serious leisure activity in the future. Stebbins (2012a, p. 373; 2014, p. 33) also gives examples of activities such as tennis, bird-watching, swimming, and piano-playing in which some people may "forever dabble" (the casual leisure form), even though they are "capable of being pursued seriously." This idea is reinforced by common usage of the term "serious" (Stebbins, 2007, p. 121): to "take an activity seriously" implies that the same activity can also be participated in as not-seriously, that is, casually. As Shen and Yarnal (2010, p. 165) put it, "serious and casual leisure pursuits can be found in practically any activity." Yet formal presentations of the SLP continue to be present seriousness as a form-specific typology rather than a continuum (e.g., Stebbins, 2015a, p. 16; 2015b, p. 13; 2016b).

Two technical features of the SLP indicate the multiform nature of activities and so undermine its internal consistency. First, even in formal presentations of the perspective, as in Figure 1, there are activity subtypes that appear in more than one leisure form: *volunteering* and *entertainment* both appear in all three forms, while *liberal arts* and *making /tinkering* appear in two forms. On the other hand, the obviously multiform nature of the key leisure activity of sport is hidden by idiosyncrasies of subtype definitions and terminology. Conversely, there are "rewards" which are common to both serious and casual leisure, namely "regeneration/re-creation"/"re-creation," and "personal relationships"/"social attraction."

Second, while the procedures for allocating an activity-experience to an SLP form are not spelled out in detail in the SLP literature, if some reasonable assumptions are made they point to uncertainties. Thus, considering the six distinguishing qualities of serious leisure, it seems unlikely that empirical work to assess their salience in a given leisure participation situation would always produce clear yes/no responses. As some of the SLP empirical research demonstrates, the strength of association between a distinguishing quality and an activity-experience varies from activity to activity, from situation to situation and from individual to individual. Some, situations or individual experiences of the same activity are likely to emerge as more serious than others, supporting the idea of a continuum.

Two other contributions to the serious leisure literature support the idea that leisure experiences lie on a continuum. First, Scott (2012) proposed a "marriage" between the SLP and recreation specialization, a field of study which, as noted above, has also developed over the last four decades and, since its inception, has been based on the idea of a continuum of experience (Lee & Scott, 2013; Scott & Shafer, 2001). In making this proposal, Scott (2012, p. 368) observed: "There is a diversity of commitment and seriousness within virtually all leisure activities" and he also coined the term "SL-CL continuum." In a response to these comments Stebbins (2012a, p. 372), while not accepting the marriage proposal, endorsed the idea of closer cross-fertilization with recreation specialization ideas, and seemed to accept the continuum concept, although its validity had "some limitations" (p. 373). He declared that "the casual leisure-serious leisure (CL-SL) (sic) continuum as it is called these days has a reasonably long history." However, the history he refers to is not of a continuum covering all leisure forms but rather his own and other researchers' subdivision of serious leisure participants into career-related subcategories: neophyte, participant, moderate devotee, and core devotee. The main limitation described is that "movement along the CL-SL continuum is by no means inevitable" (p. 373). He refers to the example of those people who "forever dabble" (i.e., participate in casual mode) in activities which can also be engaged in with a serious mode, as noted above. A second example is the converse, that in the case of activities requiring considerable up-front skills, participants may miss the dabbling-neophyte stages altogether. There are two problems with this argument. First, proponents of the use of continua in analyzing leisure experience do not suggest that all participants must *inevitably* move along it in some standard way. Indeed, Scott and Shafer (2001, p. 319), in discussing the recreation specialization continuum, observe that progression along the continuum "is not a typical career path pursued by recreation participants." Thus, while it is possible to classify participants according to varying levels or types of skill, experience, and commitment and place them at a point on a continuum, how they get to that point and where they proceed from there, if anywhere, are likely to vary across individuals, activities, and contexts. Second, Stebbins seems to ignore the point, made above, that if some people can be "forever dabblers" in activities that can also be engaged in seriously, then this places such participation on a common continuum. For example, the activity of playing football is *neither* a casual activity *nor* a serious activity; it can be participated in in either mode. Arguably, this is the case for most leisure activities. Stebbins (2014, p. 34) comes very close to acknowledging this in a recent graphic, in which casual leisure/dabbling and project-based leisure form an antecedent stage of the "SLP involvement scale."

The second additional contribution to the move to introduce a continuum to the SLP is the introduction of quantification. This involved the development of the Serious Leisure Inventory and Measure (SLIM) scale by a group of researchers of which Stebbins was a member (Gould, Moore, McGuire, & Stebbins, 2008). A comparable scale, combined with items relating to specialization, was developed independently by Tsaur and Liang (2008). These scales were based on a number of items (attitude statements) corresponding to the serious leisure distinguishing qualities, which were scored by participants using a Likert-type scale. The SLIM scale was utilized in further development of the quantification of the SLP in the form of the *structural model of serious leisure* which, introduced by another team of which Stebbins was a member (Heo et al., 2012), modeled the correlational links among serious leisure distinguishing qualities as variables. As Shen and Yarnal (2010, p. 166) point out, the use of a scale "inadvertently defies the dichotomous SL-CL conception by constructing a tool that allows for explicitly assessing the degrees to which the six purported SL dimensions may be experienced." While the SLIM scale and the structural model are confined to the serious leisure form only, the study conducted to verify the scale (Gould et al., 2008) raised the question: Is a low score on one or more serious leisure qualities an indication of casualness? A further question that might be asked is: why could not a version of these tools also be developed for casual leisure? Then, in line with the idea of a continuum spanning both serious and casual leisure, the possibility arises that a combined scale and a single model covering all three forms might be developed. Such possibilities are, however, not mentioned in the most recent discussion of future developments of the SLP (Elkington & Stebbins, 2014, pp. 197–207).

The above discussions of the SLP do not include consideration of project-based leisure. However, since it is described as "capable of generating many of the rewards experienced in serious leisure" but "does not demand long-term commitment" (Elkington & Stebbins, 2014, p. 31), it can be seen as "serious leisure lite," implicitly lending support to the continuum idea. It is therefore not given separate attention as a distinct form in the following discussion.

Given these significant developments, dating back to at least 2008 and seemingly endorsed by Stebbins, it is puzzling to find that in a recent statement on developments in the SLP since 2007 there is no mention of the existence of the SL-CL continuum, the SLIM scale, or the structural model (Stebbins, 2015c). This omission occurs in the preface to the paperback edition of the 2007 consolidating book in which the development of the SLIM scale had been keenly anticipated (Stebbins, 2007, p. 36; 2015, p. 36). The developments are also ignored in the latest consolidating book (Elkington & Stebbins, 2014). In the latter case it is possible that such matters were considered too advanced for what is designed as a student textbook, but they are not referred to even in further reading lists or in the final chapter on the future of the perspective. Stebbins (2014, pp. 31–33) acknowledges the CL-SL continuum in a recent book on careers in leisure, but this acknowledgement does not appear in the opening chapter devoted to the standard typological presentation of the SLP (pp. 3–27), so the incompatibility between the two approaches is not addressed. Meanwhile, empirical studies continue to be published using the dichotomy form of the SLP, without any reference to these continuum-related developments.

The contributors discussed above have tended not to follow their arguments to their logical conclusions, which would threaten the distinctiveness of the SLP. Shen and Yarnal

(2010,x p. 177), while using challenging terminology in the title of their paper ("blowing open the serious leisure-casual leisure dichotomy") and being quite critical of the SLP in general, are essentially reformist, describing their contribution as "an effort to advocate an alternative conception that bridges the SL-CL dichotomy." Scott (2012), while equally critical of the dichotomous nature of the SLP, nevertheless proposes a "marriage" between the SLP and his preferred framework, recreation specialization. The SLIM proposals themselves contain the seeds of a root-and-branch reform of the SLP through consideration of the implications of low scores, but these appear not to have been followed up in the eight years since publication. These analyses are presented as contributions to the further development of the SLP, but they are potentially more fundamental than that.

The discussions establish that, with the casual-serious couplet viewed as a continuum rather than two separate concepts, and with participation in virtually any leisure activity being seen as possible in varying degrees of seriousness or casualness, the notion of distinct lists of leisure activity subtypes labeled "serious," "casual," and "project-based"—as summarized in Figure 1—is not appropriate. It further follows that the three lists of distinguishing qualities could also each be seen as a continuum and be combined into a single consolidated list of qualities applicable, to a greater or lesser extent, to any leisure activity.

It would then follow that the same process of consolidation could be applied to costs/rewards. In fact, the difference between "distinguishing qualities" and "costs/rewards" is hard to sustain. The obvious illustration of this is that the second distinguishing quality of serious leisure consists of nine "durable *benefits*" that are almost identical to its "rewards." Elkington and Stebbins (2014, p. 20) explain that rewards are "antecedent conditions" for individuals deciding whether or not to participate, while durable benefits are "outcomes" for actual participants. A cursory examination of the two lists reveals that they could all, to a greater or lesser extent, be both antecedents *and* outcomes. This parallels the SERVQUAL consumer research approach comparing consumers' *anticipation of satisfaction* prior to purchase of a good or service with *actual satisfaction* during or following consumption (Williams, 1998).

The above analysis has implications for the core structure of the SLP. The discrete typology of activity subtypes disappears. A consolidated list of the 39 distinguishing qualities, costs, and rewards nevertheless remains a useful list of potential features of leisure activity-experiences. They are, however, no longer form-specific but are applicable, with varying degrees of saliency and intensity, to any leisure activity-experience. This could be studied either qualitatively or quantitatively or both. In quantitative terminology, any one person's activity-experience would be assessed, or scored, and would occupy a unique position in a multidimensional conceptual space. Some clustering of individuals with similar profiles might be found, possibly along a seriousness or some other continuum. Based on such a scenario, research on the seriousness dimension of leisure would no longer be classificatory but would be qualitative, descriptive and comparative, as much of it is, in practice, already.

Conclusions

The conclusions of the above theoretical and typological reviews of the SLP are similar: the discrete activity typology and associated form-specific distinguishing qualities and costs/rewards are not a valid representation of the leisure experience domain.

Lest this be viewed as an entirely negative exercise, however, it is appropriate to consider a potential way forward regarding the study of leisure experiences. It is not possible in this article to develop detailed proposals, but a potential direction can be indicated. Some 30 years ago, Rojek (1985, p. 4) referred to the phenomenon of "multiparadigmatic rivalry" in leisure

Table 1. Draft checklist of leisure activity-experience constructs and variables[1].

A. Activity experience qualities	B. Characteristics of participants
1. Perseverance/effort	1. Gender
2. Benefits sought/satisfied (range)	2. Age
3. Needs desired/satisfied (range)	3. Ethnicity
4. Career/stage	4. Disability
5. Specialization opportunity/stage	5. Class/Socio-economic group
6. Unique ethos/social world/tribe	6. Employment status
7. Training/knowledge/skill/experience	7. Social capital
8. Identification with activity	8. Family/household situation
9. Relationship with professionalism	9. Education/cultural capital
10. Volunteer status	10. Income
11. Commitment	11. Education/cultural capital
12. Side bets	12. Subjective health status
13. Strain on personal/family relationships	13. Life satisfaction/stress
14. Strain re work commitments	14. Lifestyle
15. Frustrations/injuries	15. Identity
16. Amount/pattern of time expended	
17. Length of (calendar) time involved	C. Context
18. Money expended	1. Organizational structure of activity
19. Marginality	2. Facilities
20. Degree of control (addiction)	3. Geographical location/place
21. Individual or group/team activity	4. Activity history/tradition
22. Focus (partner, family, friends, fitness, etc.)	5. Macro-social conditions
23. Enjoyment/satisfaction/attraction	
24. Experience of 'flow'	
25. Financial return	
26. Equipment involved	
27. Intra-personal constraints faced/overcome	
28. Inter-personal constraints faced/overcome	
29. Structural constraints faced/overcome	
30. Signification	
31. Physical exercise involved	

[1]Variables may be nominal/categorical, quantitative or qualitative, single variables or clusters/composites. Items drawn from SLP, Needs, Benefits, Specialization, Commitment, Constraints, Involvement, leisure studies generally.

theory; what is being proposed here is multiparadigmatic cooperation. As the discussion of complementary theory above indicates, there are numerous existing paradigms, frameworks, and approaches which a researcher might consider when examining leisure experiences. Six such frameworks addressing leisure experiences are listed in this article, all seeking to understand the leisure experience phenomenon. Three of the six—commitment, specialization, and involvement—are based on the idea of a continuum format, which, I argue, is the logical format for the seriousness dimension. While these frameworks often overlap, each highlights particular variables and constructs and ways of assessing them.

It is proposed that variables or constructs from these frameworks and approaches, including the SLP and key variables from the broad field of leisure studies, be considered as the starting point for research on leisure experience. A tentative draft of such a list is presented in Table 1, divided into three groups: characteristics of experiences, characteristics of individuals, and context.

The idea of drawing on features of different frameworks is not entirely original. For example, there have been proposals for linking *involvement* with *constraints* (Lee & Scott, 2009) and with *commitment* (Iwasaki & Havitz, 2004; Kim, Scott, & Crompton, 1997) and for linking the SLP with *specialization* (Scott, 2012; Cole & Scott, 1999; Lee & Scott, 2013; Lyu & Oh, 2015; Tsaur & Liang, 2008) with *constraints* (Kennelly et al., 2013; Lamont, Kennelly, & Moyle, 2015; McQuarrie & Jackson, 1996; Stalp, 2006) and with *commitment* (Tomlinson, 1993). This proposal takes these ideas a step further to consider a wider range of frameworks/constructs.

While some rationalization and refinement of the draft list of variables is likely to be possible, as is extension, it is a somewhat daunting list. However, the research literature collectively indicates that all the variables listed are candidates for consideration when seeking to describe and understand the diversity and complexity of leisure experiences. While individual existing frameworks could continue to function, awareness of variables and constructs from other frameworks might stimulate development and linkages in both conceptual and theoretical terms and in regard to qualitative and/or quantitative data collection and analysis. This remains for future consideration.

In outlining the history of the SLP, Stebbins (2007, p. 2) indicated that he had considered calling his framework the "leisure experience perspective," referring to Mannell's (1999) precedent. Shen and Yarnal (2010), in their study challenging the SL-CL dichotomy, developed a Leisure Experience Characteristic instrument, while Gallant et al. (2013), in their proposals for reform of the SLP, advocated a change of emphasis from the classification of *activities* to the study of *experiences*. It seems that there may be an emerging consensus that what is now required to progress the exploration of leisure experiences in all their diversity is a Leisure Experience Perspective, which seems a suitable label for the proposed approach.

References

Adler, M. J. (1996). *The time of our lives: The ethics of common sense* (2nd ed.). New York, NY: Fordham University Press. (Original work published 1970)

Anderson, L. (2011). Time is of the essence: An analytic autoethnography of family, work, and serious leisure. *Symbolic Interaction, 34*, 133–157.

Anderson, L., & Taylor, J. D. (2010). Standing out while fitting in: Serious leisure identities and aligning actions among skydivers and gun collectors. *Journal of Contemporary Ethnography, 39*, 34–59.

Aronowitz, S., & DiFazio, W. (1994). *The jobless future*. Minneapolis, MN: University of Minnesota Press.

Baldwin, C. K., & Norris, P. A. (1999). Exploring the dimensions of serious leisure: Love me – love my dog. *Journal of Leisure Research, 31*, 1–17.

Bartram, S. A. (2001). Serious leisure careers among whitewater kayakers: A feminist perspective. *World Leisure Journal, 43*, 4–11.

Blackshaw, T. (2010). *Leisure*. London, England: Routledge.

Blackshaw, T., & Crabbe, T. (2004). *New perspectives on sport and "deviance"*. London, England: Routledge.

Breeze, M. (2013). Analysing "seriousness" in roller derby: Speaking critically with the serious leisure perspective. *Sociological Research Online, 18*, 23. Retrieved from www.socresonline.org.uk/18/4/23.html

Brown, C. A. (2007). The Carolina shaggers: Dance as serious leisure. *Journal of Leisure Research, 39*, 623–647.

Bryan, H. (1977). Leisure value systems and recreational specialization. *Journal of Leisure Research, 9*, 174–187.

Bryan, H. (2008). *Conflict in the great outdoors* (2nd ed.). Tuscaloosa, AL: University of Alabama Press. (Original work published 1979)

Buchanan, T. (1985). Commitment and leisure behavior: A theoretical perspective. *Leisure Sciences, 7*, 401–420.

Butler, E. (2010). *Equestrianism: Serious leisure and inter-subjectivity* (Master's thesis). Fort Collins, CO: Colorado State University.

Charmaz, K. (2006). *Constructing grounded theory*. London, England: Sage.

Cole, J. S., & Scott, D. (1999). Segmenting participation in wildlife watching: A comparison of casual wildlife watchers and serious birders. *Human Dimensions of Wildlife, 4*, 44–61.

Cova, B., Kozinets, R.V., & Shankar, A. (Eds.). (2007). *Consumer tribes*. Oxford, England: Butterworth-Heinemann.

Derom, I., & Taks, M. (2011). Participants' experiences in two types of sporting events: A quest for evidence of the SL-CL continuum. *Journal of Leisure Research, 43*, 383–402.

Diener, E. (2000). Subjective well-being: The science of happiness and a proposal for a national index. *American Psychologist, 55*, 34–43.

Dilley, R. E., & Scraton, S. J. (2010). Women, climbing and serious leisure. *Leisure Studies, 29*, 125–142.

Driver, B. L., & Bruns, D. H. (1999). Concepts and uses of the benefits approach to leisure. In E. L. Jackson & T. L. Burton (Eds.), *Leisure studies: Prospects for the twenty-first century* (pp. 349–370). State College, PA: Venture.

Driver, B. L., Tinsley, H. E. A., & Manfredo, M. J. (1991). The paragraphs about leisure and recreation experience preference scales: Results from two inventories designed to assess the breadth of the perceived psychological benefits of leisure. In B. L. Driver, P. J. Brown, & G. L. Paterson (Eds.), *Benefits of leisure* (pp. 263–286). State College, PA: Venture.

Elkington, S., & Stebbins, R. A. (2014). *The serious leisure perspective: An introduction.* London, England: Routledge.

Frew, E. A. (2006). Comedy festival attendance: Serious, project-based or casual leisure? In S. Elkington, I. Jones, & L. Lawrence (Eds.), *Serious leisure: Extensions and applications* (pp. 105–122). Eastbourne, England: Leisure Studies Association.

Gallant, K., Arai, S., & Smale, B. (2013). Celebrating, challenging and re-envisioning serious leisure. *Leisure/Loisir, 37*, 91–109.

Gibson, H., Willming, C., & Holdnak, A. (2002). "We're Gators, not just Gator fans": Serious leisure and University of Florida football. *Journal of Leisure Research, 34*, 397–425.

Giddens, A. (1991). *Modernity and self-identity: Self and society in the late modern age.* Cambridge, England: Polity.

Gillespie, D. L., Lefler, A., & Lerner, E. (2002). If it weren't for my hobby, I'd have a life: Dog sports, serious leisure, and boundary negotiations. *Leisure Studies, 21*, 285–304.

Glasser, R. (1973). Leisure and the search for a satisfying identity. In M. A. Smith, S. Parker, & C. S. Smith (Eds.), *Leisure and society in Britain* (pp. 56–68). London, England: Allen Lane.

Goff, S. J., Fick, D. S., & Oppliger, R. A. (1997). The moderating effect of spouse support in the relation between serious leisure and spouses' perceive leisure-family conflict. *Journal of Leisure Research, 29*, 47–60.

Gould, J., Moore, D., McGuire, F., & Stebbins, R. A. (2008). Development of the serious leisure inventory measure. *Journal of Leisure Research, 40*, 47–68.

Gravelle, F., & Larocque, L. (2005). Volunteerism and serious leisure: The case of the Francophone games. *World Leisure Journal, 47*, 45–51.

Green, B. C., & Jones, I. (2005). Serious leisure, social identity and sport tourism. *Sport in Society, 8*, 164–181.

Haggard, L. M., & Williams, D. R. (1992). Identity affirmation through leisure activities: Leisure symbols of the self. *Journal of Leisure Research, 24*, 1–18.

Hamilton-Smith, E. (1993). In the Australian bush: Some reflections on serious leisure. *World Leisure and Recreation, 35*, 10–13.

Havitz, M. E., & Dimanche, F. (1990). Propositions for testing the involvement construct in recreational and tourism contexts. *Leisure Sciences, 12*, 179–195.

Havitz, M. E., & Dimanche, F. (1997). Leisure involvement revisited: Conceptual conundrums and measurement advances. *Journal of Leisure Research, 29*, 245–278.

Heley, J., & Jones, L. (2013). Growing older and social sustainability: Considering the "serious leisure" practices of the over 60s in rural communities. *Social & Cultural Geography, 14*, 276–299.

Heo, J., Lee, I. H., Kim, J., & Stebbins, R. A. (2012). Understanding the relationships among central characteristics of serious leisure: An empirical study of older adults in competitive sports. *Journal of Leisure Research, 44*, 450–462.

Heo, J., Lee, Y., McCormick, B. P., & Pedersen, P. M. (2010). Daily experiences of serious leisure, flow and subjective well-being of older adults. *Leisure Studies, 29*, 207–225.

Homans, G. C. (1974). *Human behavior: Its elementary forms.* New York, NY: Harcourt, Brace, Jovanovich.

Hutchinson, S. L., & Kleiber, D. A. (2005). Gifts of the ordinary: Casual leisure's contributions to health and well-being. *World Leisure Journal, 47*, 2–16.

Iwasaki, Y., & Havitz, M. E. (2004). Examining relationships between leisure involvement, psychological commitment and loyalty to a recreation agency. *Journal of Leisure Research, 36*, 45–72.

Jackson, E. L., & Henderson, K. A. (1995). Gender-based analysis of leisure constraints. *Leisure Sciences, 17*, 31–51.

Jones, I. (2000). A model of serious leisure identification: The case of football fandom. *Leisure Studies, 19*, 283–298.

Jones, I. (2006). Examining the characteristics of serious leisure from a social identity perspective. In S. Elkington, I. Jones, & L. Lawrence (Eds.), *Serious leisure: Extensions and applications* (pp. 47–60). Eastbourne, England: Leisure Studies Association.

Jun, J., Kyle, G. T., & Vlachopoulos, S. P. (2012). Reassessing the structure of enduring leisure involvement. *Leisure Sciences, 34*, 1–18.

Kane, M. J., & Zink, R. (2004). Package adventure tours: Markers in serious leisure careers? *Leisure Studies, 23*, 329–346.

Kennelly, M., Moyle, B., & Lamont, M. (2013). Constraint negotiation in serious leisure: A study of amateur triathletes. *Journal of Leisure Research, 45*, 466–484.

Kim, J., Dattilo, J., & Heo, J. (2011). Taekwando participation as serious leisure for life satisfaction and health. *Journal of Leisure Research, 43*, 545–559.

Kim, S. S., Scott, D., & Crompton, J. L. (1997). An exploration of the relationships among social psychological involvement, commitment, and future intentions in the context of birdwatching. *Journal of Leisure Research, 29*, 320–341.

Kuentzel, W. F. (2012). Comment on Scott: Is integration better? *Leisure Sciences, 34*, 375–376.

Kuentzel, W. F., & Heberlein, T. A. (1997). Social status, self-development and the process of sailing specialization. *Journal of Leisure Research, 29*, 300–319.

Kyle, G., & Chick, G. (2002). The social nature of leisure involvement. *Journal of Leisure Research, 34*, 426–448.

Lamont, M., Kennelly, M., & Wilson, E. (2012). Competing priorities as constraints in event travel careers. *Tourism Management, 33*, 1068–1079.

Lamont, M., Kennelly, M., & Moyle, B. D. (2015). Toward conceptual advancement of costs and perseverance within the serious leisure perspective. *Journal of Leisure Research, 47*, 647–654.

Lee, J.-H., & Scott, D. (2009). The process of celebrity fans' constraint negotiation. *Journal of Leisure Research, 41*, 137–155.

Lee, J.-H., & Scott, D. (2013). Empirical linkages between serious leisure and recreational specialization. *Human Dimensions of Wildlife, 18*, 450–462.

Lyu, S. O., & Oh, C. (2015). Bridging the conceptual frameworks of constraints negotiation and serious leisure to understand leisure benefit realization. *Leisure Sciences, 37*, 176–193.

Maffesoli, M. (1996). *The time of the tribes, decline of individualism in mass society*. London, England: Sage.

Mannell, R. C. (1993). High-investment activity and life satisfaction among older adults: Committed, serious leisure and flow activities. In J. R. Kelly (Ed.), *Activity and aging: Staying involved in later life* (pp. 125–145). Newbury Park, CA: Sage.

Mannell, R. C. (1999). Leisure experience and satisfaction. In E. L. Jackson & T. L. Burton (Eds.), *Leisure studies: Prospects for the twenty-first century* (pp. 235–252). State College, PA: Venture.

Martin, D. C. (2008). Review of "Serious leisure: A perspective for our time" by Robert Stebbins. *Contemporary Sociology, 37*, 274–275.

McIntyre, N. (1989). The personal meaning of participation: Enduring involvement. *Journal of Leisure Research, 21*, 167–179.

McQuarrie, F., & Jackson, E. L. (1996). Connections between negotiation of leisure constraints and serious leisure: An exploratory study of adult amateur ice skaters. *Society and Leisure, 19*, 459–483.

Organization for Economic Cooperation and Development (OECD). (2013). *OECD guidelines on measuring subjective well-being*. Paris, France: Author.

Parker, S., Hamilton-Smith, E., & Davidson, P. (1993). Serious and other leisure: Thirty Australians. *World Leisure and Recreation, 35*, 14–18.

Puddephatt, A. J. (2007). Review of "Serious leisure: A perspective for our time," by Robert Stebbins. *Canadian Journal of Sociology Online*. Retrieved from www.cjsonline/reviews/seriousleisure.html

Rifkin, J. (1995). *The end of work*. New York, NY: G.P. Putnam's Sons.

Rojek, C. (1985). *Capitalism and leisure theory*. London, England: Tavistock.

Rojek, C. (1999). Deviant leisure: The dark side of free-time activity. In E. L. Jackson & T. L. Burton (Eds.), *Leisure studies: Prospects for the 21st century* (pp. 81–96). State College, PA: Venture.

Rojek, C. (2000). *Leisure and culture*. Basingstoke, England: Macmillan.

Scott, D. (2012). Serious leisure and recreation specialization: An uneasy marriage. *Leisure Sciences, 34,* 366–371.

Scott, D., & Godbey, G. C. (1992). An analysis of adult play groups: Social versus serious participation in contract bridge. *Leisure Sciences, 14,* 47–67.

Scott, D., & Shafer, C. S. (2001). Recreational specialization: A critical look at the construct. *Journal of Leisure Research, 33,* 319–343.

Shamir, B. (1988). Commitment and leisure. *Sociological Perspectives, 31,* 238–258.

Shen, X. S., & Yarnal, C. (2010). Blowing open the serious leisure-casual leisure dichotomy: What's in there? *Leisure Sciences, 32,* 162–179.

Shinew, K. J., & Parry, D. C. (2005). Examining college students' participation in the leisure pursuits of drinking and illegal drug use. *Journal of Leisure Research, 37,* 364–386.

Siegenthaler, K. L., & O'Dell, I. (2003). Older golfers: Serious leisure and successful aging. *World Leisure Journal, 45,* 45–52.

Stalp, M. (2006). Negotiating time and space for serious leisure: Quilting in the modern U.S. home. *Journal of Leisure Research, 38,* 104–132.

Stebbins, R. A. (1979). *Amateurs: On the margins between work and leisure*. Beverly Hills, CA: Sage.

Stebbins, R. A. (1982). Serious leisure: A conceptual statement. *Pacific Sociological Review* (now *Sociological Perspectives*), *5,* 251–272.

Stebbins, R. A. (1992). *Amateurs, professionals and serious leisure*. Montréal, Canada: McGill-Queen's University Press.

Stebbins, R. A. (1997). Casual leisure: A conceptual statement. *Leisure Studies, 16,* 17–26.

Stebbins, R. A. (1998). *After work: The search for an optimal leisure lifestyle*. Calgary, Alberta, Canada: Detselig.

Stebbins, R. A. (2001). *New directions in the theory and research of serious leisure*. Lewiston, NY: Edwin Mellen Press.

Stebbins, R. A. (2005a). Project-based leisure: Theoretical neglect of a common use of free time. *Leisure Studies, 24,* 1–12.

Stebbins, R. A. (2005b). Recreational specialization: Serious leisure and complex leisure activity. *Leisure Studies Association Newsletter, 70,* 11–13.

Stebbins, R. A. (2005c). *Challenging mountain nature: Risk, motive and lifestyle in three hobbyist sports*. Calgary, Alberta, Canada: Detselig.

Stebbins, R. A. (2005d). Inclination to participate in organized serious leisure: An exploration of the role of costs, rewards and lifestyles. *Leisure/Loisir, 29,* 183–201.

Stebbins, R. A. (2007). *Serious leisure: A perspective for our time*. New Brunswick, NJ: Transaction.

Stebbins, R. A. (2012a). Comment on Scott: Recreation specialization and the CL-SL continuum. *Leisure Sciences, 34,* 372–374.

Stebbins, R. A. (2012b). *The idea of leisure*. New Brunswick, NJ: Transaction.

Stebbins, R. A. (2014). *Careers in serious leisure*. Basingstoke, England: Palgrave Macmillan.

Stebbins, R. A. (2015a). *The interrelationship of leisure and play*. Basingstoke, England: Palgrave Macmillan.

Stebbins, R. A. (2015b). *Leisure and positive psychology*. Basingstoke, England: Palgrave Macmillan.

Stebbins, R. A. (2015c). Preface to the paperback edition. In *Serious leisure: A perspective for our time* (pp. xiii–xviii). New Brunswick, NJ: Transaction.

Stebbins, R. A. (2016a). Costs, constraints, and perseverance: A rejoinder to Lamont, Kennelly, and Moyle. *Journal of Leisure Research, 48,* 1–4.

Stebbins, R. A. (2016b). Dumazedier, the serious leisure perspective, and leisure in Brazil. *World Leisure Journal*. Retrieved from http://dx.doi.org/10.1080/16078055.2016.1158205

Super, D. E. (1980). Life-span, life-space approach to career development. *Journal of Vocational Behavior, 16,* 282–298.

Tinsley, H. E. A., & Eldredge, B. D. (1995). Psychological benefits of leisure participation: A taxonomy of leisure activities based on their need-gratifying properties. *Journal of Counseling Psychology, 42,* 123–132.

Tomlinson, A. (1993). Culture of commitment in leisure: Notes towards the understanding of a serious legacy. *World Leisure and Recreation, 35*, 6–9.

Tsaur, S.-H., & Liang, Y.-W. (2008). Serious leisure and recreation specialization. *Leisure Sciences, 30*, 325–341.

Unruh, D. R. (1980). The nature of social worlds. *Pacific Sociological Review* (now *Sociological Perspectives*), *23*, 271–296.

Van Moorst, H. (1982). Leisure and social theory. *Leisure Studies, 1*, 157–170.

Veal, A. J. (1993). The concept of lifestyle: A review. *Leisure Studies, 12*, 233–252.

Williams, C. (1998). Is the SERVQUAL model an appropriate management tool for measuring service delivery quality in the UK leisure industry? *Managing Leisure, 3*, 98–110.

Worthington, B. (2006). "Getting steamed up about leisure" – aspects of serious leisure within the tourism industry. In S. Elkington, I. Jones, & L. Lawrence (Eds.), *Serious leisure: Extensions and applications* (pp. 19–31). Eastbourne, England: Leisure Studies Association.

Leisure Sciences and the Humanities

Paul Heintzman

ABSTRACT
The purpose of this research reflections paper is to explore the prevalence of the humanities in the journal *Leisure Sciences* over the last 40 years, since its inception. During this period has the prevalence of the humanities increased or decreased? An analysis of papers published in *Leisure Sciences* indicates that just over 3% have focused on the humanities (philosophy, history, ethics, the arts). There was an increase in humanities papers from 1985 to 1999; however, only one humanities paper has been published in the last 10 years. Implications for the next 40 years of leisure research include emphasizing the humanities in leisure studies education and encouraging special journal issues and conference themes focused on the humanities.

The year 2017 marks the 40th anniversary of the journal *Leisure Sciences* and the 40th anniversary of the beginning of my undergraduate education in leisure studies. The Statement of Editorial Policy in the first issue of *Leisure Sciences* stated:

> *Leisure Sciences* is conceived as an interdisciplinary social and administrative sciences journal devoted to publishing scholarly and substantive articles in the fields of leisure, recreation, natural resources, and the related environments. The central criteria for publication are that the material be germane to the above topics, be theoretically and/or empirically based, and be substantive in the sense of proposing, discovering, or replicating something. (p. 1)

The term "interdisciplinary" and the phrase "theoretically and/or empirically based" suggest the journal was not limited to social scientific empirical studies but was also open to other disciplinary approaches including those from the humanities. The interdisciplinary nature of the journal was further reinforced in the Information for Authors in the first issue, which stated "*Leisure Sciences* provides a forum for the interdisciplinary presentation of leisure studies…" This approach to the study of leisure was consistent with my first-year introductory leisure studies course in fall of 1977 taught by Dr. Tom Goodale at the University of Ottawa in which I read large sections of Kerlinger's (1973) *Foundations of Behavioral Research* as well as all of Bronowski's (1965) *Science and Human Values* and a small section of Newman's (1852/1959) *The Idea of a University*. A major theme of this undergraduate course was that both the social sciences and humanities are necessary for a satisfactory understanding of leisure and related phenomena.

Forty years later, is *Leisure Sciences* as open to interdisciplinary perspectives? Currently, the Aims and Scope of *Leisure Sciences* as stated on Taylor and Francis's web page for the journal includes the following: "*Leisure Sciences* presents scientific inquiries into the study of leisure, recreation, parks, travel, and tourism from a social science perspective. Published articles theoretically and/or methodologically advance the understanding of leisure behavior." These initial sentences of the Aims and Scope seem to suggest that *Leisure Sciences* emphasizes social scientific research approaches. However, the Aims and Scope subsequently states that "The journal also features...philosophical and policy treatises..." and that there is "an interdisciplinary diversity of topics." These phrases appear to imply that the journal continues to be open to papers arising from the humanities. The purpose of this research is to determine the prevalence of the humanities in *Leisure Sciences* over the last 40 years. Furthermore, during this period has the prevalence of humanities papers increased or decreased?

Literature review

Concerns about an overreliance on empiricism

For more than 25 years concerns have been raised about an over reliance on empiricism within the study of leisure. Pronovost and D'Amours (1990) were critical of the excessive empiricism, both quantitative and qualitative, of leisure research. Sylvester (1990) noted that most leisure researchers believe "that empiricism is the most positive and progressive way to understand leisure...leisure studies has embraced the rationality of empiricism to the near exclusion of moral understanding" (p. 294). Elsewhere, Sylvester (1991) wrote that leisure science "considers empiricism the answer for the 'problems which trouble us,' most of which are moral rather than technical" (p. 452). Hemingway (1990) claimed that "the dominance within leisure studies of a single research framework, namely a combination of empiricism and social psychology, has led to shortcomings in both our investigation and understanding of leisure" (p. 303).

Within this context, Dustin, Schwab, and Rose (2012), like Sylvester (1991), recommended *phronesis*, a practical wisdom that involves judgments and decisions based on ethical deliberations about values associated with practice. Since the Enlightenment, *phronesis* has faded into the background as instrumental rationality, that is, a focus on how to reach an end rather than why or the value of the end, has become the dominant position informing science. In contrast, value rationality focuses on the value of an end. As a result science has addressed "is" questions, for the most part uninformed by "ought" questions. Dustin et al. gave an example from Bronowski's (1965) *Science and Human Values*–an example I am familiar with due to my reading of this book in my first year introductory recreation class–that describes the development of the atomic bomb with little consideration given to the moral question associated with using it. Dustin et al. argued for adopting an applied *phronesis* perspective in leisure science. Such an approach is seen in Dustin et al. (2011) *Stewards of Access/Custodians of Choice* that applies Bronowski's thinking to the park, recreation, and tourism field.

More recently in a review of de Grazia's (1962) *Of Time, Work and Leisure*, which I was also exposed to in my first year of undergraduate study 40 years ago, Sylvester (2013) noted that "the discipline of leisure studies has never had much of an ear or rhythm for the humanities" (p. 257). Citing authors such as Dare, Welton, and Coe (1987), Fain (1991), Hemingway (1988), Hunnicutt (1990), and Goodale & Godbey (1988), Sylvester observed that there was a brief period in the late 1980s and early 1990s where the humanities partially flourished in leisure studies, before they faded into obscurity about the time that the NRPA Leisure Research Symposium moved to organizing sessions by thematic tracks rather than disciplines. Sylvester's observation parallels Goodale's (1990) comment that critical, interpretive, historical and ethical papers had begun to appear in both *Leisure Sciences* and the *Journal of Leisure*

Research, in the years prior to his 1990 paper suggesting a trend toward more pluralistic ways of knowing.

Previous research

A few studies have examined the disciplinary content of papers published in leisure journals. In a study to determine the nature of leisure research, Ng (1985) examined papers from three journals, *Journal of Leisure Research, Leisure Sciences*, and *Recreation Research Review* (a predecessor of the current journal *Leisure/Loisir*) during the seven-year period from 1977 to 1983. Sixty-one percent were practical problems; 37% were conceptual, theoretical, or philosophical problems; and 2% were policy problems. Of note, 85% of papers in *Recreation Research Review* were practical problems, while 53% of papers in *Leisure Sciences* were conceptual, theoretical, or philosophical problems.

In 1987, Burton and Jackson (1990) conducted an international survey of leisure scholars which included a question that asked respondents what they thought had been the dominant themes in leisure research during the previous 20 years. Historical studies were ranked 15th, and although philosophical studies were not mentioned they possibly comprised part of the theme of concepts and theories which was tied for eighth. The survey also asked participants to identify the main three priorities for leisure research in the next 10 years. In this list historical studies dropped to 17th, and concepts and theories jumped to first.

More recently, Long (2013) investigated the content of two U.S.-based journals (*Journal of Leisure Research* and *Leisure Sciences*) and two U.K.-based journals (*Leisure Studies* and *Managing Leisure*) in terms of their disciplinary base and the research methods used. Recognizing the difficulty of reducing the complexity of research into a finite number of categories, papers were placed into one of nine groups based on their primary discipline: geography, environmental/urban studies, planning; sociology and social policy; economics, management and business; political science; psychology; history; philosophy; pedagogy, education studies; and unassigned. A sample of journal volumes was selected beginning with the two most recent volumes (2010, 2011) and their equivalents in each decade (1991, 1990, 1981, 1980) with the exception of 1982 for *Leisure Studies*, because that was the first volume of this journal, and beginning with 2000 for *Managing Leisure*. Long's study demonstrated the significance of psychology in the U.S. journals, sociology in *Leisure Studies*, and economics, management, and business in *Managing Leisure*. Of relevance to this paper, Long suggested that the decision to have separate categories for history and philosophy was not well-founded given the small number of papers in these categories. One percent of papers in the *Journal of Leisure Research* were philosophical while there were no historical papers in this journal, 1% of papers in *Leisure Sciences* were philosophical while 1% were historical, and 4% of papers in *Leisure Studies* were philosophical while 1% of papers were historical. There were no philosophical or historical papers in *Managing Leisure*. Thus philosophical and historical papers were more prevalent in *Leisure Studies* than the other journals. However, as Long points out, this was a partial picture as only selected journal volumes were included in the study. A more complete picture of the content of these journals is needed. The 40th anniversary of *Leisure Sciences* provides a good occasion for examining the content of this journal.

Method

What is the prevalence of the humanities in the journal *Leisure Sciences* over the last 40 years? During this period has the prevalence of the humanities papers increased or decreased? To answer these questions, an analysis was conducted of the papers published in *Leisure Sciences* to determine if they were quantitative social scientific, qualitative social scientific, conceptual (definition of a concept or the relationship between concepts for the purpose of use in social scientific research), an essay that advanced an argument, a review paper that synthesized empirical research, or humanities (historical, ethical, philosophical, arts). Unlike the Long (2013) study for which only selected volumes were examined, all papers published from the first issue in 1977 to the last issue of 2016 were included to give a comprehensive assessment. For each paper the title, abstract and keywords were read and then the paper was classified according to one of the above categories. If the category of the paper was unable to be determined from the title, abstract and keywords, then the paper was perused further to determine the category it fit into. In a few cases, a paper overlapped more than one category and in these cases the paper was placed in the category that predominated.

Results

The results indicate that just over 3% of the 807 papers published in *Leisure Sciences* from 1977 to 2016 focus on the humanities. The frequency of humanities papers published in *Leisure Sciences* was much greater during the middle decades of the journal's history compared to the first and last decades. From 1977 to 1986 there were three humanities papers; from 1987 to 1997, 17; from 1998 to 2007, 13; and from 2008 to 2017 there was only one humanities paper. Furthermore, 60% of the humanities papers published in *Leisure Sciences* were published in the 15-year period between 1985 and 1999. Although history and philosophy overlaps in some papers there were roughly the same number of history and philosophy papers and fewer ethical and arts papers. Clearly the most prevalent author of humanities papers in *Leisure Sciences* was Charles Sylvester with four papers published.

Another finding from the analysis of the content was that humanities papers tended to be associated with special issues or featured and invited papers that were followed by a number of responses or commentaries. For example, an invited historical paper titled "Listening for a Leisure Remix" (Fox & Klaiber, 2006) was followed by several response papers.

Discussion and implications for the next 40 years of leisure research

The findings of this analysis concerning the small percentage of humanities papers published in *Leisure Sciences* compared with empirical papers provides documented evidence obtained through systematic analysis for what some writers have previously observed anecdotally. The current study's finding of an increased number of humanities papers in *Leisure Sciences* between 1985 and 1999 confirms both Sylvester's (2013) and Goodale's (1990) observations. However, this increase was not sustained and the publication of humanities papers has declined since then and quite dramatically in the last decade with only one humanities paper published.

The findings of the current analysis indicate a neglect of humanities research published in *Leisure Sciences*. The evidence does not seem to support the Aims and Scope of the journal that state "the journal also features …philosophical and policy treatises …" and that there is "an interdisciplinary diversity of topics." It is possible, as suggested by Long's (2013) study which found that *Leisure Studies* published four times as many philosophical papers as *Leisure Sciences* and as the *Journal of Leisure Research*, that authors submit humanities manuscripts to other journals such as *Leisure Studies* since there may be a greater likelihood that humanities papers will be accepted in these other journals. However, it must be remembered that Long's study was based on selected volumes and the percentage of humanities papers in his study may be higher than the percentage if all volumes had been included in the study. Based on the current study if all the *Leisure Sciences* volumes are considered, the difference between the current study's finding concerning humanities papers (3%) in *Leisure Sciences* and Long's finding concerning philosophical and historical papers (5%) in *Leisure Studies* is minimal. Furthermore one might question why North American authors should have to send their humanities papers to a British journal for publication, especially given the current Aims and Scope of *Leisure Sciences* outlined above. This neglect of the humanities needs to be addressed in a number of ways in order for the humanities to thrive and contribute to the understanding of leisure in the next forty years: education, special issues, and conference themes.

Leisure studies education

Sylvester (2013) claimed that vocationalism in leisure studies curriculum leaves little room or reason for a study of the humanities. He concluded that "sadly, without the humanities, leisure studies, consisting as it does of human beings, will be unable to hear its collective soul talking to itself, or assist other individuals to listen [to] their own. It would be ironic, as well, because that was one of the purposes of classical leisure" (p. 257). In a paper relevant to leisure studies, Caton (2014) identified a desperate need of a shift in tourism education to include the humanities:

> The humanities are often dismissed as frivolous, something which can easily be dispensed with in an era of economic challenges . . . , and so our programs become more and more technically focused, with the emphasis placed on building skills to solve the problems of the moment. In truth, however, what the humanities offer us are the fundamental building blocks of approaching life as a human being, using the full capacities that set us aside from other creatures: the ability to reason logically and independently about our circumstances, the capacity to care and to feel compassion for others, the imagination to dream up alternative futures, and the moral compass to move us in the direction we want to go. (p. 31)

Incorporating humanities into leisure research begins by incorporating the humanities into undergraduate leisure studies education. I was fortunate that my research benefited from professors and courses that emphasized both the social sciences and the humanities.

Special issues

One of the findings of this study was that humanities papers sometimes tend to be published as a special issue that includes a featured or invited paper followed by responses by multiple authors (e.g., Fox & Klaiber, 2006). Editors of leisure journals such as *Leisure Sciences* need to be proactive and look for opportunities to encourage the publication of humanities papers through such special issues and feature papers followed by response papers.

Leisure and humanities as conference themes

From early in its history until 2009, the Leisure Research Symposium, which began in 1978 one year after the inaugural volume of *Leisure Sciences,* included a humanities topical area, although its name changed from time to time. For example, both the 1982 and 1983 symposiums had a "Philosophical, Historical, Cultural and Economic Aspects of Leisure and Recreation" session. By the 1986 and 1987 symposiums, the name was "Philosophical and Historical Aspects of Leisure." In 1988 it was changed slightly to "Philosophical, Historical and Cultural Aspects of Leisure Behavior." The 1998 symposium had the topical area of "Leisure Research and the Humanities" which by the time of the 2000 symposium was changed to "Leisure and the Humanities" and continued until this topical area was discontinued in 2010. Although the "Leisure and the Humanities" topical area continued until 2009 for the submission of abstracts, in the 1990s there was a shift where papers were grouped together for presentation at the symposium based on themes and thus all the humanities papers were not necessarily presented in the same session as previously. Between 1987 and 2009 I presented seven papers at the Leisure Research Symposium—three humanities papers and four social scientific papers. No doubt the presentation of my humanities papers was facilitated by the fact that there was a humanities topical session to submit my abstracts to.

Perhaps it is coincidental that the first Research Institute of The Academy of Leisure Sciences (TALS) took place in the same year that *Leisure Sciences* celebrates its 40th anniversary. A possible way to encourage more humanities papers is to incorporate a humanities topical area or stream into future TALS Research Institutes similar to the Humanities Topical area that existed up until 2009 at the Leisure Research Symposium. Of course, the same practice is also desirable at other leisure studies conferences.

Conclusion

Returning to *Science and Human Values* that I read 40 years ago in my introductory leisure studies class, Bronowski (1965) claimed that the distinction between science and art is not as prominent as many think it to be. Nevertheless as demonstrated by this study, the humanities have been neglected in leisure sciences, especially in the last ten years. In the next forty years may *Leisure Sciences* be more successful in accepting and encouraging of the humanities.

Acknowledgment

The author would like to thank Carl Nienhuis for his work as a research assistant on this project.

ORCID

Paul Heintzman ◉ http://orcid.org/0000-0002-6603-4778

References

Bronowski, J. (1965). *Science and human values* (rev. ed.). New York, NY: Harper & Row.
Burton, T. L., & Jackson, E. L. (1990). On the road to where we're going: Leisure studies in the future. *Loisir et Société / Society and Leisure, 13*(1), 207–227.
Caton, K. (2014). Underdisciplinarity: Where are the humanities in tourism education? *Journal of Hospitality, Leisure, Sport & Tourism Education, 15*, 24–33.
Dare, B., Welton, G., & Coe, W. (1987). *Concepts of leisure in western thought: A critical and historical analysis*. Dubuque, IA: Kendall Hunt.
De Grazia, S. (1962). *Of time, work, and leisure*. New York, NY: The Twentieth Century Fund.
Dustin, D., McAvoy, L., Schultz, J., Bricker, K., Rose, J., & Schwab, K. (2011). *Stewards of access/Custodians of choice: A philosophical foundation for parks, recreation, and tourism*. Urbana, IL: Sagamore.
Dustin, D., Schwab, K., & Rose, J. (2012). Toward a more *phronetic* leisure science. *Leisure Sciences, 34*, 191–197.
Fain, G. S. (1991). *Leisure and ethics: Reflections on the philosophy of leisure*. Reston, VA: American Association for Leisure and Recreation.
Fox, K. M., & Klaiber, E. (2006). Listening for a leisure remix. *Leisure Sciences, 28*(5), 411–430.

Goodale, T. L. (1990). Perceived freedom as leisure's antithesis. *Journal of Leisure Research, 22*(4), 296–302.
Goodale, T. L., & Godbey, G. C. (1988). *The evolution of leisure: Historical and philosophical perspectives.* State College, PA: Venture.
Hemingway, J. L. (1988). Leisure and civility: Reflections on a Greek ideal. *Leisure Sciences, 10,* 179–191.
Hemingway, J. L. (1990). Opening windows on an interpretive leisure studies. *Journal of Leisure Research, 22*(4), 303–308.
Hunnicutt, B. K. (1990). Plato on leisure, play, and learning. *Leisure Sciences, 12,* 211–227.
Kerlinger, F. N. (1973). *Foundations of behavioral research* (2nd ed.). Montreal, QC, Canada: Holt, Rinehart & Winston.
Long, J. (2013). Research positions, postures and practices in leisure studies. In T. Blackshaw (Ed.), *Routledge handbook of leisure studies* (pp. 82–96). Florence, England: Routledge.
Newman, J. H. (1852/1959). *The idea of a university.* Garden City, NY: Image Books.
Ng, D. (1985). La nature des problèmes et des hypothèses de recherche en loisir, *Loisir et Société /Society and Leisure, 8*(2), 349–358.
Pronovost, G., & D'Amours, M. (1990). Leisure studies: A re-examination of society. *Loisir et Société / Society and Leisure, 13*(1), 39–62.
Sylvester, C. (1990). Interpretation and leisure science: A hermeneutical example of past and present oracles. *Journal of Leisure Research, 22*(4), 290–295.
Sylvester, C. (1991). Recovering a good idea for the sake of goodness: An interpretive critique of subjective leisure. In T. L. Goodale & P. A. Witt (Eds.), *Recreation and leisure: Issues in an era of change* (3rd. ed., pp. 441–454). State College, PA: Venture.
Sylvester, C. (2013). Fiftieth anniversary: "Of time, work, and leisure." *Journal of Leisure Research, 45*(2), 253–258.

Research on Race, Ethnicity, Immigration, and Leisure: Have We Missed the Boat?

Monika Stodolska

ABSTRACT
The goal of this essay is to offer a critical look at the past 40 years of research on race, ethnicity, immigration, and leisure and to pose some provocative questions about the future of this subdiscipline. In particular, the article examines the main strands of research on this topic, reviews suggestions for future study offered by some key manuscripts and book chapters, and examines their relevance vis-á-vis current social and political discourse in North America and beyond. Are these research questions still relevant or does the new reality of North American and European societies necessitate refocusing of our scholarship?

Research on leisure behavior among members of racial and ethnic minorities has significantly developed and matured in the last 50 years. Much of this literature has been inspired by the unprecedented growth in the ethnic and racial minority population in the United States, which more than tripled in size between 1950 and 2016. The current demographic forecasts predict that by 2044 more than half of all Americans will belong to a minority group, and by 2060 nearly one in five Americans will be foreign-born (Colby & Ortman, 2015). However, changes in the public sentiments toward ethnic and religious groups and the resurgence of open racism both in the United States and Europe (Wike, Stokes, & Simmons, 2016) beg the question: Is our research still relevant? Or, should we ask new questions, explore new topics, and adopt new theoretical perspectives? What should these questions be and what roles can the leisure and recreation field play in the new era of race and ethnic relations in the United States? The goal of this essay is to offer a critical look at the past five decades of research on race, ethnicity, immigration, and leisure and to pose some provocative questions about the future of this subdiscipline. In particular, this article will 1) provide a brief overview of the main strands of research on the topic, 2) review suggestions for future study offered by some key manuscripts and book chapters published between 2000 and 2016, and 3) examine their relevance vis-á-vis current social and political trends in North America and beyond.

The existing research on ethnicity, race, and leisure

The beginnings of research on race, ethnicity, immigration, and leisure date back to the classic Outdoor Recreation Resources Review Commission (ORRRC) studies of the 1960s, but the in-depth investigations of the factors conditioning leisure behavior among ethnic and racial minorities have not begun until the early 1990s. Since then, a number of special issues of our main disciplinary journals (e.g., *Journal of Leisure Research* in 1998 and 2009, *Leisure Sciences* in 2002, *Leisure/Loisir* in 2007, *Leisure Studies* in 2015, *World Leisure Journal* in 2015) have been devoted to this topic, and the book *Race, Ethnicity, and Leisure* (Stodolska, Shinew, Floyd, & Walker) was published in 2014. The existing studies have explored a plethora of subjects, including leisure needs and motivations among minority populations (e.g., Walker, Deng, & Dieser, 2001), leisure constraints and constraints negotiation (e.g., Shores, Scott, & Floyd, 2007), discrimination in leisure contexts (e.g., Sharaievska, Stodolska, Shinew, & Kim, 2010), and issues of social justice, power, privilege, and whiteness (e.g., Arai & Kivel, 2009; Mowatt, 2009). Moreover, topics such as cultural change and leisure (e.g., Tirone & Goodberry, 2011), and leisure behaviors among minorities in the context of various environments and activities (e.g., nature, urban settings, physical activity, music and art) (e.g., Gobster, 2002; Lashua & Fox, 2006) have also been examined.

A growing number of theoretical approaches and methodological tools have been applied to study leisure behavior among ethnic and racial groups (Floyd & Stodolska, 2014; Lee & Stodolska, 2017; Henderson & Walker, 2014). Although the majority of research has focused on leisure experiences of African Americans and Latinos, numerous studies on Asian Americans and, to a lesser extent, European Americans and American Indians have also been conducted (Lee & Scott, 2013; McAvoy, 2002; Stodolska & Jackson, 1998; Walker & Wang, 2009). Floyd, Walker, Stodolska, and Shinew (2014) argued that although "both the quantity and qualitative content of studies focused on racial and ethnic minority groups have markedly increased" (p. 306) and the "theory and concepts used to explain and understand racial and ethnic patterns in leisure are becoming more diverse and comprehensive" (p. 298), our field will be challenged to respond to the new dynamics of race relations and the changing racial and ethnic composition of our societies.

Suggestions for future research proposed in key review manuscripts

The 40th anniversary issue of *Leisure Sciences* offers a convenient departure point to reevaluate the suggestions for future research on race, ethnicity, and leisure proposed by key review manuscripts and book chapters published between 2000 and 2016. Moreover, it provides an opportunity to discuss to what extent these recommendations are still relevant considering the changing nature of North American and European societies. In this article, I selected what I believed to be the key review articles published in *Journal of Leisure Research* by Allison (2000) and by Floyd, Bocarro, and Thompson (2008), in *Leisure Sciences* by Shinew et al. (2006), in *Leisure/Loisir* by Stodolska and Walker (2007), and the concluding chapter in the book on *Race, Ethnicity and Leisure* by Floyd, Walker, Stodolska, and Shinew (2014). It needs to be taken into account that some of these texts are now more than a decade old, so the perspectives that they present should be considered within the context of the time period when they were written.

Allison (2000) advocated for the use of social justice paradigm (Young, 1990) in exploring issues of race and ethnicity. She argued that in comparison to research on gendered leisure, "race and ethnicity leisure-based research has focused less on justice-related issues and more heavily on the influence of race/ethnicity on participation patterns" (p. 4). Allison claimed that research on barriers to access and discrimination experienced by ethnic/racial minorities is limited and that future research should explore topics such as environmental justice, institutional racism, program/agency nonresponsiveness, and violence. Allison believed that in order for social change to occur, leisure research needs to help understand the institutional conditions, properties, processes, conflicts and constraints that foster exclusion.

Shinew et al. (2006) cited Eduardo Bonilla-Silva's (2002) provocative theory that the United States is moving toward a three-tier racial structure and questioned how this new structure would impact leisure opportunities and constraints among minority groups. Bonilla-Silva claimed that in this new hierarchy, inequality would be based on the phenotype and skin tone rather than on a rigid "black-white" color line. Whites along with white Latinos, select multiracial groups, and a few Asian groups will maintain their highest-tier position. A middle stratum will consist of light skinned Latinos, Asian Americans, people from the Middle East, and most people of mixed racial origin. The lowest tier will be occupied by African Americans, including Black immigrants, Native Americans residing on reservations, dark skinned Latinos, and Southeast Asians. Shinew et al. also cited Hiemstra (2005), who had predicted that racial divisions will lose significance in the future and would be replaced by the legality of residence as a marker of social status. They posed a question "to the extent that such new structures are emerging, how will they impact leisure opportunities and constraints?" (pp. 404–405). In terms of future research, Shinew et al. argued that studies should examine factors that facilitate and constrain leisure experiences of ethnic/racial groups, intergroup interactions in public leisure spaces, and explore how minorities negotiate limited leisure resources. They also advocated for more research on the contributions of leisure to a sense of place and community in diverse neighborhoods.

Stodolska and Walker's (2007) review outlined what they believed were the major shortcomings of the existing leisure research on ethnicity and race, including its focus on a small number of well-established groups without explicitly acknowledging their immigration status, generational tenure or legality of residence, and ties to their communities of origin. They argued that broader societal issues need to be acknowledged by leisure researchers and called for cross-national comparison studies that would examine the integration of minorities in societies with different political systems. They echoed Shinew et al.'s (2006) belief that the changing makeup of minority groups in the U.S. and Canada may lead to the emergence of a new social hierarchy. Stodolska and Walker expressed concern that future national or global crisis may lead to new sources of conflict, discrimination, and exclusion by the mainstream population. They argued that such conflicts may "play out in leisure settings, concern recreation space and resources, or affect people's ability to participate in free time activities" (p. 16). They also called for more attention to the processes of globalization of leisure cultures and more research on the transnational nature of ethnic populations.

Floyd, Bocarro, and Thompson (2008) provided a systematic review of research on race and ethnicity published in five major leisure journals and argued that future studies should examine underdeveloped themes and emerging issues such as children and youth, immigration, environmental justice, and physical activity among ethnic and racial populations. They also encouraged scholars to provide systematic assessments of literature and "integrative research reviews and analysis of theories, populations, and findings" (p. 18).

In their concluding chapter to the book on *Race, Ethnicity and Leisure*, Floyd et al. (2014) argued that future research should focus on macro processes at the societal- and global-levels and, in particular, pay more attention to the globalization issues, the mobility of minority populations, and the possible realignment of racial hierarchies. They also argued that more focus needs to be placed on issues of resistance and trajectories of success and advancement among ethnic and racial groups and that researchers should move beyond examining factors that affect leisure participation and explore outcomes of leisure engagements. More research on topics such as happiness, life satisfaction, and subjective wellbeing among members of racial/ethnic groups is needed. They echoed Floyd, Bocarro, and Thompson's (2008) call for examinations of leisure among minority children and teenagers and argued that more research should examine their use of expressive arts. Floyd et al. (2014) believed that more research should focus on the unique leisure experiences and leisure needs among young families who are often affected by unstable living arrangements, language barrier, economic constraints, discrimination and fear of deportation. Floyd et al. (2014) also called for more research on minority older adults and cautioned against homogenizing ethnic and racial groups. They argued that more focus needs to be placed on similarities *across* ethnic populations and differences *within* them based on subcultures and acculturation levels. They believed that future research should acknowledge and embrace people's multiple intersecting identities shaping their leisure experiences and that development of new theories and more theoretical integration in leisure studies are needed.

Are these research questions still relevant in light of the social and political trends?

Shifts in immigration patterns

While most scholars of ethnicity and race have predicted continued relevance of such research given the current demographic trends (Murdoch, 2014), few expected the extraordinary shifts in the social, cultural and geopolitical situation brought by the massive migration crisis that has swept Europe in 2015–2016. In 2015 alone, European Union (EU) Member States experienced a record number of over 1.2 million asylum seekers (Eurostat, 2016). An additional 359,000 applications for refugee status were processed in 2016 (United Nations High Commissioner for Refugees [UNHCR], 2016a), mostly from people from the war-torn regions of Syria, Afghanistan, Iraq, and North and East Africa. At the end of 2016, the UN Refugee Agency released a statement that "we are now witnessing the highest levels of displacement on record" with "unprecedented 65.3 million people around the world [who] have been forced from home" (UNHCR, 2016b). UNHCR statistics show that, as a result of conflict or persecution, nearly 34,000 people are forcibly displaced every day. Over half of these refugees are children under the age of 18.

Such unprecedented migration flows led to a global humanitarian crisis and contributed to the emergence of exclusionary policies, confrontation tactics, and the rise of far-right movements in many destination countries in Europe and North America (Payne, 2016). For instance, according to a recent PEW report, almost two-thirds of the surveyed Dutch and Italians agreed that "Refugees will increase the likelihood of terrorism in our country," and 72% of Greeks, 65% of Italians and 53% of French concurred with a statement that "Refugees are a burden on our country because they take our jobs and social benefits" (Simmons & Stokes, 2016). Similar anti-immigration sentiments have dominated much of the 2015–2016 election campaign in the United States and the postelection period in early 2017.

In light of these trends, Stodolska and Walker's (2007) cautionary words about the rise of intergroup conflicts sparked by the global crisis, increased migratory flows, and problems with securing borders are salient more than ever. It is hard to ascertain to what extent such conflicts will play out in leisure settings and how the rapid increase in the number of refugees in Europe and other Western countries will affect the utilization of local recreation resources. What we know, however, is that the existing research shows leisure can be a vehicle for coping with the stress of dislocation among the migrants and can facilitate their integration into host societies (Peters, 2010; Rishbeth & Finney, 2006). For instance, the existing studies have shown that visiting urban parks for leisure can give immigrants an insight into the culture of the host society (Rishbeth & Finney, 2006) and allow for interracial interactions, which can contribute to the development of place attachment, cross-cultural understanding, and positive integration (Leikkilä, Faehnle, & Galanakis Peters, 2010). Participation in leisure activities that carry significant cultural components (e.g., tae-kwon-do) can promote cultural understanding (Kim, Heo, King, & Kim, 2014; Rishbeth & Finney, 2006). Studies have also shown that recreational sport participation can facilitate "intergroup harmony" because of its unique ability to foster intergroup contacts and friendships, and thus reducing prejudice and hostility (Lee & Scott, 2013, p. 268). In the coming decades, research on the roles of leisure in reducing stress and loneliness among displaced persons, defusing conflicts, reducing intergroup tensions, bridging the gap between refugees and their host societies, and promoting their integration will be of utmost importance (Mohadin, 2015; Troop, 2015). More studies on the global trends that sparked these migratory flows, their long-term consequences, and on the ways immigrants' leisure is shaped by the broader societal and political discourses will also be needed (Floyd et al. 2014).

Continued significance of race and racism

Over the last 16 years, many researchers have assumed the inevitability of the slow march toward the equality for all and some even heralded the end of the significance of race and ethnicity in shaping people's leisure opportunities and choices (Hutchinson, 2005). In 2014, however, Bonilla-Silva challenged the notion of the postracial society and argued that racial progress has stagnated and even regressed since the 1980s. He claimed that in the last 40 years, we have witnessed the rise of the "color-blind racism" and that racial inequality is a persistent problem in America. Bonilla-Silva argued that the overt racism of the past has been "swiped under the carpet" and that people are no longer free to express their true racial attitudes in a society that shuns overt expressions of racism.

The divisive dialogue that accompanied the 2015–2016 election in the United States and the postelection period, and the campaign that led to the eventual Brexit vote in the United Kingdom made it clear that the overtly prejudicial attitudes are no longer reserved to the fringe element of society but are now common among large portions of the North American and European populations. At the dawn of 2017, many mainstream Americans no longer feel constrained to voice their opinions on the issues of undocumented immigration and the U.S. immigration policy. Executive Orders 13769 (issued on January 27, 2017) and 13780 (issued on March 6, 2017) titled Protecting the Nation from Foreign Terrorist Entry into the United States restricted admission and halted new visa applications of citizens from Iran, Libya, Somalia, Sudan, Syria, and Yemen for 90 days and suspended the U.S. Refugee Admissions Program for 120 days (WhiteHouse.gov, March 6, 2017). Although both executive orders have been stopped by the courts on the grounds of violating the Establishment Clause, the challenge against 13780 and other executive orders and legislations is likely to continue in the foreseeable future. Arrests of undocumented immigrants increased 32.6% in the first weeks of the new administration (Sacchetti, 2017). Not only anti-immigration sentiments have been common at the dawn of 2017, but confrontations between Black protesters and the police that play out in urban settings deepen the mistrust between the law enforcement and the communities of color.

Such hostile climate will lead to further division of communities and is likely to have an effect on how people will interact in leisure settings, and how leisure services will be provided to people of color. In light of these trends, issues of racism, including its institutional forms and processes that lead to exclusion (Allison, 2000) should be the front-center of future leisure research. We have elaborated on this issue in more detail elsewhere (Floyd & Stodolska, In press). Moreover, examinations of intergroup interactions in public spaces and the roles of leisure in creating a sense of community in diverse neighborhoods (Shinew et al., 2006) will be clearly needed. With respect to the predictions of Bonilla-Silva (2002), cited by Shinew et al. (2006), Stodolska and Walker (2007), and Floyd et al. (2014), the racial hierarchy based on the skin color has certainly *not* disappeared but became augmented by divisions along the lines of the legality of status and religious affiliation (Hiemstra, 2005). We are yet to see if the three-tier racial hierarchy will materialize, but the "black-white" color line that divides U.S. society is more visible than ever.

Social justice

Allison (2000) argued that more emphasis on social justice is necessary if we are to achieve equality for all. This line of research has received significant attention in recent years (e.g., Arai & Kivel, 2009; Bocarro & Stodolska, 2013; García, 2013; Johnson & Parry, 2015; Parry, Johnson, & Stewart, 2013; Stewart, 2014), but more focus on this area is needed. Parry et al. (2013) called for embracing critical theories as an effective path to social justice and contended that "leisure is a context where people can create changes that may bring about a more socially just world" (p. 83). Stewart (2014) added that lines of inquiry grounded in the social justice perspective "are motivated by needs to end various kinds of oppression and marginalization related to gender, race, ethnicity, sexual identity, ability, and socioeconomic status within leisure-related contexts" (p. 325). Such research perspective that shares a commitment to challenging and breaking down social structures (Stewart, 2014) is ideally positioned to critically examine the ways in which poverty, structural racism, white hegemony, and migration regimes condition lives, including leisure, among immigrants and people of color. Embracing the social justice framework could also lead to a much-needed shift among the existing race/ethnicity scholarship from the largely descriptive accounts of variations in leisure patterns among minorities to more explanatory investigations of the *reasons* for the existing differences and providing possible *solutions* to achieve social change (Arai & Kivel, 2009; Stewart, 2014).

Evolving structure, characteristics, and adaptation pathways among minority populations

As Floyd et al. (2014) argued, contemporary migration trends and higher (although currently decreasing) (Colby & Ortman, 2015) fertility rates among some immigrant groups led to changes in the age structure of the U.S. population. These trends prompted both the authors of the concluding chapter in *Race, Ethnicity and Leisure* (Floyd et al. 2014) and the 2008 review article (Floyd et al. 2008) to call for examinations of leisure among minority children and youth, with a particular focus on Latino and African American populations. Current projections confirm that the diversity among U.S. children and youth will grow in the future. As Colby and Ortman (2015) argued, "The total population [of the United States] is projected to be 17% Hispanic in 2014 and 29% Hispanic in 2060. In contrast, nearly one-quarter (24%) of the child population is projected to be Hispanic in 2014, and this group's share is projected to increase to 34% in 2060" (p. 11). According to the authors, by 2060, 64% of children in the United States will belong to racial and ethnic minorities. Given the current and projected geographic distribution of minority groups, some regions of the country are likely to be affected by these demographic shifts more than others (Peake, 2012). These statistics alone should serve as a reminder to leisure researchers and practitioners that the population they will be serving in the next 40 years will be markedly different from their current constituents. We should not, however, lose sight of the fact that the majority of these children and youth will comprise of second or third generation ethnics whose life experiences, aspirations, and challenges will be markedly different from their foreign-born counterparts (Portes, Fernandez-Kelly, & Haller, 2009; Portes & Rumbaut, 2007). Despite strong cultural influences of their families and ethnic communities, they will face strong acculturative pressures from their peers and the American educational system. It will be a challenge for leisure researchers to determine to what extent leisure participation patterns, needs, aspirations and constraints of U.S.-born minority children are different from the first generation youth, what societal-, community-, family-, and individual level factors condition their leisure experiences, and how to best serve their leisure needs.

Current demographic predictions also alert us to the emerging trend of the aging of the foreign-born population in the United States. As Colby and Ortman (2015) argued, "in 2014, the majority of the foreign-born [were] concentrated in the ages 20–60. By 2060, the core of the foreign-born population is projected to expand to include the ages between 60 and 80" (p. 8). These changes will be the most pronounced among the foreign-born population 65 and older, which is expected to double from 13% in 2014 to 26% in 2060. In light of these trends, Floyd et al. (2014) appeal for more examinations of leisure among minority older adults is clearly warranted. Calls for a better understanding of the leisure needs of older adults in the United States have been made for decades (Gibson & Singleton, 2012). What we will need to explore, however, is how to provide leisure services to older adults from populations with cultural backgrounds and life experiences different from the "mainstream".

The concepts of "mainstream," "majority" and "white" population will also need to be reexamined. According to the U.S. Census (2015) projections, non-Hispanic Whites will cease to be the majority group by 2044. PEW Research Center estimated that the United States will reach this milestone in 2055 (PEW, 2015). As of 2010, four states (California, Hawaii, New Mexico, and Texas) and the District of Columbia have already attained the "majority minority" status (U.S. Census, 2011). The proportion of non-Hispanic Whites is likely to decrease in many states in the near future (e.g., the Hispanic population of California is projected to increase from 39% in 2016 to 46% in 2060 with a concomitant decrease in the non-Hispanic White population from 38 to 31%) (State of California, 2017). Moreover, the definitions of racial categories and people's self-identification are likely to change. The growing multiracial population in the United States has been termed "the leading edge of a vast change in the way Americans view their cultural and genetic heredity" (Kunkle, 2015). According to a recent PEW report, views on racial identity among young Americans are shifting, formerly fixed boundaries of gender, age, and race are becoming more fluid, and "our standard demographic categories are falling apart" (Kunkle, 2015).

Not only Floyd et al. (2014) and Stodolska and Walker (2007), but researchers as far back as 20 years ago (e.g., Floyd, 1998) also called for more nuanced examinations of minority groups and acknowledging their internal heterogeneity. As we move toward the future, this topic will be more important than ever. Much of the existing leisure research has been quite deterministic and far too often portrayed minority populations as underprivileged, homogenous entities. In contrast, ethnic populations are extremely diverse, both in terms of their socio-economic status and cultural traits, and the adaptation pathways among the second- and third-generation ethnics can follow a number of distinct trajectories (Portes et al. 2009). While some members of minority groups follow "downward assimilation into poverty, unemployment, and deviant lifestyles" (Portes et al. 2009, p. 1080), many others embrace the path of upward mobility and achievement of a middle-class status. Some of the recent sociological models predict that factors such as parental human capital, modes of incorporation, family structure, racial discrimination, bifurcated labor markets and inner-city subcultures determine the assimilation pathways among the U.S.-born ethnics (Portes et al. 2009). Our field is in a unique position to contribute to this discourse by examining to what extent leisure-related choices and experiences affect the trajectories of success and advancement versus lead to downward socio-economic adaptation among ethnic and racial groups. Answering the question of how leisure can assist underprivileged populations in achieving successful outcomes should be a priority.

Moreover, I argue that we have retired Washburne's (1978) marginality thesis far too soon. Instead, we should revisit the socio-economic marginality as an explanatory variable to people's leisure experiences. Future research should better elucidate the mechanisms that contribute to the persistence of poverty enclaves and examine how social and economic dynamics of high-poverty neighborhoods shape their residents' leisure opportunities and choices (Jargowsky, 2009). The last 40 years of research since the publication of Washburne's thesis clearly showed that it is not the matter of either-or but that *both* the socio-economic disadvantage *and* culture affect people's leisure behavior. Now is time to clearly operationalize and understand these concepts (Floyd, 1998) and provide in-depth investigations of the mechanisms through which they shape leisure experiences of people of color.

Theoretical developments and interdisciplinary approaches

More interdisciplinary endeavors will be needed to explore these new research avenues. The pursuit of new leisure-specific theoretical frameworks advocated by Floyd et al. (2014) should not stand it the way of leisure researchers' adopting cutting-edge theoretical frameworks from the allied disciplines such as ethnic and migration studies, sociology, geography, and anthropology. Overall, we are doing a much better job than a decade ago in cross-pollinating social-science fields by placing our work in the journals of our cognate disciplines. However, still much needs to be done to make others appreciate the critical role leisure plays in the human condition, success, and quality of life.

Conclusions

As Shinew et al. (2006) argued in their essay:

> Understanding the leisure behavior of ethnic and racial minorities is an important area of inquiry that has evolved over time. Progress has been made, but we have far to go. ... There is no doubt that we live in an extraordinarily complex society where cultural, religious, political, social, and economic forces are constantly at play. It is our responsibility to identify, understand, and appreciate these forces and incorporate them into our research. (p. 407)

These words are as current in 2017 as they were in 2006. In the climate of increased racial and ethnic tensions, the rise in global migration flows and increasing diversity of our societies, our role as leisure scholars, educators, and practitioners will be more important than ever before. Overall, my assessment is that our predictions from the last 16 years have *not* missed the boat, but the new events and trends have created opportunities and necessitated research on subjects that go far beyond of what scholars of leisure, ethnicity, and race have previously advocated.

References

Allison, M. T. (2000). Leisure, diversity and social justice. *Journal of Leisure Research*, 32, 2–6.

Arai, S., & Kivel, B. D. (2009). Critical race theory and social justice perspectives on whiteness, difference(s) and (anti)racism: A fourth wave of race research in leisure studies. *Journal of Leisure Research*, 41, 459–473.

Bocarro, J., & Stodolska, M. (2013). Researcher and advocate: Using research to promote social justice change. *Journal of Leisure Research*, 46, 2–6.

Bonilla-Silva, E. (2002). We are all Americans!: The Latin Americanization of racial stratification in the USA. *Race & Society*, 5, 3–16

Bonilla-Silva, E. (2003/2014). *Racism without racist: Color-blind racism and the persistence of racial inequality in America*. Plymouth, England: Rowman & Littlefield.

Colby, S. L., & Ortman, J. M. (2015). *Projections of the size and composition of the U.S. population: 2014 to 2060*. U.S. Department of Commerce. Economics and Statistics Administration. U.S. Census Bureau. Retrieved from https://www.census.gov/content/dam/Census/library/publications/2015/demo/p25-1143.pdf

Eurostat (2016). *Asylum in the EU member states*. Retrieved from http://ec.europa.eu/eurostat/documents/2995521/7203832/3-04032016-AP-EN.pdf/790eba01-381c-4163-bcd2-a54959b99ed6

Floyd, M. F. (1998). Getting beyond marginality and ethnicity: The challenge for race and ethnic studies in leisure research. *Journal of Leisure Research*, 39(1), 3–22.

Floyd, M. F., Bocarro, J. N., & Thompson, T. D. (2008). Research on race and ethnicity in leisure studies: A review of five major journals. *Journal of Leisure Research*, 40, 1–22.

Floyd, M. F., & Stodolska, M. (2014). Theoretical frameworks. In M. Stodolska, K. J. Shinew, M. Floyd, & G. Walker (Eds.), *Race, ethnicity, and leisure*, 9–18. Champaign, IL: Human Kinetics.

Floyd, M. F., & Stodolska, S. (In press). Scholarship on race and ethnicity: Assessing contributions to leisure theory and practice. *Journal of Park and Recreation Administration*.

Floyd, M. F., Walker, G., Stodolska, M., & Shinew, K. J. (2014). Conclusion: Emerging issues. In M. Stodolska, K. J. Shinew, M. Floyd, & G. Walker (Eds.), *Race, ethnicity, and leisure*, 297–306. Champaign, IL: Human Kinetics.

Garcia, R. (2013). Social justice and leisure: The usefulness and uselessness of research. *Journal of Leisure Research*, 46(1), 7–22.

Gibson, H., & Singleton, J. (2012). *Leisure and aging: Theory and practice*. Champaign, IL: Human Kinetics.

Gobster, P. (2002). Managing urban parks for a racially and ethnically diverse clientele. *Leisure Sciences*, 24, 143–159.

Henderson, K. A., & Walker, G. J. (2014). Methods. In M. Stodolska, K. J. Shinew, M. Floyd, & G. Walker (Eds.), *Race, ethnicity, and leisure*, 21–36. Champaign, IL: Human Kinetics.

Hiemstra, N. A. (2005, April). *Latino immigrants, spaces of intersection, and the politics of being illegal in Leadville, CO*. Paper presented at the 2005 Annual Meeting of the Association of American Geographers, Denver, CO: Association of American Geographers.

Hutchinson, R. (2005). The racialization of leisure: Comments on Stodolska's discrimination model. *Leisure Sciences*, 27(1), 29–36.

Jargowsky, P. A. (2009). Immigrants and neighborhoods of concentrated poverty: Assimilation or stagnation? *Journal of Ethnic and Migration Studies*, 35(7), 1129–1151.

Johnson, C. W., & Parry, D. C. (2015). *Fostering social justice through qualitative inquiry: A methodological guide*. New York, NY: Routledge.

Kim, J., Heo, J., King, C., & Kim, S. (2014). Cultural understanding and personal growth through Taekwondo as cross-cultural activity. *Journal of Humanistic Psychology*, 54, 3–27.

Kunkle, F. (2015). *Pew: Multiracial population changing the face of the U.S.* Retrieved from https://www.washingtonpost.com/news/local/wp/2015/06/11/pew-multiracial-population-changing-face-of-u-s/

Lashua, B., & Fox, K. (2006). Rec needs a new rhythm cuz rap is where we're livin'. *Leisure Sciences, 28*(3), 207–283.

Lee, K. J., & Scott, D. (2013). Interracial contact experiences during recreational sports: Korean American males' perspectives. *Journal of Leisure Research, 45*, 267–294.

Lee, K. J., & Stodolska, M. (2017). Asian North Americans' leisure: A critical examination of theoretical frameworks used in research and suggestions for future study. *Leisure Sciences, 39*(6), 524–541.

Leikkilä, J., Faehnle, M., & Galanakis, M. (2013). Promoting interculturalism by planning urban nature. *Urban Forestry & Urban Greening, 12*, 183–190.

McAvoy, L. (2002). American Indians, place meanings and the old/new west. *Journal of Leisure Research, 34*, 383–396.

Mohadin, A. (2015). "Here to stay here to play": The soccer teams in Europe composed entirely of refugees. *Quartz*. Retrieved from https://qz.com/521980/here-to-stay-here-to-play-the-soccer-teams-in-europe-composed-entirely-of-refugees

Mowatt, R. A. (2009). Notes from a native son: Expanding an understanding of Whiteness in leisure. *Journal of Leisure Research, 41*(4), 509–526.

Murdoch, S. H. (2014). Foreword. In M. Stodolska, K. J. Shinew, M. F. Floyd, & G. Walker (Eds.), *Race, ethnicity, and leisure*, 7–10. Champaign, IL: Human Kinetics.

Parry, D. C., Johnson, C. W., & Stewart, W. (2013). Leisure research for social justice: A response to Henderson. *Leisure Sciences, 35*, 81–87.

Payne, A. (2016). MAPPED: The growth of the far-right in Europe. *Business Insider* (3/20/2016). Retrieved from http://www.businessinsider.com/map-shows-far-right-growth-across-europe-2016-3?r=UK&IR=T

Peake, R. (2012). *Mapping 2010 Census*. Redlands, CA: Esri Press.

Peters, K. (2010). Being together in urban parks: Connecting public space, leisure, and diversity. *Leisure Sciences, 32*(5), 418–433.

PEW Research Center. (2015). *Modern immigration wave brings 59 million to U.S., driving population growth and change through 2065*. Retrieved from http://www.pewhispanic.org/2015/09/28/modern-immigration-wave-brings-59-million-to-u-s-driving-population-growth-and-change-through-2065/

Portes, A., Fernandez-Kelly, P., & Haller, W. (2009). The adaptation of the immigrant second generation in America: Theoretical overview and recent evidence. *Journal of Ethnic and Migration Studies, 35*(7), 1077–1104.

Portes, A., & Rumbaut, R. G. (2007). Introduction: The second generation and the children of immigrants longitudinal study. *Ethnic and Racial Studies, 28*, 983–999.

Rishbeth, C., & Finney, N. (2006). Novelty and nostalgia in urban greenspace: Refugee perspectives. *Tijdschrift voor Economische en Sociale Geografie, 97*, 281–295.

Sacchetti, M. (2017, April 16). ICE immigration arrests of noncriminals double under Trump. *Washington Post*. Retrieved from https://www.washingtonpost.com/local/immigration-arrests-of-noncriminals-double-under-trump/2017/04/16/98a2f1e2-2096-11e7-be2a-3a1fb24d4671_story.html

Sharaievska, I., Stodolska, M., Shinew, K. J., & Kim, K. J. (2010). Discrimination in leisure settings in Latino urban communities. *Leisure/Loisir, 34*, 295–326.

Shinew, K. J., Stodolska, M., Floyd, M., Hibbler, D., Allison, M., Johnson, C., & Santos, C. (2006). Race and ethnicity in leisure research: Where have we been and where do we need to go? *Leisure Sciences, 28*, 403–408.

Shores, K. A., Scott, D., & Floyd, M. K. (2007). Constraints to outdoor recreation: A multiple hierarchy stratification perspective. *Leisure Sciences, 29*, 227–246

Simmons, K., & Stokes, B. (2016). *Populism and global engagement: Europe, North America and Emerging Economies*. Washington, DC: PEW Research Center. Retrieved from http://www.pewglobal.org/2016/12/15/populism-and-global-engagement-europe-north-america-and-emerging-economies

State of California (2017). *Department of Finance releases new state population projections.* Retrieved from http://www.dof.ca.gov/Forecasting/Demographics/Projections/documents/P_PressRelease.pdf

Stewart, W. (2014). Leisure research to enhance social justice. *Leisure Sciences, 36*(4), 325–339.

Stodolska, M., & Jackson, E. L. (1998). Discrimination in leisure and work experienced by a white ethnic minority group. *Journal of Leisure Research, 30,* 23–46.

Stodolska, M., & Walker, G. J. (2007). Ethnicity and leisure: Historical development, current status, and future directions. *Leisure/Loisir, 31,* 3–26.

Tirone, S., & Goodberry, A. (2011). Leisure, biculturalism, and second-generation Canadians. *Journal of Leisure Research, 43,* 427–444.

Troop, W. (2015). This non-profit group in Italy uses soccer to give migrants hope. *Arts, Culture & Media.* Retrieved from https://www.pri.org/stories/2015-10-08/non-profit-group-italy-uses-soccer-give-migrants-hope

U.S. Census (2011). *2010 Census shows America's diversity.* Retrieved from https://www.census.gov/newsroom/releases/archives/2010_census/cb11-cn125.html

U.S. Census. (2015). *New Census Bureau report analyzes U.S. population projections.* Retrieved from https://www.census.gov/newsroom/press-releases/2015/cb15-tps16.html

Walker, G. J., Deng, J., & Dieser, R. (2001). Ethnicity, acculturation, self-construal, and motivations for outdoor recreation. *Leisure Sciences, 23,* 263–283.

Walker, G. J., & Wang, X. (2009). The meaning of leisure for Chinese/Canadians. *Leisure Sciences, 31,* 1–18.

Walseth, K. (2016). Sport within Muslim organizations in Norway: Ethnic segregated activities as arena for integration. *Leisure Studies, 35*(1), 78–99.

Washburne, R. F. (1978). Black under-participation in wildland recreation: Alternative explanations. *Leisure Sciences, 1,* 175–189.

WhiteHouse.gov (March 6, 2017). *Executive order protecting the nation from foreign terrorist entry into the United States.* Retrieved from https://www.whitehouse.gov/the-press-office/2017/03/06/executive-order-protecting-nation-foreign-terrorist-entry-united-states

Wike, R., Stokes, B., & Simmons, K. (2016). *Europeans fear wave of refugees will mean more terrorism, fewer jobs.* Washington DC: PEW Research Center. Retrieved from http://www.pewglobal.org/2016/07/11/europeans-fear-wave-of-refugees-will-mean-more-terrorism-fewer-jobs/

UNHCR. (2016a). *Refugees/migrants response—Mediterranean.* Retrieved from http://data.unhcr.org/mediterranean/regional.php

UNHCR. (2016b). *Figures at a glance.* Retrieved from http://www.unhcr.org/en-us/figures-at-a-glance.html

Young, I. (1990). *Justice and the politics of difference.* Princeton, NJ: Princeton University Press.

The Case of the 12-Year-Old Boy: Or, The Silence of and Relevance to Leisure Research

Rasul A. Mowatt

ABSTRACT
A 12-year-old boy is shot in a public park on the grounds of being a threat, yet despite the locational relevance there was a silence within leisure research. With this in mind, the aim of this manuscript is a manifesto on the manner that leisure-related research on race, social justice, quality of life, and leisure studies (more broadly, as an academy) must confront the silence with dealing with racism as structural and systematic. If we are to advocate in varying ways on the right of populations to enjoy the life sustaining opportunities that are afforded to them as citizens through leisure, then we must also hold ourselves accountable when those very leisure settings fail to deliver on that promise, and become life-threatening. Tamir Rice, is a case of the duality of silence on the structural nature of racism while also an opportunity to assert a social relevance for leisure research.

c. 3:30pm on November 22, 2014, a 12-year-old boy lay on the grass that was lightly covered with snow after sustaining gunshots from a police officer's gun.

The grass that he laid in was in a public park, Cudell Commons, located in the greater Cleveland, Ohio, area, in close proximity to the Cudell Recreation Center (CRC). The two officers were responding to a 911 dispatch call requesting available units to respond to a Code 1 at the CRC that simply stated, "Cudell Rec Center … there's a black male sitting on a swing …pulling a gun out of his pants and pointing it at people" (Cuyahoga County Sheriff's Office, 2015, p. 3).

According to the Cuyahoga County Prosecutor and Sheriff Office's 224-page five-month investigative report of the City of Cleveland Division of Police use of deadly force, the marked police department vehicle accessed the park area, moved passed the playground area ("swing set"), and then "came to rest between the gazebo and wooden vehicle barriers located on the grass between the gazebo and the parking lot" (p. 3).   Within two seconds, two rounds were fired into the abdomen of the 12-year-old boy "at a distance between than 4.5 feet and 7 feet" (p. 4). "3.5 minutes" after the officers' initial arrival, a request for Emergency Medical Service was sent by one of the two officers, although no medical assistance was given by the officers on the scene prior to the paramedics' arrival. The 12-year-old boy, Tamir Elijah Rice, "expired" at 12:54 am on November 23, 2014.

The aim of this manifesto

Tamir Rice, a 12-year-old boy, was shot in a public park, near a municipal recreation center, and yet there was a silence within leisure research. What is presented here is a manifesto on the manner that leisure-related research on Race,[1] social justice, quality of life, and leisure studies (more broadly as an academy) must be confronted on that silence. As a field we argue and advocate in varying ways on the right of populations to enjoy the opportunities that are afforded through leisure experiences and that those opportunities can be life-sustaining. However, what happens when those opportunities do not succeed? What happens when those very settings become life-threatening? This manifesto is rooted in the *racial threat theory* (also known as the power threat theory) and the *color-blind racial ideology* while posing significant questions on how leisure settings can be proponents of the very structural and systematic nature of racism while envisioning ways to hold the field accountable in thinking of solutions.

This treatise is intended to reassert social advocacy on societal injustices within leisure services and leisure scholarship. By taking the case of Tamir Rice and rightfully situating it

---

[1] Scholars on race contend that the term "Race" should be capitalized since it represents a concrete structure, an institution rather than a generic term that hold several meanings (such as how it is defined in a dictionary). This is an extension of the capitalization of Black, White, etc., when referring to racial categories within the *APA Publication Manual*, 6th edition.

within leisure scholarship, it becomes a tool to advocate and give voice to the voiceless. By seeing the death of Tamir Rice in a public park as related to this field, it becomes not only a tool to affirm empowerment to individuals who are alive but also to those who are dead. The death of someone, especially a child in a location of play, should be disturbing enough to shock and remind us of the very real, the very structural, and the very systematic nature of racism and that unlike racial discrimination, racism is quite legal. As a result we overlook the structural nature of racism, as if some other form of solution other than policy can address its existence (Parham-Payne, 2014). Thus, the initial question of "why should the death of Tamir Rice be relevant to leisure research?" should be correctly altered to "why doesn't leisure research focus on the structural and systematic nature of racism and the violence against populations of color in public recreation and leisure spaces?"

What has preceded and follows is not a study of the legalities in the case of Tamir Rice's death. Rather, we present ways that *racial threat theory* (Blalock, 1967) with an attention to media via media inquiry and media analysis can grant leisure researchers far more immediate ways to inform their line of questioning and study the examples of the structural nature of racism. But a greater awareness of the *color-blind racial ideology* (Frankenberg, 1993) also allows us as researchers to be far more mindful of the current state of affairs of Race in society, and our role in those affairs.

Racial threat theory

The silence from leisure researchers is part and parcel to the silence of many others in society who had a glancing familiarity with the case of Tamir Rice through media outlets since "what we consciously believe and do is tied to many aspects of reality maintenance" that rests on a "stocks of knowledge" of reality (Altheide & Schneider, 2013, p. 13). Because of this stock knowledge, many bring into their perceptions of his shooting varying degrees of impressions of his appearance being less of a boy and more the appearance of a man, or that his erratic playing with a toy gun was far too violent. Viewing the structural nature of racism, Blalock (1967) asserted a theoretical explanation for the existence of racial disparities in the outcomes of the criminal justice system that emphasized that the state-control of populations of color was necessary. In White-dominated societies, power is exerted through institutional practices to protect existing power and privileges. Blalock's theory posited three forms of racial threat: *economic threat* (racialized threats to job availability and stability), *political threat* (racialized threats to political positions of authority), and *symbolic threat* (racialized threats in social conduct and to the social order).

It is the last of his three forms of racial threat that relates most to the case of Tamir Rice in that the very presence of the Black body denotes deviancy and criminality. Through various mechanisms of social construction that create and fabricate conceptions of Black people, a partially media-informed stock knowledge is created of a Black body that engenders a response when encountered in the public sphere. However, within *racial threat theory* or power threat theory this engendered response does not stop with revulsion or disapproval but results in bodily elimination either through arrest, detention, or summary execution. Media is one of the chief tools that Race and racism are socially constructed and maintained. The use of intentional visuals, wordplay, language, and even the frequency of the delivery of information shape our understanding of one racialized incident while preparing us for the next racialized incident.

As a result, we never see racism in the long form, but only in abstract haikus, disjointed excerpts, and unfamiliar snippets that fabricate our conceptions of the deviant behavior that exists in all Black youth, and by extension, all youth of color. Even upon his death a cascade of images from his Facebook page showed him with air pistols and other hand gestures as characterizations and indictments of non-existent gang activity that was worthy of eventual incarceration or execution. Tamir Rice was a threat in the park, he was a threat prior to the park, and he would be a threat to the park in the future. But also, it is not just that Tamir Rice was/is a threat; it is every youth who resembles him, and as a result every youth conjures the same need to call upon state-sanctioned social control and violence. A racially structured society requires a racial ideology,

> not simply a "superstructural" phenomenon (a mere reflection of the racialized system), but becomes the organizational map that guides the actions of racial actors in society. It becomes as real as the relations it organizes. (Bonilla-Silva, 1997, p. 470)

The racial ideology is then rhetorically deployed via dominant narratives that normalizes the White domination of Black (and Brown) bodies. *Symbolic threats*, not human beings, must then be neutralized and put down.

Relevance and silence of a Boy's death

Why should the Tamir Rice incident be relevant to leisure research? What about the incident merits further study? What do we talk about in leisure research when we talk about Race? We have talked about various programmatic initiatives, usage patterns, visitation rates, and aspects of neighborhood conditions, but not the nature of space—leisure spaces as locations that reify the racial social order and maintain the structural nature of racism. Kelly-Pryor and Outley (2014) stated, despite arguing for the subversions of spaces for justice work, "the production of space by the powerful are discursively bound" (p. 276). Pendleton (2000) warned that "in the absence of a leisure setting model of crime and enforcement" the response to crime in leisure settings is "shaped by conventional views of crime and police" (p. 112).

The Cuyahoga County Sheriff's (2015) Department report contained several relevant snippets of information:
- The decedent (Tamir Rice) "per CRC records/witnesses…spent approximately 4 to 5 days a week at the CRC" (p. 8);
- The "911 caller" "was seated in the gazebo area and noticed an African American male with a gun…described male as "probably" a juvenile waving a "fake" gun…claims that the person was "acting gangster" in a witness interview on conducted on March 5, 2015 (p. 9);
- A Recreational Instructor Level 1 at the CRC "remembered [the 12-year-old boy] coming to the CRC that afternoon" (p. 10) and later received a phone call from her manager that "one of her volleyball players' brother just got shot at the recreation center…" (p. 138);
- A "Supervisor for 'Old Tymers' basketball team at the CRC" saw the "young male" pointing a gun at the ground and that no one else was present (p. 11), and that he was 81 years old and a 34-year consultant and "teacher in physical education and recreation" (p. 152); and
- Another interview of an associate (to Tamir) that "occasionally would play basketball with [Tamir Rice] and commented that he wasn't that good of a basketball player…the guys at the CRC liked to pick on [Tamir Rice] and bully him" (p. 140).

Much of this counters all initial coverage and preponderant understanding of what transpired on November 22, 2014, not because the information had been withheld but instead had been packaged in such way that prevents a larger view. As Morales (2013) contended

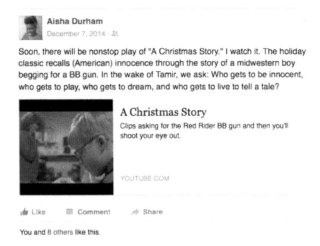

Figure 3. Post from noted feminist scholar Aisha Durham (Durham, 2014).

on myth construction and meaning making in a mediated culture, "it is very easy to see how a particular presentation of data in the media can become a common belief around people" (p. 40). Throughout the various forms of media coverage, official reports, social media commentary, etc., the words park, playground, play, toy, commons, recreation, center, basketball, volleyball, and sport spring forth like intentional keywords meant for a search.

For over a year, information began to be leaked or officially released on this case. In the public arena and through various local, national, and international news agencies conducted their own investigations and subsequent commentaries. Each presented their perspective on the incident of Tamir Rice's shooting and packaged that information based on their audiences' demographic profile and agency mission. Various publicly known individuals, including one professional football wide receiver based in Cleveland, stepped forward and added their voice to the incident, sometimes with support, and most times with disgust and condemnation. As Johnson, Richmond, and Kivel (2008) stated that "narratives seem to strip away the power and at times punish those characters who symbolically represent hegemonic masculinity," and despite his status a professional football player he became publically marginalized for standing on a position (p. 308).

Once the news of his shooting and death, organizers and activists planned various protests throughout the city of Cleveland. In this age of social media, others chimed in various ways on Tamir Rice's death presenting Facebook posts directly after the video was released. Cultural studies/critical feminist scholar Aisha Durham (2014) questioned, "who gets to be innocent, who gets to play, who gets to dream, and who gets to live to tell a tale…" (see Figure 3). Twitter in particular became a location for users of color who wished to employ the brevity and feedback mechanisms inherent in the digital platform to grieve, discuss, and plan since Twitter has sometimes been seen as a venue for civic activism in the public sphere (Brock, 2012). While returning to the usage of Facebook, others presented posts after the announcement that the two officers would not be indicted, a little over a year after the first video was released (see Figure 4; Pinckney, 2015). A leisure scholar of color from Clemson, HP Pinckney IV (2015) posted:

> A Black male [and female] in this country…cannot simply walk to the local gas station or convenience store for a snack. They cannot simply enjoy a leisurely drive with friends while listening to their favorite artist on full blast. They cannot play with toy guns.

Figure 4. Post from a leisure scholar Harrison Pinckney (Pinckney, 2015).

However, Durham's 2014 social media posting is coupled with a voice in academic spaces through her 2015 follow-up article "_____ While Black: Millennial Race Play and the Post-Hip-Hop Generation" in *Cultural Studies ↔ Critical Methodologies*. Analysis and articulation of a social critique within other fields exists both in academic and social media spaces. Within certain disciplines in social behavioral sciences (sociology, psychology), the humanities (cultural studies, history), and professional fields (criminal justice, public policy) voice overwhelms any chance for a silence on a current or enduring phenomenon. Does the field of leisure research have any mechanisms or outlets for these types of discussions? Does the field of leisure research inhibit this type of discussion? The silence seems to perpetuate a lack of knowing that is crucial to the structural nature of racism and its racial ideological underpinnings. The racial ideology that operates in the United States is a racial contract and "cognitive model that precludes self-transparency and genuine understanding of social realities …an invented delusional world, a racial fantasyland, a "consensual hallucination" …though this particular hallucination is located in real space" (Mills, 1997, p. 18). Racial ideologies rely on not knowing and not being reflexive about empirical exemplars of racism (the case of Tamir Rice). So the silence in leisure research could be both an outcome of this incognizance as well as a perpetrator of it. The lack of the presence of research and discussions on the structural nature of racism begets further lack of knowing and blindness to the effects of racism.

Color-Blind racial ideology

Despite the overwhelming use of leisure related terminology and the fact that the very location of the shooting took place in a public park, there had been a perceived overwhelming silence in leisure related online discussion forums (e.g., TALS—The Academy of Leisure Sciences, CALS—Canadian Association for Leisure Studies), and, sessions at official gatherings (National Recreation and Park Association 2015 Congress) since the shooting, death, and grand jury ruling. Why has there been a silence within The Academy of Leisure Sciences?

Neville, Awad, Brooks, Flores, and Bluemel (2013) empirically contended that a *color-blind racial ideology* consisted of two salient domains: 1) *color-evasion* (denial of Race and racial differences in society while emphasizing sameness) and 2) *power-evasion* (denial of Racism, and the impact of racism while highlighting the significance of various examples of equal opportunity). *Color-evasion* emphasizes in the idea of sameness as a conscious way to reject "the idea of white racial superiority," and that there is White-dominance in society (Frankenberg, 1993, p. 147). *Color-evasion* reduces incidents of racial discrimination to isolated circumstances of bad actors acting badly, rather than normal exertions of White actors acting White. While *power-evasion*, in the context of this ideology, denotes that "any failure to achieve [or succeed in society] is therefore the fault of people of color themselves" (Frankenberg, p. 14). *Power-evasion* completely denies that racism can/is structural, has a history, and is maintained at a macro-level by institutions. At best for the color-blinded individual, racism is a phenomenon of simple racial slurs and sentiments levied at a person, and that racism can be weeded out of society by trying harder and doing better as people.

The dangers of racism that resulted in the shooting of Elenor Bumpurs, Malice Green, Aiyana Stanley-Jones, Rekia Boyd, Trayvon Martin, Tamir Rice, and others are countless isolated circumstances. Each is a horrible case to think of in relationship to the loss of life, but none of the slain merit the slightest supposition on our part as observers and researchers that the incidents are interconnected acts of state-control. Within a *color-blind racial ideology*, each action can be broken down to actions that should or should not have been done by the victim. Media sources assist in framing each shooting into a racial ideology of normalcy. But media are also created by people who come into their roles as journalists, reporters, or producers with their preexisting racial ideologies of normalcy. The evasiveness in a *color-blind racial ideology* is both a tool and by-product in the phenomenon of racism.

Indications of the structural nature of racism

This phenomenon of positing the dangers, control, and potential elimination of the Black body should not be regulated to discussions within sociology, political science, criminology, or any other field. According to Swaine, Laughland, Lartey, and McCarthy (2015), although Black males between the ages of 15 and 34 comprise only 2% of the U.S. population, they "comprised more than 15% of all deaths …Paired with official government mortality data …one in every 65 deaths of a young African American man …is a killing by police." When the occurrences of these deaths by law enforcement are in a park or engaged in recreation, as was the case of Tamir Rice, our conception of the sanctity of green space and the benefits of recreation are called into question.

Although Cudell Commons and the CRC seemed to present a fairly moderate if not successful provision of space, facility, and programming, since both Tamir Rice and his sister were engaged in structured and unstructured activities quite often (City of Cleveland, n.d.). However, the presence of the park-owned-and-operated surveillance system seems to go well beyond Scott's (2013) call to increase safety to encourage access to parks and community facilities. On page 174 of the Cuyahoga County Sheriff's Office (2015) report, a total of 10 cameras were operational at all times by the CRC manager. As Scott (2013) and Stodolska, Shinew, Acevedo, and Roman (2013) noted, fear of crime is frequent and high in communities of color and communities experiencing high volume of concentrated poverty. As a result, "fear of crime is among the most frequently reported reasons why many poorer Americans do not make greater use of community leisure facilities near where they live" (Scott, p. 7), which may explain that through viewing the 30-minute video the park is quite empty besides Tamir and the few of people who interacted with him. But what do these calls for increased surveillance, policing, police presence, and tough-on-crime tactics beget within communities of color and on people of color?

It is of increasing importance to not lose sight of how city development strategies and the privatization of public spaces are playing out in the context of which communities will have the ease of access to leisure spaces throughout the United States. Positively, we see some parks and emerging greenways serving as social catalysts for prosocial cross-racial interaction due to their fluid programmable nature and the geographical pattern of weaving through racially and ethnically segregated neighborhoods (Coutts & Miles, 2011). Negatively, it is also crucial to think about the role of police in regulating and determining who has access to spaces for recreation and who is empowered to enjoy those spaces.

In scanning for other such cases in leisure settings or engaging in recreation, one has to wonder about what the empirical does not tell us about the presence of the structural nature of racism and the systematic ways that certain populations are eliminated when posing a (symbolic) threat. We can search and find the following: 1) deaths of 36-year-old Miguel Espinal in Tibbetts Brook Park in the Bronx (Fenton & Cohen, 2015) and 29-year-old Jason Moland in Beyer Park in Modesto, California (Recede, 2015) by law enforcement officers; 2) choking death of 39-year-old Jonathan Sanders after being detained while driving a horse drawn buggy (exercising the horse) in Clarke County, Mississippi (Swaine, 2015); 3) death of 26-year-old Jordan Baker who was apparently simply riding a bike and window shopping in Houston, Texas (Dia, 2014); 4) death of 20-year-old D'Andre Berghardt Jr., at hands of Bureau of Land Management agents after he asked several passersby for water near Red Rock Canyon National Conservation Area (Goldstein, 2014); and lastly, the death of 22-year-old Darren Nathaniel Hunt while engaged in Anime Cosplay with a toy sword (Hathaway, 2014).

Ta-Nehisi Coates (2015), in the critically praised *Between the World and Me*, remarked to his young son,

> Now I personally understood my father and the old mantra—"Either I can beat him or the police…that is a philosophy of the disembodied, of a people who control nothing, who can protect nothing, who are made to fear not just the criminals among them but the police who lord over them with all the moral authority of a protection racket. (p. 82)

This is a phenomenon that merits leisure studies' attention. As even in seeking formal complaints we begin to see racial disparities, according to Shifflett, Scheller, Alecci, and Forster (2015), communities have attempted to speak for themselves through the filing of complaints, they go mostly unheard. Shifflett et al. reported that in Chicago,

> of 10,500 complaints filed by black people between 2011 and 2015, just 166—or 1.6%—were sustained or led to discipline after an internal investigation. Overall, the authority sustained just 2.6% of all 29,000 complaints. Nationally, between 6 and 20% of citizen-initiated complaints are sustained.

Leisure research and recreation programming must acknowledge the ways that the structural nature of racism destroys the lives of youth of color, in particular Black youth, far greater than they "destroy" themselves which runs counter to the ways we have articulated "at-risk" youth programming over the decades (Witt & Caldwell, 2010). As Stacey Patton (2014) commented, "Black America has again been reminded that its children are not seen as worthy of being alive...not seen as children at all, but as menacing threats to white lives." Crime as an infestation in certain communities thereby establishes the myth of the Black-on-Black crime epidemic that remains in our thinking. As both media consumers and as researchers, and despite never dealing with actual empirical evidence that states otherwise, through a color-evasive approach we perpetuate the structural phenomenon of the deprived and dangerous "Black community/ghetto" while never highlighting the structural nature of the society that erects Race and racism (Black homicides have the sharpest rate of decrease than all other racial demographics in the states; according to Jackson, 2013). Our cognition of crime simultaneously strips the usage of outright racial overtones as a product of a greater society, while subverting our senses with underwritten racialized undertones through the imagery (the Black perpetrator) and wordplay ("urban," "at-risk," "inner-city") of location specific acts of crime (the Bronx, Southside of Chicago, Compton, Liberty City–Miami, South Philadelphia, etc.).

Do all lives, really, matter?

Who has a right to leisure? Who has a right to leisure spaces, and who does not? Pendleton (2000) further warned that "an uninformed rush to adopt an urban based understanding of crime and subsequent enforcement promises to be inappropriate to many if not most leisure settings" (p. 115). The *symbolic threat* of Black youth informs macro-level patterns of police use of force (Parker, MacDonald, Jennings, & Alpert, 2005). Differences in neighborhoods determine policing style (Weitzer, 2000), and communities with higher levels of poverty and disadvantage increase the likelihood of the use of force (Barlow & Barlow, 2000; Terrill & Reisig, 2003).

Far and wide, some variation of concept/term quality of life is used within the mission statements of parks and recreation agencies, independent recreation centers, and numerous nonprofit facilities. Furthermore, it is the often go-to phrasing for leisure scholars to frame and discuss research. Yet we continue to see stark realities based on Race, and/or the combination of Race and class-in-leisure services, in the allocation of resources (Corner & Skraastad-Jurney, 2008; García, 2013; Wolch, Wilson, & Fehrenbach, 2005), the lack of dearth in the offerings of youth programming that is culturally relevant and supportive of youth of color (Floyd & Mowatt, 2014; Kelly-Pryor & Outley, 2014; Pinckney, Outley, Blake, & Kelly, 2011; Shinew, Mowatt, & Glover, 2007), and the absence and need for policy related to the acknowledgment of social inequity within communities of color (McKenzie, Moody, Carlson, Lopez, & Elder, 2013; Scott, 2013).

As mentioned earlier, Durham's (2015) "____ While Black: Millennial Race Play and the Post-Hip-Hop Generation" is of special note as she looked at the various Internet memes that were created about the next dead Black body as a new form of virtual pleasure, entertainment, and leisure. Durham posited that, "from the mobile game to blackface memes, new media Race play dictates White pleasure [that] can trump Black pain" (p. 4). Quality of life is not a naturally occurring reality. The idea of it must recognize the forces that are at play that prevent various peoples from not fully enjoying it. In many ways, quality of life may be important, just not everyone's quality of life.

In 2000, Pendleton warned leisure researchers and practitioners that "as the Millennium approaches it seems possible that crime and enforcement may become a defining part of an evolving leisure experience that has not been fully recognized and explored" (p. 111). He contended that "crime is a part of the leisure setting" (Pendleton, 2000, p. 112) and that we need to be cautious in how we refurbish spaces to no longer be civil or social (Pendleton, 1998). Despite his 1998 warning, communities have been overpoliced and populations of color that are oversurveilled continue to be in 2016, as individuals no matter where they roam, move, or recreate. But as Cobb (2015) opined, these are not matters of police and policing since in numerous cases the police were responding to dispatch calls informed by "the perceptions of callers who saw armed black men [and women] and deduced a criminal threat. The police became simply the final and most lethal vectors of a much broader public suspicion."

Making black lives matter in leisure research

Whose quality of life matters? Where do they matter? When do they matter, and when do they not? García (2013) acknowledged that "there may be a concern that advocacy "taints" research" (p. 8). However, he sees research and advocacy in having the opportunity for a great partnership in terms of social justice in leisure. Taking his discussion further, advocacy or the "act of pleading or arguing ...[for a] cause, idea, or policy; active support" (García, 2013, p. 8). Within a mediated culture, we become dependent on media to guide us in processing, organizing, and categorizing information for us. We can read a headline and bypass the report because it does not fit in our cognitive newsfeed. We no longer are scavengers seeking news in a plethora of location; we simply wait for it to be given to us by like-minded "friends" and easily rendered reliable sources. The realities of people of color and their safety in leisure spaces and while engaging in recreation is threatened not only by law enforcement enforcing social policy but also by every citizenry that act as vigilantes and informed citizens. The following news-related occurrences further accentuate the ways that the structural and systematic nature of racism are performed by a variety of racial actors.

The hanging "suicide" of lennon lacy on a swing set

Just as Tamir Rice's death lost its temporal resonance, the death of 17-year-old Lennon Lacy of Bladenboro, North Carolina, probably never even came for most of us.

The news of it simply went away in spite of the questionable nature of his death, which was ruled a mystery since his body was found hanging from a playground swing set (see Figure 5; Pilkington, 2014). In a town of 1,700, his death conjures up a state history "in which 86 black

Figure 5. The swing set where Lennon Lacy was found hanging from in a trailer park in the rural town of Bladenboro, North Carolina (Craft, 2014; photo credit Andrew Craft: www.acraftphoto.com).

people were lynched between 1882 and 1968" for the small black community (Pilkington, 2014). Despite being a neighborhood "good kid," a narrative quickly emerged that sexually linked him to a 31-year-old White woman who lived across from the Lacy family. Wordplay and language describing Black children becomes problematic, criminal, and dangerous. Goff, Jackson, Di Leone, Culotta, and DiTomasso (2014) noted that across four studies testing three hypotheses, Black boys were consistently seen as older, less innocent, not childlike, associated with apes, and were appropriate targets for police violence.

The craig ranch pool party and the right of access

As in 2015, we witnessed another incident of national attention related to pool access and Race in McKinney, Texas, when a cop threw down a Black girl while also preparing to unholster his firearm on a Black boy who approached him (Bouie, 2015). Bouie concluded with a historical account of similar incidents throughout American history when he noted that

> every part of this incident—from the setting of a private pool in a predominantly White suburb to the angry neighbors and eventual violence—is informed by this fraught history of Race and swimming. Whether they realize it or not, each participant—from the kids to the residents to the police—was playing an old part in an even older story of anger and confrontation.

The valley swim club revoking campers of color

The pool incident of 2015 goes alongside a tradition of Race and swimming (as Bouie indicated). But another incident in 2009 involved a large number of campers of color who were denied access to a private pool, although their summer camp program had paid for their access. When this group of day campers from "inner city" Philadelphia traveled to a suburb just outside the city limits, they were quickly met with hostility and restriction. Members of the private pool raised issued with staff because "there was concern that a lot of kids would change the complexion … and the atmosphere of the club" (Lattinzio, 2009). The campers, predominantly of color, conjured up an immediate discursive meaning of disdain and potential deviancy that led to the need for control mechanisms to be instituted for their removal. The micro-level incident should not be seen as an isolated case, but more indicative of a phenomenon of how the macro-level nature structural racism exists, and more importantly exists within leisure (Lewis, Mowatt, & Yuen, 2016).

The irony of eric garner's life

We were bombarded with the audio sounds and visual imagery of Eric Garner exclaiming 11 times that he could not breathe when New York City officers sought to detain him while he stood hanging out in front of a business he frequented (allegedly selling single cigarettes). As he gasped his last breath from being held in a chokehold, more questions were raised about what Mr. Garner could have done to elicit such a response from the officers rather than questioning the unnecessary ferocity of the officers present. Ross Gay (recorded by PBS Newshour), scholar and poet, quickly responded with answering the question of what Eric Garner did not on that city block but in his life (Segal, 2015, www.splitthisrock.org/poetry-database/poem/a-small-needful-fact):

A Small Needful Fact

Is that Eric Garner worked

for some time for the Parks and Rec.

Horticultural Department, which means,

perhaps, that with his very large hands,

perhaps, in all likelihood,

he put gently into the earth

some plants which, most likely,

some of them, in all likelihood,

continue to grow, continue

to do what such plants do, like house

and feed small and necessary creatures,

like being pleasant to touch and smell,

like converting sunlight

into food, like making it easier

for us to breathe.

Advocating for change, calling for solutions

This manifesto is to appeal to leisure scholars, as Johnson et al. (2008) remarked to challenge the "White" experience that is dominant in leisure research. This manifesto seeks to highlight the voice and power of those who have been most impacted by the systematic structure of racism. Has leisure research in not viewing the case of Tamir Rice as relevant, regulated him and others like him as a population of people who are not to be heard? Has leisure research deemed him and others like him as non-existent, unimportant, or even difficult to access emotionally and intellectually?

A return to soft enforcement policies in leisure settings

Taking a cue from older enforcement strategies within the national park system, the use of soft enforcement in urban parks, and other leisure settings might be a plausible response to crime or perceptions of criminal activity (Pendleton, 1998). The underlying philosophy of soft enforcement is the use of "informal methods of education, prevention and community relations" (p. 552). This counters the philosophy of hard enforcement that arrests, doles out citations, and necessitates the use of force. More importantly, the use of soft enforcement ensures that the primary mandate of the park of "public enjoyment" is coupled with the second mandate of protection. Further, the need to return to soft enforcement in leisure settings increases community stability while encouraging residents to increase their visitation of those locations. Sadly, Pendleton (1998) remarked that little research had been done (and is still the case) on the transition from soft enforcement to hard enforcement, much less the ramifications of such a transition.

Concentrated poverty with pockets of peace

As Leech (2015) studied, the narrow focus on "pockets of crime" have completely ignored the "pockets of peace" where virtually no crime exists nor do the traditionally structured deterrents to crime (e.g., churches, recreation programming) are also present. The existence of "pockets of peace" challenges the prevailing myth of Black neighborhoods as being crime ridden and the overfocus of crime that does occur in those neighborhoods. As with any neighborhood there is nuance, and research on neighborhoods needs to show that nuance, since "among neighborhoods dealing [with] delinquency, those with higher rates of homeownership experiences fewer misdemeanor and felony charges" (Leech, p. 10). It also challenges us as researchers and practitioners from solely investing in formal forms of youth supervision and programming to address delinquent behavior. Informal forms of youth supervision from neighbors and neighborhood block clubs have shown some signs of lower rates of criminal activity for adolescence.

Expanding the idea of the public trust doctrine

The public trust doctrine became a part of common law in the United States on public lands in 1892. Over the past 50 years, there has been resurgence in invoking the principles of the doctrine in Canada and the United States. The doctrine stresses that public lands ought to remain the right of access to all over the exclusive use by private interest. Although much of the resurgence has revolved around access to waterways and shorelines (Negris, 1986; Pentland, 2009), the fundamental notion of public access is what is most important with the doctrine.

As questions about access and citizenship seem to be increasing in fervor, the need to advocate for the use of public space by the full public is more than warranted. It is also imperative to think about the ways Race is operating within questions of access. Who has access? Who belongs? Who is allowed? Each question and how an answer is conceived determines access to public, privatized, and privately funded public spaces; and to the very role of police in controlling those spaces and how policy makers have conscripted police to operate in a certain way.

A concluding stance

Floyd (2014) remarked, "when we do not speak up, we are in effect contributing to the very same inequalities and injustices we seek to undo" (p. 383). Further, "researchers working in the social justice arena must be willing to take intentional and unequivocal positions that place them well beyond the line separating research and activism and advocacy," since the social problems that communities of color face are not just socially unacceptable but also life threatening (Floyd, p. 385).

Rather than seeing our role as researchers as limited to only whether we should conduct research on communities or in partnership with communities, maybe the question of our role is about conducting research as a member of a community (Leech & Potts, 2010). Sadly being a member of a community also poses the very real, the very systematic, and the very structural nature of racism that makes it more than likely as a scholar of color to be seen as a *symbolic racial threat* and become a victim like Tamir Rice or as a "fortunate" survivor like Mark Clements (survivor of torture tactics; Sharp, 2014). As a member of a community, there is not a distance to overcome related to studying and research the structural nature of racism. We need to question the apprehension of "bias" in research in order to determine how it maintains a hidden *color-blind racial ideology* that prevents us from taking part in social change. We as researchers should see ourselves as another advocate with other members of a community for self-determination.

Yet Tamir Rice is a dual case of the silence and relevance of leisure research in dealing the structural nature of racism. It shows on one hand, the complicity of us as leisure research to wrestle with difficult subject matter that is fundamentally associated with the literature. While on the other hand, it grants leisure research a way that it can be relevant in the public sphere and in our classrooms. As Stacey Patton (2014) concluded that "the legions of young people protesting the Ferguson travesty in schools, on social media and in the streets are [simply] trying to ensure that children of color get to be children — and that they live to see adulthood, too." Thus, as we continue to research and advocate for the improved quality of life of communities, we are absolutely saying that Black lives do matter, because Tamir was simply playing in the park as was his right to.

References

Altheide, D. L., & Schneider, C. J. (2013). *Qualitative media analysis*. Thousand Oaks, CA: Sage.
Barlow, D., & Barlow, M. (2000). *Police in a multicultural society*. Prospect Heights, IL: Waveland.
Blalock, H. M. (1967). *Toward a theory of minority-group relations*. New York, NY: Wiley and Sons.
Bonilla-Silva, E. (1997). Rethinking racism: Toward a structural interpretation. *American Sociological Review*, 62, 465–480.
Bouie, J. (2015). Our segregated summers: The police misconduct in McKinney, Texas is part of America's long, fraught history of race and swimming. *The Slate*. Retrieved from http://www.slate.com/articles/news_and_politics/politics/2015/06/mckinney_texas_police_misconduct_at_swimming_pool_party_america_s_ugly_history.html
Brock, A. (2012). From the blackhand side: Twitter as a cultural conversation. *Journal of Broadcasting & Electronic Media*, 56(4), 529–549. doi:10.1080/08838151.2012.732147
City of Cleveland. (n.d.). Cudell recreation. *City of Cleveland Recreation Home Page*. Retrieved from http://www.city.cleveland.oh.us/node/5320
Colorofchange.org. (2015, December 30). We won't be silent #BlackAugust #HeyMeg. *Colorofchange.org: Changing the color of democracy*. Retrieved from http://colorofchange.org/campaign/we-wont-be-silent-blackaugust-heymeg/original_email/
Corner, J. C., & Skraastad-Jurney, P. D. (2008). Assessing the locational equity of community parks through the application of geographic information systems. *Journal of Park and Recreation Administration*, 26(1), 122–146.
Coates, T. (2015). *Between the world and me*. New York, NY: Spiegel & Grau.
Cobb, J. (2015, December 29). Tamir Rice and America's tragedy. *The New Yorker*. Retrieved from http://www.newyorker.com/news/daily-comment/tamir-rice-and-americas-tragedy
Coutts, C., & Miles, R. (2011). Greenways as green magnets: The relationship between the race of greenway users and race in proximal neighborhoods. *Journal of Leisure Research*, 43(3), 317–333.

Craft, A. (2014, October 9). The swing set where Lennon Lacy was found hanging from in a trailer park in the rural town of Bladenboro, North Carolina *The Guardian*. Retrieved from http://www.theguardian.com/us-news/2014/oct/09/-sp-north-carolina-teenager-suspicious-death-lennon-lacy

Cuyahoga County Sheriff's Office. (2015, June 2). *Synopsis of CCSD Case #15–004 use of deadly force incident*. Northeast Ohio Media Group. Retrieved from http://www.cleveland.com/metro/index.ssf/2015/06/911_caller_was_frightened_tami.html

Dia, H. (2014). Mom of Houston man shot dead speaks out. *Newsone*. Retrieved from http://newsone.com/2852332/jordan-baker-houston/

Durham, A. (2014, December 7). In *Facebook* [Personal Profile]. Retrieved from https://www.facebook.com/aisha.durham?fref=ts

Durham, A. (2015). ____ While Black: Millennial race play and the post-hip-hop generation. *Cultural Studies <->Critical Methodologies*, 15(4), 253–259.

Fenton, R., & Cohen, S. (2015). NYPD cops fatally shoot suspect after wild car chase. *New York Post*. Retrieved from http://nypost.com/2015/12/08/nypd-chase-of-armed-suspects-ends-in-wild-crash/

Floyd, M. F. (2014). Social justice as an integrating force for leisure research. *Leisure Sciences*, 36(4), 379–387. doi:10.1080/01490400.2014.917002

Floyd, M. F., & Mowatt, R. A. (2014). Leisure and African Americans: A historical overview. In M. Stodolska, M. Floyd, K. J. Shinew, & G. J. Walker (Eds.), *Race, ethnicity, and leisure* (pp. 53–74). Champaign, IL: Human Kinetics.

Frankenberg, R. (1993). *White women, race matters: The social construction of whiteness*. Minneapolis, MN: University of Minnesota Press.

García, R. (2013). The George Butler lecture: Social justice and leisure. *Journal of Leisure Research*, 46(1), 7–22. doi:http://dx.doi.org/10.18666/JLR-2013-V45-I1-2940

Goff, P. A., Jackson, M. C., Di Leone, B. A. L., Culotta, C. M., & DiTomasso, N. A. (2014). The essence of innocence: Consequences of dehumanizing Black children. *Journal of Personality and Social Psychology*, 106(4), 526–545. doi:10.1037/a0035663

Goldstein, S. (2014, February 19). Shocking video shows cops in Nevada shoot man several times after he enters police vehicle. *New York Daily News*. Retrieved from http://www.nydailynews.com/news/national/video-cops-shoot-man-dead-nevada-highway-article-1.1620564

Hathaway, J. (2014, October 29). Autopsy: Cops shot Black anime cosplayer four times in the back. *Gawker*. Retrieved from http://gawker.com/autopsy-cops-shot-black-anime-cosplayer-four-times-in-1652268367

Jackson, M. (2013, July 29). The myth of the Black-on-Black crime epidemic. *Demos Policy Shop*. Retrieved from http://www.demos.org/blog/7/29/13/myth-black-black-crime-epidemic

Johnson, C. W., Richmond, L., & Kivel, B. D. (2008). "What a man ought to be, he is far from": Collective meanings of masculinity and race in media. *Leisure/Loisir*, 32(2), 303–330.

Kelly-Pryor, B. N., & Outley, C. (2014). "Just spaces": Urban recreation centers as sites for social justice youth development. *Journal of Leisure Sciences*, 46(3), 272–290.

Lattinzio, V. (2009, July 10). Swim club members: "Nothing to with race." *NBC News10*. Retrieved from http://www.nbcphiladelphia.com/news/archive/Swim-Club-Members-Nothing-to-Do-With-Race.html

Leech, T. G. J. (2015). Beyond collective supervision: Informal social control, prosocial investment, and juvenile offending in urban neighborhoods. *Journal of Research on Adolescence*, 26(3), 418–431. doi:10.1111/jora.12202

Leech, T. G. J., & Potts, E. (2010). Community empowerment through an academic product: Implications for social-justice oriented scholar. *Journal of African American Studies*, 14, 75–86. doi:10.1007/s12111-009-9108-3

Lewis, S. T., Mowatt, R. A., & Yuen, F. (2016). Chapter 9: Working through difference: Acknowledging power, privilege, and the roots of oppression. In E. Sharpe, H. Mair, & F. Yuen (Eds.), *Community development: Application for leisure*. State College, PA: Venture Publishing.

McKenzie, T. L., Moody, J. S., Carlson, J. A., Lopez, N. V., & Elder, J. P. (2013). Neighborhood income matters: Disparities in community recreation facilities, amenities, and programs. *Journal of Park and Recreation Administration*, 31(4), 12–22.

Mills, C. (1997). *The racial contract*. London, England: Cornell University Press.

Morales, S. S. (2013). Myth and the construction of meaning in mediated culture. *KOME – An International Journal of Pure Communication Inquiry*, 1(2), 33–43.

Negris, K. A. (1986). Access to New Jersey beaches: The public trust doctrine. *Columbia Journal of Law and Social Problems, 20*, 437–460.

Neville, H. A., Awad, G. H., Brooks, J. E., Flores, M. P., & Bluemel, J. (2013). Color-blind racial ideology: Theory, training, and measurement implications in psychology. *American Psychologist, 68*(6), 455–466. doi:10.1037/a0033282

Northeast Ohio Media Group. (2015, January 7). *Extended Tamir Rice shooting video shows officers restrained sister* [Screen shot #1 from public released Video]. Retrieved from http://www.cleveland.com/metro/index.ssf/2015/01/extended_tamir_rice_shooting_v.html

Parham-Payne, W. (2014). The role of the media in the disparate response to gun violence in America. *Journal of Black Studies, 45*(8), 752–768.

Parker, K. F., MacDonald, J. M., Jennings, W. G., & Alpert, G. P. (2005). Racial threat, urban conditions and police use of force: Assessing the direct and indirect linkages across multiple urban areas. *Justice, Research and Policy, 7*(1), 53–79.

Patton, S. (2014, November 26). In America, Black children don't get to be children. *The Washington Post*. Retrieved from https://www.washingtonpost.com/opinions/in-america-black-children-dont-get-to-be-children/2014/11/26/a9e24756-74ee-11e4-a755-e32227229e7b_story.html

Pendleton, M. (1998). Policing the park: Understanding soft enforcement. *Journal of Leisure Research, 30*, 552–571.

Pendleton, M. R. (2000). Leisure, crime and cops: Exploring a paradox of our civility. *Journal of Leisure Research, 32*(1), 111–115.

Pentland, R. (2009). *Public trust doctrine: Potential in Canadian water and environmental management*. POLIS Discussion Paper 09–03. Victoria, BC, Canada: POLIS Project on Ecological Governance.

Pilkington, E. (2014, October 9). Teenager's mysterious death evokes painful imagery in North Carolina: "It's in the DNA of America." *The Guardian*. Retrieved from http://www.theguardian.com/us-news/2014/oct/09/-sp-north-carolina-teenager-suspicious-death-lennon-lacy

Pinckney, H. P., Outley, C., Blake, J. J., & Kelly, B. (2011). Promoting positive youth development of Black youth: A rites of passage framework. *Journal of Park and Recreation Administration, 29*(1), 98–112.

Pinckney, H. P. (2015, December 29). In *Facebook* [Personal Profile]. Retrieved from https://www.facebook.com/profile.php?id=8358987&fref=ts

Recede, K. (2015, April 20). Off-duty Ceres police officer accused of shooting man loses job. *Fox 40*. Retrieved from http://fox40.com/2015/04/20/off-duty-ceres-police-officer-accused-of-shooting-man-loses-job/

Scott, D. (2013). Economic inequality, poverty, and park and recreation delivery. *Journal of Park and Recreation Administration, 31*(4), 1–11.

Segal, C. (2015, July 20). A detail you may not have known about Eric Garner blossoms in poem. *PBS Newshour*. Retrieved from http://www.pbs.org/newshour/poetry/small-needful-fact-eric-garner/

Sharp, D. (2014, December 29). Reparations for victims of police torture. *The Root*. Retrieved from http://www.theroot.com/articles/culture/2014/12/chicago_activists_push_for_reparations_for_victims_of_police_abuse.html

Shifflett, S., Scheller, A., Alecci, S., & Forster, N. (2015, December 7). Police abuse complaints by Black Chicagoans Dismissed nearly 99 percent of the time. *The Huffington Post*. Retrieved from http://data.huffingtonpost.com/2015/12/chicago-officer-misconduct-allegations

Shinew, K., Mowatt, R., & Glover, T. (2007). An African American community recreation center: Participants' and volunteers' perceptions of racism and racial identity. *Journal of Parks and Recreation Administration, 25*(2), 84–106.

Stodolska, M., Shinew, K. J., Acevedo, J. C., & Roman, C. G. (2013). "I was born in the hood": Fear of crime, outdoor recreation and physical activity among Mexican American urban adolescents. *Leisure Sciences, 35*, 1–15.

Swaine, J. (2015, July 15). Unarmed Mississippi man died after 20-minute police chokehold, witnesses say. *The Guardian*. Retrieved from http://www.theguardian.com/us-news/2015/jul/15/jonathan-sanders-mississppi-chokehold

Swaine, J., Laughland, O., Lartey, J., & McCarthy, C. (2015, December 31). Young Black men killed by U.S. police at highest rate in year of 1,134 deaths. *The Guardian*. Retrieved from www.theguardian.com/us-news/2015/dec/31/the-counted-police-killings-2015-young-black-men

Terrill, W., & Reisig, M. D. (2003). Neighborhood context and police use of force. *Journal of Research in Crime and Delinquency, 40,* 291–321.

Weitzer, R. (2000). Racialized policing: Residents' perceptions in three neighborhoods. *Law and Society Review, 35,* 129–155.

Witt, P. A., & Caldwell, L. L. (2010). The rationale for recreation services for youth: An evidence-based approach. *National Recreation and Park Association Research Series.* Retrieved from http://www.nrpa.org/uploadedFiles/nrpa.org/Publications_and_Research/Research/Papers/Witt-Caldwell-Full-Research-Paper.pdf

Wolch, J., Wilson, J. P., & Fehrenbach, J. (2005). Parks and park funding in Los Angeles: An equity-mapping analysis. *Urban Geography, 26*(1), 4–35.

Evocative Words and Ethical Crafting: Poetic Representation in Leisure Research

Sandra Sjollema and Felice Yuen

ABSTRACT
In recent years, leisure scholars have increasingly used creative analytic practice (CAP). Poetic representation is one form of CAP that allows researchers to synthesize findings and represent the data while highlighting the emotional aspects of the lived experience. Despite the increased use of CAP in leisure research, little has been written about the process of using poetry as a form of representation. This article focuses on the process and experiences of creating poems to represent data from a study about leisure and Aboriginal women's healing. It describes how researcher location and subjectivity can impact ethical practice, as well as the aesthetic and epistemological tensions that can occur. It introduces the term "Ethical Crafting," which denotes that aesthetic attention to detail is at the same time an ethical practice. Finally, this article highlights the importance of researcher intuition and emotion, and argues for a reflexive practice to negotiate the tensions experienced in the poetic process.

when you do
this body map
you are putting
everything out there
you are being
an Indian woman

I'm ready and willing
to share who I am
the courage to tell
be an example

Over the last 40 years, in an effort to re-vitalize qualitative social science inquiry, academics have begun incorporating the arts into their research (Cole & Knowles, 2010). For these researchers (e.g., Denzin, 2000; Dillard, 2001; Finley, 2003), using art in research is not a question of replacing one form of representation with another. Rather, it is about changing the way we relate to the world (Eisner, 2010). For example, in contrast to Western scientific thought, where *truth* is often reduced to *the* truth (Eisner, 2010), qualitative research that embraces artistic methods can offer us multidimensional and complex views on the human condition (Cole & Knowles, 2010; Denzin, 2000; Dillard, 2001; Eisner, 2010; Finley, 2003; Grumet, 1978). Sociologist Laurel Richardson (1994), who conceived the term creative analytic practice (CAP), expressed this diversity of truths by using the metaphor of a crystal, where what we see differs according to angle or approach.

For nearly a decade, the field of leisure studies has embraced CAP as both a method of analysis and representation. According to Parry and Johnson (2007), expressing research findings through arts-based techniques enables researchers to present the complex personal and social meanings of experiences rather than simplified generalizations. CAP contextualizes leisure practices and embraces the complexity of lived experiences (Parry & Johnson). In addition, CAP facilitates an alternative understanding of data. Examples of CAP in the field of leisure studies include narrative vignettes or short stories (Johnson & Samdhl, 2005; Glover, 2007; Hayes, 2012; Lewis & Johnson, 2011; Mair, 2009; Parry, 2007), screenplays (Berbary, 2011), and, notably in the context of this article, poetry (Gilles, 2007; Hayes, 2012; Yuen, 2011; Yuen, Arai, & Fortune, 2012).

The use of poetry to represent data is increasing in qualitative research (Hordyk, Ben Soltane, & Hanley, 2013). The process of interviewing participants and using the resulting transcripts to craft poems is referred to as *found poetry* or *poetic representation* (Clarke, Febbraro, & Hatzipantelis, 2005; Glesne, 1997; Reilly, 2013). Poetic representation is one means of using poetry in a field of investigation known as poetic inquiry (Prendergast, 2009). Like other forms of art, poetic knowing is different from rationally-informed means of knowledge derived from prosaic text (Dancer, 2009; Faulkner, 2009; Leggo, 2010; Prendergast, 2009; Willis, 2002). Poetic knowing, often qualified as "imaginal" or "expressive" (Willis, 2002, p. 1), can allow us to understand social phenomena in refreshing ways (Faulkner, 2009). Poetic representation is pertinent because poetry's oral aspects "privilege the importance of orality in historically marginalized cultures" (Calafell, 2004, p. 180). This form of representation can also allow the body to listen "and in this listening, dualisms, such as mind-body, intellect-emotion, self-other, researcher-researched…are collapsed" (Richardson, 1993, p. 706). In short, using poetry as a form of representation enables researchers and their audience to think and feel the experience, which facilitates a complex understanding of the data (Sparkes & Douglas, 2007).

Poetry was chosen as a method of representation for this study because of its ability to evoke emotion (Leggo, 2010). Other researchers have emphasized the embodied and affective experience of poetry (e.g., Hordyk et al., 2013; Yuen, Arai, & Fortune, 2012). Hordyk and her colleagues (2013), who conducted a study about homeless immigrant women in Montreal, state that poetic representation allowed for "a three-dimensional, embodied voice to women who were invisible, marginalized, and silenced" (p. 205). Yuen and her colleagues (2012), who carried out research among female inmates, used poetic representation because it allowed them to synthesize findings while keeping the data close to emotion that is important to women's experience.

A pertinent issue when carrying out poetic representation concerns the ability to craft good poetry and conduct or produce good research[1] at the same time (Faulkner, 2007, 2009). While aesthetics may concern the poet, establishing ethical relationships with participants, including authentically re-creating participant experience and emotion in representation, can preoccupy the researcher (Butler-Kisber, 2002; Faulkner, 2009). Further, ethical and aesthetic concerns cannot be separated from epistemology (Denzin, 2000). In other words, what we

---

[1]Please see Faulkner (2009) as to what constitutes good poetry/good research and how to combine the two criteria.

know is intimately connected with *how* we know and with our relationship with research participants (Guba & Lincoln, 2005). While issues of poetic ways of knowing, debates over evaluating research poetry (as both poetry and research), and guidelines for conducting poetic representation have been deliberated by numerous poetic inquiry scholars (e.g., Butler-Kisber; 2002; Dancer, 2009; Dillard, 2001; Faulkner, 2007; Hordyk et al., 2013; Leggo, 2010), few academic sources speak to the hands-on process of poetic representation from the location of both researcher and poet. In addition, few sources comment on the researcher-participant relationship, the type of knowing this creates, and how this knowing influences the process of poetic representation.

In this article, we will describe how researcher location and subjectivity can impact ethical practice and the researcher-participant relationship. In addition, we will discuss how the process of research representation can produce tension and can ultimately help a researcher-poet experience integration between the two aspects of self. The discussion follows the journey of Sandy[2], who carried out the poetic representation exercise in this study, and her experiences of researcher reflexivity, including journaling, research poems, and discussion, and considers how she used these means as strategies to identify and negotiate the tensions experienced as a researcher-poet.

From ethical practice to ethical crafting

In this article, ethical practice is conceived as establishing an ethic of care among researcher and participants (Finley, 2003) that implies responsibility and connectedness within the research (Munford, Sanders, Veitch, & Conder, 2008). We argue that ethical practice requires researchers to assume personal accountability for their location and subjectivity. Corbyn Dwyer and Buckle (2009) describe researcher location as being the identity, social position or membership in groups in which researchers locate themselves or are located in. This personal perspective ultimately influences the choices they make in the research process (Guba, 1990) and affects their relationships with participants (Guba & Lincoln, 2005).

An ethical practice also assumes that researchers must reflect upon the nature of power within the researcher-participant relationship (Furman, Langer, Davis, Gallardo, & Kulkarni, 2007) and critically reflect on the self during all stages of the research process (Guba & Lincoln, 2005). Of course, such reflection can prove difficult for researchers because personal insights can be uncomfortable and researchers might be hesitant to admit mistakes, such as asking misguided questions (Finlay, 2002). At the same time, researchers need to take care to not let their reflections take up too much space and block out participants' voices (Finlay, 2002). As leisure scholars have acknowledged, engaging in reflexivity is challenging (Sharpe, 2011), disruptive and destabilizing (Cohen, 2013), and embarrassing (Trussell, 2014), which can leave us feeling vulnerable (Dupuis, 1999; Yuen, 2011). Nonetheless, these scholars acknowledge that is it our responsibility to interrogate our location and subjectivity as it leads to a more holistic and richer understandings of lived experiences.

Another aspect of engaging in ethical practice in research includes being in touch with one's emotions. An exploration of one's own emotions can help researchers develop sympathetic understanding and empathetic awareness towards participants (Hewitt, 2007). Denzin (1992) and Ronai (1992)[3] are two examples of scholars who detail the importance of

---

[2]The study's principal investigator is Felice. Sandy is a PhD. student who worked as the research assistant on this project.
[3]These two authors are contributors to a book called *Investigating Subjectivity: Research on Lived Experience* (C. Ellis & M.G. Flaherty, Eds.).

researchers' emotions as a means of subjectivity and reflexivity and their links to ethical practice. Incorporating an ethical practice into our research is part of our obligation to interrogate who we are. As argued by Fine, Weis, Weseen, and Wong (2000), this interrogation means working the hyphens of self-other relations and "coming clean" at the hyphen (p. 123). They argue we have "a responsibility to talk about our identities, why we interrogate what we do, what we choose not to, how we frame our data, [and] on whom we shed our scholarly gaze" (p. 123).

In the case of poetic representation, a number of poetic inquiry scholars (Butler-Kisber; 2002; Prendergast, 2009; Washington, 2009) advise researchers to never lose sight of their own subjectivity, including their emotional responses to the text (Prendergast, 2009), when engaging in the practice since it can influence both the choice of words selected from the original text and the crafting of poems. The term *ethical crafting* was created in the context of this study to signify the need for researchers to take responsibility for their subjectivity while engaging in the poetic representation process. In addition, this term was conceived due to the need for researchers to go beyond, as Prendergast (2009) suggests, "the first ordinary word that comes to mind, the easy cliché" (p. xxvi) when creating poems. Therefore, *ethical crafting* also means, in line with Prendergast's conception, making hard-won aesthetic choices that "honour(ing)...individuals" and therefore are "an ethical choice" (p. xxvi). Notably, ethical practice and aesthetic considerations are not mutually exclusive at a conceptual level; however, in practice the sense that a dichotomy exists between the ethical and the aesthetic can prevail. The context in which we engaged in the ethical crafting of poetry is described in the following section.

Journey women: Aboriginal women's healing

The process of poetic representation described in this article is part of a larger research project called *Journey Women*, which was done in collaboration with Minwaashin Lodge, an Aboriginal women's support center located in Ottawa, Ontario, Canada. *Journey Women* was founded upon Indigenous methodologies and participatory action research: the project was embedded in a process of decolonization, whereby we sought to support and empower Aboriginal peoples to be agents of their own lives and healing journey (see journeywomen.org for more detail).

In Canada, Aboriginal women are more likely to be a victim of a violent crime than non-Aboriginal women (Native Women's Association of Canada, 2015; Royal Canadian Mounted Police, 2015). According to Statistics Canada's 2004 General Social Survey (as cited by Native Women's Association of Canada, 2015), Aboriginal women reported spousal assault three times more than non-Aboriginal women. Statistics Canada also reported that forms of family violence, such as having a gun or knife used against them, being beaten, choked, or sexually assaulted, are reported by 54% of Aboriginal women compared to 37% of non-Aboriginal women. These statistics highlight the disproportionate number of Aboriginal women and girls who suffer from acts of violence. Given that these numbers are taken from reported incidents, the actual numbers are likely higher. The impact of this violence is embedded in a history of colonization, residential schools, racism, and discrimination.

Residential schools were publicized by the Canadian government as noble efforts to prepare Aboriginal children for mainstream society — to educate and to give them a future they would otherwise lack. As reported by the Truth and Reconciliation Commission of Canada (2015), these schools were a major contribution to the cultural genocide of Aboriginal peoples. More than 150,000 First Nation, Inuit and Métis children were removed from their communities and forced to adopt Christianity and speak English or French. Couched within a mission to "civilize," children in residential schools experienced severe punishment for speaking their language, living their spirituality and cultural traditions, and seeking out family. Sexual, physical, and emotional abuses were not uncommon. The artists interviewed for this study are survivors of the aforementioned; however, in keeping with the guidance of Indigenous scholar Tuhiwai Smith (1999), *Journey Women* sought to emphasize strengths rather than seek out what is dysfunctional.

As a part of emphasizing and celebrating Aboriginal women's strength and courage, part of the *Journey Women* project consisted of a three-day body mapping workshop[4] and a week-long public exhibit of their body maps at a local art gallery. The art exhibit, as held in conjunction with Woman Abuse Awareness Month, included a day-long celebration and ceremony and an artist talk by the workshop participants. The data discussed in this article were collected using telephone interviews with five of six artists who participated in the art exhibit.[5] The purpose of these interviews was to explore how the art exhibit impacted the women's healing. The interviews were 30–50 minutes in length and audio-recorded. Artists were given a choice of using pseudonyms or their real names in articles and presentations related to dissemination, thus both pseudonyms and real names are used in this article.

A different kind of analysis

Given that the project was founded on principles of participatory action research and Indigenous methodologies, the Aboriginal community played a significant role in all aspects of the research. In terms of data analysis, the artists participated in a process known as *witnessing* in art therapy. Witnessing involves seeing with presence and suspended judgment (Learmouth, 1994) while supporting and acknowledging the artist and her story. As the group walked around each canvas, words and phrases that described the body-map were said out loud. At the end of the viewing, each woman filled out a short form based on Solomon's (2007) work with body-mapping. The form consisted of one fill-in-the-blank sentence. The two examples below contain the words of women as they reflected upon the body-maps of others:

> When I see Roberta's body map and I hear her story, I see a person living with transformation and hope.

> When I see Bape-Ando-Kwe's body map and I hear her story, I see a person living with fun, journey and pain.

Transformation, hope, oppression, fun journey, and *pain*, along with other words on the forms, were then used to inform the subsequent forms of analysis. For example, both oppression and pain helped identify and confirm one of the four final themes, *challenge*. This process of witnessing as a form of analysis was chosen after a conversation with the artists before the workshop when they indicated that there were not interested in participating in conventional

---

[4]Body-mapping, adapted from Solomon's (2007) work with individuals in East Africa and Southern Africa living with AIDS and HIV, was used as a process to map out Aboriginal women's experiences of healing and identifying with positive and affirming aspects of themselves and their culture, besides pain, hurt, abuse, violence, and cultural assimilation. Please see Lu and Yuen (2012) for more details about the process.

[5]The artist who was not interviewed was willing to participate, but ended up not being available at the scheduled time. Unfortunately, we were unable to reschedule the interview.

methods of analysis (i.e., thematic analysis). This preliminary analysis was conducted with artists on the last day of the body-mapping workshop.[6]

Analysis of the telephone interviews was conducted by Felice and another research assistant using N-Vivo 10 and Strauss' (1987) open and axial coding process. During this process, the following four themes were identified: *challenge, discovery, release,* and *collective responsibility.* However, continuing the analysis in this manner, where themes may be further broken down or merged together, and representing the data as quotations to describe the theme, no longer seemed the appropriate method to use. Healing is an emotional process and conventional methods of analysis and representation seemed to remove the emotion that was important to the experience. After a long period of reflection, exploration, and even paralysis, Felice felt that poetic representation would be a better method to represent Aboriginal women's experiences of leisure and healing. It is at this point where Felice asked Sandy to create poems from the themes. Ultimately, these poems would serve as the method to illustrate the data as a way to represent each theme.

The poetic representation process undertaken by Sandy resulted in four data poems (Prendergast, 2009) representing the four themes. To create these data poems, Sandy followed suggestions laid out by Glesne (1997) and Butler-Kisber (2002) regarding poetic representation, and she used poetic techniques described by Ioannou (2000), Ellis (2000), and Sullivan (2009). Specifically, she first highlighted words or phrases in the texts that she felt best represented the themes or the participants' voices and that were descriptive and emotionally evocative (Butler-Kisber, 2002; Glesne, 1997). She also looked for examples in the texts of poetic technique such as repetition or metaphor (Ioannou, 2000). For example, in one of the coded texts from the analysis of the telephone interviews, the word *art* was repeated: *Expression with art, I love performing arts, empowerment using art*, which Sandy incorporated into the data poem. Preference was also given to words that concretely described a situation rather than using abstract words, thus adhering to the poetic principle of *showing and not telling* (Ellis, 2000; Sullivan, 2009). For example, instead of using the word *shame* in the poem used to represent the theme *discovery*, Sandy used the following description:

You're supposed to be
in a potato sack
paint that all in black,
keep your eyes on the floor
be circumspect

As recommended by Glesne (1997), Sandy proceeded to extract the highlighted words and phrases exactly as they appeared in the original text respecting their chronological order. She then took the extracted excerpts and "experimented with the words" (Butler-Kisber, 2002, p. 233) to create rhythms, accentuations, and stop points. She aimed for sound quality through rhyming or by repeating certain consonant or vowel sounds (Ioannou, 2000). For example, in the data poem representing the theme *discovery*, the *a* sound is repeated:

we had to paint body maps
about stuff from the past,
we were forced back

Similar to Glesne, Sandy engaged in poetic license by playing with the order of words, changing verb tenses, repeating certain words, and by dropping or adding word endings (*e.g.,*

---

[6]While the artists in this project were part of the dissemination process (through conference presentations and art exhibits), none were interested in being involved in data analysis beyond what was done in the workshop or in taking part in the poetic representation process.

ing, s, ly). In some instances, she borrowed words that related to the theme she was writing about from the other thematically-analyzed texts.

As poetry has an auditory and performance dimension (Butler-Kisber, 2002), an important aspect of this representation included frequently reading the poetry out loud to get a sense of how it resonated on an embodied level (i.e., Did the words sound good together? Did anything sound discordant or out of place?). Sandy was able to fine tune the poems by reading them out loud in this manner (Butler-Kisber, 2002). As we discuss the ethical practice and tensions experienced in the creation of the data poems, the remainder of this article will focus on Sandy's experience and the process she followed as she created these poems.

Ethical practice or how to reflect as a researcher and poet

To ensure an ethical practice, Sandy enacted suggestions put forth by researchers concerning researcher reflexivity (Hordyk et al., 2013). First, she kept a journal to document how and why she was making various choices, also noting any questions or reflections. Second, she continually revisited and revised the data poems. Other social science scholars, for example, Washington (2009) and Glesne (1997), have detailed their experiences of reflection as they engaged in the poetic representation exercise, which in their case included asking questions of themselves and about the sometimes difficult aspects of their relationships with their participants. Additionally, Sandy wrote a research poem as means of critical reflection. Research poems as a tool for reflection have also been used by many social science scholars (e.g., Arai, 2011). Using poetry as a form of reflexivity permitted Sandy to experience her emotional reactions to the data in an intense manner (Furman et al., 2007), to embrace them, and to describe them with concision (Furman, 2006). Overall, writing research poems as a form of reflexivity allowed for a greater inclusion of Sandy's emotions into the research process (Yuen, 2011). Some of Sandy's reflections are included in this article to illustrate the tensions she experienced. In order to differentiate from the main text, her reflections are written in italics. Excerpts from the research poem that are featured in this article are also written in italics.

Positionalities, relationships, and other ways of knowing

For scholars who use poetic inquiry as a methodology, there is much consideration and discussion about the ways in which researchers self-identify. While some do not refer to themselves as poets because they feel they lack the artistic skills to do so (e.g., Willis, 2002), others employ this title (e.g., Faulkner, 2009). In order to develop artistic skills, Butler-Kisber (2002), along with Faulkner (2007) and Sullivan (2009), suggest that researchers, especially those with no previous poetry writing experience, take workshops or courses in poetry writing and that they read different types of poetry. A common term used in the field of poetic inquiry is *researcher-poet* (Faulkner, 2007; Furman et al., 2007), signifying that the researcher identifies with both of these positions. Sandy felt comfortable using this term because she locates herself as both poet and researcher. In graduate school she conducted research; she has also studied poetry at the undergraduate level, authored three chapbooks and has published widely, for example, in the *Journal of Poetry Therapy* (2012, 2013), *The Canadian Author's Association Montreal Anthology* (2009), and in *Retort Magazine* (2007), a literary journal based in Australia.

As researchers, reflecting on our social position(s) is important because it allows us to consciously choose the manner in which we interact with study participants and with the research process overall (Furman et al., 2007). In this study, Sandy was very aware on her position as a white Canadian and granddaughter of settlers in British Columbia. She was conscious of how she, as a white Canadian, was in a position of privilege in regards to the Aboriginal women who were the participants in this study. Acknowledging one's position in relation to the people and community we are working with is essential to Indigenous methodologies. As Kovach (2009) contends, Indigenous research is bound by the relational. In the same regard, Wilson (2001) argues that Indigenous methodology is about relational accountability. Specifically, he states:

> As a researcher you are answering to *all your relations* when doing research. You are not answering questions of validity or reliability or making judgments of better or worse. Instead you should be fulfilling your relationships with the world around you. So your methodology has to ask different questions: Rather than asking about validity or reliability, you are asking how am I fulfilling my role in this relationship? What are my obligations in this relationship? (emphasis in original, p. 177)

The recognition of her social position in relation to the Aboriginal women in the study and her obligation to them as a white researcher allowed Sandy to take this privilege into consideration during the process of poetic representation.

In addition to her white privilege, Sandy's distance from research participants was also due to the fact that she was at another university completing her Masters during the data collection phase of the study. As such, she never had the chance to meet the five Aboriginal women whose words she was to craft into poems. Prior to engaging in the act of poetic representation, Sandy, like other researchers (e.g., Lu & Yuen, 2012), felt some trepidation about being a non-Aboriginal person involved in research regarding Aboriginal women and about reasserting neo-colonial practices through poetic representation. In addition, due to her late arrival in the project and consequential reliance on written text, she felt a sense of disjointedness in her relationship with the women. Overall, Sandy's location as a white researcher and lack of relationship to the women led to a strong sense of discomfort. This feeling in turn led Sandy to write a research poem where she attempted to establish some kind of connection with the women:

> *I wasn't there*
> *with you at the healing lodge*
> *painting of the body maps*
> *public exhibition*
>
> *wish I would have been*
> *have smudged with sweet grass before*

After writing this poem, Sandy realized that she addressed the women directly (i.e., using *you*) because it gave her some sense of talking to them even if she had never met them. As a result, she began to feel some connection to the women. However, she continued to experience uneasiness as a white researcher having a one-way conversation with Aboriginal women. Even though her intentions were to respect the experiences of the women, she felt like she was replicating the colonial dynamic in Canada where white society often talks *at* rather than *with* Aboriginal people. Sandy's reflections regarding this socio-historical context echo the need for researchers to discuss race and white privilege as part of the power dynamic within the researcher-participant relationship (Arai & Kivel, 2009) and to continually take into consideration "the universalizing...pull of whiteness" (McDonald, 2009, p. 18) during the research process. To engage in poetic representation from a disconnected relationship brought up an important issue for Sandy: How could she, as a white researcher, honor her relationship with the Aboriginal women involved in the study even if she had not met them? Sandy was aware of holistic approaches to knowing in both Aboriginal culture, which feature emotional, intellectual, spiritual, and physical aspects (Wilson, 2008) as well as poetry, which involve embodied, cognitive, affective, and spiritual ways of knowing (Dancer; 2009; Faulkner, 2009; Leggo, 2010). With this is mind, she asked Felice to send her the audio recordings of the interviews with the women. Listening to the interviews provided Sandy with a holistic basis from which to engage in the poetic representation exercise and influenced the way she wrote the poems: She often heard the women speaking the words and this helped her decide how to form certain lines, which words to emphasize etc. This listening process was also included in Sandy's research poem:

> *I listened*
> *recordings*
> *bouts of laughter,*
> *patterns of speech*
> *each of you spoke in your own voice*

After writing and re-reading this poem, Sandy realized that listening to the recordings was a good antidote to her being the one to address the women in this research poem. In other words, this time Sandy was doing the listening, not the talking. During this listening process, Sandy put into practice the principles of embodied interpretation from Galvin and Todres (2009). These principles emphasize paying attention to one's physical clues and emotional resonance. She therefore noted any physical or emotional reactions she encountered, which included crying. This encounter was reflected in the research poem:

> *I cried when you said*
> *you had a chance to feel proud*
> *came in touch*
> *with your own artist*
>
> *that the word 'Aboriginal'*
> *means beauty*
> *means art*

By listening to the recordings, Sandy gained an embodied and affective knowledge of the women not only through their diction but also through the volume, intonation, and cadence of their voices. Consequently, she felt closer to them and more attuned to their lived experience (Prendergast, 2009), and she gained a better sense of who they are.

Poetic representation and the dance of the researcher-poet

Sandy began to experience another set of tensions and once again felt a sense of discomfort upon embarking on the poetic representation exercise. This time the disquiet was a result of reacting to the text from what felt like two distinct positions: the researcher and the poet. While she identified her researcher side as being concerned with issues of accurately depicting the participants' experience, Sandy identified the poet within as the part of her that desired to create evocative poems. Sandy experienced this struggle, which occurred in the writing of the four data poems, as a tension between ethical considerations (a concern of the researcher) and aesthetics (a concern of the poet):

> *I kept on asking myself if I was re-arranging or cleaning up the data too much in the name of 'good' poetry. Had my emphasis on succinctness (saying more with less) – which reflects my own style as*

a poet – gone too far? Was I letting the poet in me take over the process? Was the end result truly representative of the experiences of the Aboriginal women in their healing process? If not, how could I speak of being ethically accountable to their experiences?

The following excerpt is an example of the tension and struggle Sandy experienced in the poetic representation process. It is a rough draft of a data poem based on the theme of *release*. In the first stanza, the body mapping exercise is clearly the context of the experience. Notably, the "chance to be seen" described in the second stanza might lead the reader to assume that this chance is within the context of the body mapping experience. In the third stanza, the reader would likely assume that what the participant is willing to share is her view of herself as a beautiful person:

when you do
this body map
you are putting
everything out there
you are being
an Indian woman

I felt a part
of something
chance to be seen

I'm ready and willing
I can share that
beautiful person
the courage to tell
to be an example

In terms of the excerpt from the poem above, Sandy expressed the following concerns and questions:

Was the form in the second stanza too concise, had it cut too much of the original text? Did the removal of the word "exhibition" found in the original text take away too much from the experiences of the women? Did the placement of the words "beautiful person" after "I can share that" (in the original text these two lines were not back to back) in the third stanza respect the relationship between these two ideas as expressed in the original text? It was clear to me that my motivations for arranging the words as such – for example, to be explicit that the participant thought of herself as a beautiful person – came from a place of empathy or solidarity with the women. However, I wondered if the end result (i.e., the data poem), was representative enough for the sake of authentic research.

Finally, Sandy decided to leave the rough draft of the data poems alone for several days to gain a bit of distance and to be able to look at them anew. In the meantime, she spoke to Felice and shared her concerns. They had a discussion about representation within the poetic representation experience that helped Sandy to go back and take another look at the poems, this time viewing the data more from a researcher's perspective than that of a poet. The excerpt below reveals how the data poem was revised. The reflection following these excerpts explains why she made the changes that led to the final poem:

when you do
this body map
you are putting
everything out there

you are being
an Indian woman

I felt really part
of something
didn't feel like that was an exhibition
felt like that was just a chance to be seen

I'm ready and willing
to share who I am
the courage to tell
be an example

I allowed for more of the original dialogue to be expressed starting with "I felt really part" and also added the word "exhibition" from the original data so that the context of being seen would be explicit. I left the original chronological order of words intact in "I am ready and willing/to share who I am" because by this point in the poem (these stanzas represent the tail end of the poem), the reader would have an idea as to how the participant sees herself. The words "who I am" were used rather than "that beautiful person" because this is, in fact, what the woman actually said after "I'm ready and willing to share." As well, from a poetic perspective, "who I am" is in and of itself a very potent statement. In this sense, the poem was more representative of the actual context of the women's healing, was clearer, and at the same time, ethically speaking, was more faithful to the Aboriginal women's experiences.

This period of reflexive thought, which included the creation of a research poem, writing in her journal, and having an open conversation about her experiences with Felice, enabled Sandy to acknowledge the tensions she was experiencing. This acknowledgement and reflexive process also helped her to work through the tensions she felt as a research-poet and ultimately allowed her to gain a sense of integration. In other words, the reflexive process allowed the poet and researcher "to find each other" (Richardson, 1992, p. 35). Notably, when Sandy included more of the original dialogue to ensure that the context was clear and the women's voices were heard, she did not have to push aside the poet in her: Indeed, using the statement, *"who I am"* satisfied both the poet and researcher within.

The recursive turn and the art of integration

The process of poetic representation is not an easy one. Practically having to carve out the essence of what is being said in a succinct manner from pages of data is no small feat. In addition, to express the words and worlds of participants in ways that are evocative can add to the pressure of being concise. Ideologically, striving for accurate representation can be challenging when one's personal position in life is vastly different from the individuals we are working with as researchers. At the same time, researchers may be exposed to worlds and words very different from their own, and yet must still listen and take in the information in a nonjudgmental way (Lashua, 2011; Lu & Yuen, 2011). When writing data poems based on the experiences of marginalized populations, such as Aboriginal women, researchers must also be mindful of feelings of empathy which may cause them to overly compensate for negative stereotypes portrayed in mainstream society. At the same time, producing poems that can act as a counter narrative to dominant discourse is an important endeavor, especially when the poetry speaks of the experiences and emotions of those who are often the most silenced (Foster, 2012).

Rather than provide a how-to guideline to conduct poetic representation, this article has put the emphasis on the role that researcher reflexivity plays in this process and has shown that intuition, embodied reaction, and emotion are important aspects of researcher reflexivity. Indeed, in many instances during poetic representation process in this study, Sandy listened to and acted upon on her intuition. For example, she especially relied on intuition and embodied reaction when she read out loud the rough drafts of the data poems and could "feel" if they sounded right or not. To be able to trust this process, she has to confront the fact that she could not necessarily explain why she was making certain choices. She had to come to terms with the fact that it was sometimes only in retrospect that reasons became apparent, or that in some cases the reasons never became explicit. This lack of concrete answers flies in the face of the scientific process that demands explanations and conclusions (Willis, 2002). Although other poetic inquiry researchers (e.g., Glesne, 1997) have mentioned the role of intuition in the poetic representation process, it was not until Sandy underwent the process herself that she saw how important the role of the intuition can be in this exercise. It was also through this exercise that Sandy was able to see how much her experience as a poet helped her trust and value her intuition and embodied reactions, and that she could draw on them as a means of knowing as a researcher (Dancer, 2009; Leggo, 2010; Willis, 2002). Notably, it was the reflexive process that enabled Sandy to investigate her intuition and engage in the scientific process. As demonstrated earlier, there were occasions where her reflexivity lead to the realization that her poetic side may have initially overshadowed the researcher within. Further, her conscious and deliberate reflexivity also enabled her to question her emotions, chosen words, and the creation of the poems in general. Undoubtedly, reflexive practice is an important component of poetic representation, as demonstrated by other scholars who have detailed their reflective process through the poetic representation process (Glesne, 1997; Washington, 2009).

Sandy also was in tune with her emotions and trusted her feelings during the representation process. The main feeling throughout was one of discomfort or tension. First, Sandy felt estranged from the Aboriginal women in the study due to having never met them and having only (initially) thematic text from which to craft poems. This feeling was compounded by a feeling of trepidation that resulted from the power dynamic in the researcher-participant relationship. Sandy also felt a sense of disquiet when crafting the data poems and having to take into account both poetic and research criteria.[7] Using both prose and poetry as a means of reflection about these feelings allowed Sandy to adopt two strategies: 1) listening to audio recordings, a technique suggested by other poetic inquiry scholars (e.g., Prendergast, 2009), and 2) poetic revision.

The entire process allowed Sandy to see that researcher emotion, rather than being an obstacle in the research process, is an important part of this process that can lead researchers to engage in an ethical practice by creating a stronger connection with those whose experiences we are honoring. Furthermore, acknowledging and investigating emotional response has the potential to provide powerful understandings of lived experiences (Vannini & Taggart, 2013). In this particular instance, emotion was a tool used to understand the artists' experiences of healing. That is, an understanding of Aboriginal women's healing was produced through an affective and embodied process. As Thrift (2008) suggests, "affect is a different kind of intelligence about the world, but it is intelligence nonetheless, and previous attempts to either relegate affect to the irrational or raise it up to the level of the sublime are both equally mistaken" (p. 175). The poetic representation process in this study involved many layers of reflection and took three different forms: Journaling, research poetry (with revision), and open discussions with colleagues. It involved both listening and speaking: That is, listening to oneself

---

[7]For a full discussion of poetic and research criteria, see Faulkner (2009).

and to the women's voices, and speaking by performing the research and data poems. Moving between listening, writing, speaking, and revision involved an ongoing recursive process (Prendergast, 2009). As a poet, Sandy is well versed in the back-and-forth process between the writing, speaking, reflection, and revision of poetry that can sometimes last for months or even years. As a well-known saying about poetry states, "a poem is never finished, only abandoned" (Valéry, 2015, A poem is never finished, only abandoned, para.1).

Poetry then, and by extension poetic representation, can not only resolve a crisis in representation (Yuen et al., 2012) that allows for research findings to be represented in evocative and fresh ways, but it also has much to teach researchers about researcher reflexivity. That is, it emphasizes the value of researcher intuition and emotion, holistic ways of knowing, and having patience with the recursive process and all it entails. This type of reflexivity also ultimately means establishing an ethic of care, first with participants, by allowing emotion to guide us into an empathic understanding of them, and also with ourselves by honouring our own emotions and alternative ways of knowing.

Conclusion: Forging new research paths with poetry

This article highlights the use of CAP, and more specifically poetic representation in leisure research. It discusses two advantages of using poetry as a form of representation: 1) its ability to evoke and express emotion and 2) its capacity to represent the complexity of lived experience in refreshing ways. At the same time, this article presents tensions a researcher can experience during the process of poetic representation. The tensions experienced include issues of ethical practice and research relationships, as well as epistemological and aesthetic concerns. While researcher location and subjectivity can contribute to such tensions, engagement in a reflexive practice, and paying particularly close attention to the researcher's intuition and emotional response, can help develop strategies to navigate and negotiate these tensions. Of course, developing such intuition is a process that comes with time and practice.

This study also reveals that some tensions simply cannot be resolved within the context of certain research designs and, more specifically, within poetic representation. In this study, for example, conducting poetic representation from thematic analysis ultimately became a source of discomfort for Sandy, who joined the project after the data were collected. In response to this uneasiness, Sandy, after listening to the audio recordings, also read the interview transcripts. As such, she was able to connect with the individual voice of each woman which contributed to an intimate understanding of the woman's lived experience. Consequently, the data poem Sandy created to represent the experience of one of the artists — simply an experimental exercise — also had less separation from the original context, the individual being interviewed, and the depth of emotions expressed. In other words, the thematic analysis that took place in this particular study created a level of separation — contextually, relationally, and emotionally — for an individual who was not involved in the research prior to analysis. Consequently, in addition to the option of using poems to represent data that are thematically categorized, we also encourage readers to consider creating data poems directly from interview transcripts, thereby using poetry as a form of both analysis and representation. While one cannot control the timing of a research project with the admission and hiring of a graduate student, it would have been ideal to have Sandy involved at the beginning of the project so she would have had the opportunity to establish a direct relationship with the participants. The decision to use poetry for representation or for both analysis and representation depends on how you want to answer your research question. It is important to note that Felice, Lucy (the co-facilitator and art therapist from Minwaashin Lodge), and a couple of the Aboriginal artists read Sandy's data poems, crafted from thematically categorized texts, and felt the poems appropriately represented the experience of the workshop and exhibit. If these individuals had felt a disconnect between the poems and what they had experienced, we would have re-created the poems directly from the transcripts. While we cannot offer specific guidelines for which approach to take — nor do we propose one be created — we strongly encourage researchers to consider their emotions and intuition through a reflexive practice during the analytic and representation process to help them decide which method to use. As Dancer (2009) contends, poems are "epiphanies of life [that] elude form" (p.39). Breaking free of form, using poetry in research can lead to alternative research designs, questions, and knowledge that can shed new light on the words and worlds of those who have long been made invisible and silenced.

References

Arai, S. (2011). What will you assume about my difference? In K. Paisley & D. Dustin (Eds.), *Speaking up & speaking out for social and environmental justice through parks, recreation, and leisure* (pp. 21–30). Champaign, IL: Sagamore.

Arai, S., & Kivel, D. B. (2009). Critical race theory and social justice perspectives on whiteness. *Journal of Leisure Research, 41*(4), 459–471.

Berbary, L. A. (2011). Poststructural writerly representation: Screenplay as creative analytic practice. *Qualitative Inquiry, 17*(2), 186–196.

Butler-Kisber, L. (2002). Artful portrayals in qualitative inquiry: The road to found poetry and beyond. *Alberta Journal of Educational Research, 48*(2), 229–239.

Calafell, B.M. (2004). Disrupting the dichotomy: Yo Soy Chicana/o in the New Latina/o South. *The Communication Review, 7*(2), 175–204.

Clarke, J., Febbraro, A., Hatzipantelis, M., & Nelson, G. (2005). Poetry and prose: Telling the stories of formerly homeless mentally ill people. *Qualitative Inquiry, 11*(6), 913–932.

Cohen, S. A. (2013). Reflections on reflexivity in leisure and tourism studies. *Leisure Studies, 32*(3), 333–337.

Cole, A., & Knowles, J. G. (2010). Arts-informed research. In J. G. Knowles & A. Cole (Eds.), *Handbook of the arts in qualitative research* (pp. 55–70). Thousand Oaks, CA: Sage.

Corbyn Dwyer, S., & Buckle, J. L. (2009). The space between: On being an insider–outsider in qualitative research. *International Journal of Qualitative Methods, 8*(1), 54–63.

Dancer, A. (2009). The soundscape in poetry. In M. Prendergast, C. Leggo, & P. Sameshima (Eds.), *Poetic inquiry: Vibrant voices in the social sciences* (pp. 31–42). Rotterdam, the Netherlands: Sense Publishers.

Denzin, N. (1992). The many faces of emotionality: Reading persona. In C. Ellis & M. G. Flaherty (Eds.), *Investigating subjectivity* (pp. 17–30). London, England: Sage.

Denzin, N. (2000). Aesthetics and the practice of qualitative inquiry. *Qualitative Inquiry, 6*, 256–265.

Dillard, C. (2001). Enacting life notes: Endarkened epistemologies as deeply cultured knowing and inquiry. In L. Neilsen, A. Cole, & G. Knowles (Eds.), *The art of writing inquiry* (pp. 228–235). Halifax, NS, Canada: Backalong Books.

Dupuis, S. L. (1999). Naked truths: Towards a reflexive methodology in leisure research. *Leisure Sciences, 21*, 43–64.

Eisner, E. (2010). Art and knowledge. In J. G. Knowles & A. Cole (Eds.), *Handbook of the arts in qualitative research* (pp. 3–12). Thousand Oaks, CA: Sage.

Ellis, C. (2000). Creating criteria: An ethnographic short story. *Qualitative Inquiry, 6*, 273–277.

Faulkner, S. L. (2007). Concern with craft: Using Ars Poetica as criteria for reading research poetry. *Qualitative Inquiry, 13*(2), 218–234.

Faulkner, S. (2009). *Poetry as method: Reporting research as verse.* Walnut Creek, CA: Left Coast Books.

Fine, M., Weis, L., Weseen, S., & Wong, L. (2000). For whom? Qualitative research, representations, and social responsibilities. In N. K. Denzin & Y. S. Lincoln (Eds.), *Handbook of qualitative research* (2nd ed., pp. 107–132). Thousand Oaks, CA: Sage.

Finlay, L. (2002). "Outing" the researcher: The provenance, process, and practice of reflexivity. *Qualitative Health Research*, *12*(4), 531–545.

Finley, S. (2003). Arts-based inquiry in QI: Seven sources from crisis to guerrilla warfare. *Qualitative Inquiry*, *9*(2), 281–296.

Foster, V. (2012) What if? The use of poetry to promote social justice. *Social Work Education, The International Journal*, *31*(6), 742–755.

Furman, R. (2006). Poetic forms and structures in qualitative health research. *Qualitative Health Research*, *16*(4), 560–566.

Furman, R., Langer, C. L., Davis, C. S., Gallardo, H. P., & Kulkarni, S. (2007). Expressive research and reflective poetry as qualitative inquiry: A study of adolescent identity. *Qualitative Research*, *7*, 301–315.

Galvin, K., & Todres, L. (2009). Poetic inquiry & phenomenological research: The practice of embodied interpretation. In M. Prendergast, C. Leggo, & P. Sameshima (Eds.), *Poetic inquiry: Vibrant voices in the social sciences* (pp. 307–316). Rotterdam, the Netherlands: Sense Publishers.

Gilles, J. (2007). Staying grounded while being uprooted: A visual and poetic representation of the transition from university to community for graduates with disabilities. *Leisure Sciences*, *29*(2), 175–179.

Glesne, C. (1997). That rare feeling: Re-presenting research through poetic transcription. *Qualitative Inquiry*, *3*(2), 202–221.

Glover, T. D. (2007). Ugly on the diamonds: An examination of white privilege in youth baseball. *Leisure Sciences*, *29*(2), 195–208.

Grumet, M. (1978). Songs and situations. In G. Willis (Ed.), *Qualitative evaluation* (pp. 274–315). Berkeley, CA: McCutchan.

Guba, E. G. (1990). The alternative paradigm dialogue. In E.G. Guba (Ed.), *The paradigm dialogue* (pp.17–27). Newbury Park, CA: Sage.

Guba, E.G., & Lincoln, Y.S. (2005). Paradigmatic controversies, contradictions, and emerging confluences. In N. K. Denzin & Y. S. Lincoln (Eds.), *SAGE handbook of qualitative research* (3rd ed., pp. 191–215). Thousand Oaks, CA: Sage.

Hayes, L. (2012). Leisure–pleasure=well-being, wellness, or survival? *Cultural Studies↔ Critical Methodologies*, *12*(1), 55–59.

Hewitt, J. (2007). Ethical components of researcher—researched relationships in qualitative interviewing. *Qualitative Health Research*, *17*(8), 1149–1159.

Hordyk, S. R., Ben Soltane, S., & Hanley, J. (2013). Sometimes you have to go under water to come up: A poetic, critical realist approach to documenting the voices of homeless immigrant women. *Qualitative Social Work*, *13*(2), 203–220.

Ioannou, S. (2000). *A magical clockwork: The art of writing the poem*. Toronto, Canada: Wordwrights Canada.

Johnson, C. W., & Samdahl, D. M. (2005). "The night they took over": Misogyny in a country western gay bar. *Leisure Sciences*, *27*(4), 331–348.

Kovach, M. (2009). *Indigenous methodologies: Characteristics, conversations, and contexts*. Toronto, ON, Canada: University of Toronto Press.

Lashua, B. D. (2011). Are you listening? In K. Paisley & D. Dustin (Eds.), *Speaking up & speaking out for social and environmental justice through parks, recreation, and leisure* (pp. 73–82). Champaign, IL: Sagamore.

Learmouth, M. (1994). Witness and witnessing in art therapy. *Inscape*, *1*, 19–22.

Leggo, C. (2010). Astonishing silence: Knowing in poetry. In A. L. Cole & J. G. Knowles (Eds.), *Handbook of the arts in qualitative social science research* (pp. 165–174). Thousand Oaks, CA: Sage.

Lewis, S. T., & Johnson, C. W. (2011). "But it's not that easy": Negotiating (trans)gender expressions in leisure spaces. *Leisure/Loisir*, *35*(2), 115–132.

Lu, L., & Yuen, F. (2012). Journey women: Art therapy in a decolonizing framework of practice. *The Arts in Psychotherapy*, *39*, 192–200.

Mair, H. (2009). Club life: Third place and shared leisure in rural Canada. *Leisure Sciences*, *31*(5), 450–465.

McDonald, M. G. (2009). Dialogues on whiteness, leisure and (anti)racism. *Journal of Leisure Research*, *41*(1), 5–21.

Munford, R., Sanders, J., Veitch, B. M., & Conder, J. (2008). Ethics and research: Searching for ethical practice in research. *Ethics and Social Welfare, 2*(1), 50–66.
Native Women's Association of Canada. (2015). *You are not alone: A toolkit for Aboriginal women escaping domestic violence*. Retrieved from http://www.nwac.ca/wpcontent/uploads/2015/05/Fact_Sheet_Missing_and_Murdered_Aboriginal_Women_and_Girls.pdf
Parry, D. C. (2007). "There is life after breast cancer": Nine vignettes exploring dragon boat racing for breast cancer survivors. *Leisure Sciences, 29*(1), 53–69.
Parry, D. C., & Johnson, C. W. (2007). Contextualizing leisure research to encompass complexity in lived leisure experience: The need for creative analytic practice. *Leisure Sciences, 29*(2), 119–130.
Prendergast, M. (2009). Introduction: The phenomena of poetry in research: 'Poem is what?' Poetic inquiry in social science research. In M. Prendergast, C. Leggo, & P. Sameshima (Eds.), *Poetic inquiry: Vibrant voices in the social sciences* (pp. xix–xlii). Rotterdam, the Netherlands: Sense Publishers.
Reilly, R. C. (2013). Found poems, member checking and crises of representation. *The Qualitative Report, 18*(15), 1–18.
Richardson, L. (1993). Poetics, dramatics, and transgressive validity: The case of the skipped line. *The Sociological Quarterly, 34*(4), 695–710.
Richardson, L. (1992). The consequence of poetic representation: Writing the other, rewriting the self. In C. Ellis & M.G. Flaherty (Eds.), *Investigating subjectivity* (pp. 125–137). London, England: Sage.
Richardson, L. (1994). Writing: A method of inquiry. In N. K. Denzin & Y. S. Lincoln (Eds.), *The Sage handbook of qualitative research* (pp. 516–529). Thousand Oaks, CA: Sage.
Ronai, C. R. (1992). The reflexive self through narrative: A night in the life of an erotic dancer/researcher. In C. Ellis & M.G. Flaherty (Eds.), *Investigating subjectivity* (pp. 102–124). London, England: Sage.
Royal Canadian Mounted Police. (2015). *Missing and murdered Aboriginal women: 2015 update to the national operational overview*. Retrieved from http://www.rcmp-grc.gc.ca/pubs/abo-aut/mmaw-fada-eng.pdf
Sharpe, E. (2011). Are you awake yet? The conscientization process. In K. Paisley & D. Dustin (Eds.), *Speaking up and speaking out. Working for social and environmental justice through parks, recreation, and leisure* (pp. 15–20). Urbana, IL: Sagamore.
Solomon, J. (2007). *"Living with X" — a body mapping journey in the time of HIV and AIDS — a facilitators guide*. Retrieved from https://www.repssi.org/living-with-x-a-body-mapping-journey-in-the-time-of-hiv-and-aids/
Sparkes, A., & Douglas, K. (2007). Making the case for poetic representations: An example in action. *Sport Psychologist, 21*(2), 170–189.
Strauss, A. L. (1987). *Analysis for social scientists*. Cambridge, UK: Cambridge University Press.
Sullivan, A. (2009). On poetic occasion in inquiry: Concreteness, voice, ambiguity, tension, and associative logic. In M. Prendergast, C. Leggo, & P. Sameshima (Eds.), *Poetic inquiry: Vibrant voices in the social sciences* (pp. 111–126). Rotterdam, the Netherlands: Sense Publishers.
Thorpe, H., & Rinehart, R. (2010). Alternative sport and affect: Non-representational theory examined. *Sport in Society, 13*(7–8), 1268–1291.
Thrift, N. (2008). *Non-representational theory: Space, politics, affect*. New York, NY: Routledge.
Trussell, D. (2014). Dancing in the margins. *Journal of Leisure Research, 46*(3), 342–352.
Truth and Reconciliation of Canada. (2015). *Truth and reconciliation commission of Canada: Calls to action*. Retrieved from http://www.trc.ca/websites/trcinstitution/File/2015/Findings/Calls_to_Action_English2.pdf
Tuhiwai Smith, L. (1999). *Decolonizing methodologies*. New York, NY: Palgrave.
Valery, P. (2015). *A poem is never finished, only abandoned*. Retrieved from http://quotes.lifehack.org/quote/paul-valery/a-poem-is-never-finished-only-abandoned/
Vannini, P., & Taggart, J. (2013). Doing islandness: A non-representational approach to an island's sense of place. *Cultural Geographies, 20*(2), 225–242.
Washington, R. D. (2009). Tornadoes, transformations and textures: Twisting poetry research. In M. Prendergast, C. Leggo, & P. Sameshima (Eds.), *Poetic inquiry: Vibrant voices in the social sciences* (pp. 325–332). Rotterdam, the Netherlands: Sense Publishers.
Willis, P. (2002). Don't call it poetry. *Indo-Pacific Journal of Phenomenology, 2*(1), 1–14.

Wilson, S. (2001). What is indigenous research methodology? *Canadian Journal of Native Education*, *25*(2), 175–179.

Wilson, S. (2008). *Research is ceremony: Indigenous research methods*. Winnipeg, Canada: Fernwood Publishing.

Yuen, F. (2011). Embracing emotionality: Clothing my "naked truths." *Critical Criminology, 19*, 75–88.

Yuen, F., Arai, S., & Fortune, D. (2012). Women in prison, community dislocation and reconnection through leisure: A poetic representation of incarcerated women's experiences of leisure and connection to community. *Leisure Sciences, 34*(4), 1–17.

Questions for Postqualitative Inquiry: Conversations to Come

Brian E. Kumm and Lisbeth A. Berbary

ABSTRACT
The past 40 years of leisure sciences affirms not only the urgency of diversely informed investigations of leisure phenomena but also the field's commitment to forward contributions of social relevance, methodological innovation, and insightful critique. This legacy owes a considerable debt to qualitative researchers who reimagined the paradigmatic purview and methodological possibilities for leisure scholarship. At the threshold of the next 40 years, we leverage postqualitative inquiry to pry a modest space for continued intellectual and methodological diversity. Specifically, we revisit Berbary and Boles's (2014) proposed ~~scaffolding~~ sous erasure (Derrida, 1974) for humanist, qualitative research to explore points of departure for postqualitative inquiry. We question the implications such a departure may hold for "data," "theory," "analysis," and "representation" within non-humanist onto-epistemologies of post-qualitative research. Ultimately, we argue for postqualitative research as a promising, humane, and hopeful trajectory for our future, adding to our already rich legacy.

We begin with the hard question, the inescapable, basic question that always haunts our research: *Why?* Why do we do what we do? Why conduct research, level critique, generate theory, engage concepts, ask questions, and form provisional answers regarding ourselves, our communities, and our world? Why bother or care? Doubtless, the variety of responses to this question would match the plurality of perspectives, worldviews, and paradigms that proliferate our highly interdisciplinary field. To be sure, the questions of "what" and "how" are often more than enough to preoccupy our endeavors.

The past 40 years of leisure sciences bears witness to vast variegation regarding the "what" of leisure and the "how" of methodology. Particularly commendable are efforts to move our discourse beyond merely circumscribing definitional, conceptual boundaries of leisure toward understanding individual leisure experience and critiquing broader social issues of leisure behavior within power disparities in leisure contexts (e.g., Parry, Johnson, & Stewart, 2013; Stewart, 2014). As researchers grew discontent with the removed, omnipotence of an "objective" researcher, the past 40 years has given us research exemplarily of activism and advocacy for marginalized groups (e.g., Arai, 2011; Berbary, 2012; Floyd, 2014; Lewis & Johnson, 2011; Glover, 2007; Kivel, 2011; Lashua & Fox, 2007; Mair, 2011; Mowatt, 2012; Parry, 2007; Samdahl, 2011; Shaw, 2001). Likewise, we celebrate *Leisure Sciences* for embracing the plurality of qualitative methodologies, promoting creative analytic and arts-based representational practices (Parry & Johnson, 2007), and engaging broader philosophical debates informing the complexity of qualitative research endeavors (Berbary & Boles, 2014; Henderson, 2011; Neville, 2013; Parry, Johnson, & Stewart, 2013). While many fields still struggle to legitimatize qualitative work within their disciplinary purviews, *Leisure Sciences* has cultivated innovation, pushing the boundaries of research to encompass broader possibilities at a much quicker pace.

This legacy of diverse investigations of leisure phenomena, contributions of social relevance, methodological innovation, and insightful critique allows us to celebrate this 40th anniversary; however, this legacy also indicates something significant about our collective values and commitments, conferring a partial answer to the various "why" questions posed above. From our readings of the current literature, it is not an overstatement to describe our discipline as variously committed to improving our individual and collective lives, our communities, and the larger world. This commitment to improving our collective existence attest to the prevalence of humanism[1] as a principal force informing research conducted over the past 40 years. Much of the innovative, relevant, and insightful work published in *Leisure Sciences* is positioned with/in humanist onto-epistemologies (e.g., realism, structuralism, constructionism) as well as humanist theories (e.g., interpretivist and Critical theories). Although these various onto-epistemologies and theories may contribute to our paradigmatic proliferation (Parry, Johnson, & Stewart, 2012), particularly in relation to qualitative methodologies, our discipline is nonetheless grounded firmly within humanism (Berbary, 2017).

Although humanism bears many positive characteristics recognizable within our literature (e.g., well-being, happiness, freedom, egalitarian democracy, shared experience, and social justice), it is not without its shortcomings. Also attributable to humanism are notions of essentialism, the proverbial "tree of knowledge," universal/meta-narratives of human progression, binary structures, capturable reality, common sense, the agentic subject, and foundational *Truth*(s) (Deleuze & Guattari, 2011; Barad, 2007; Braidotti, 2013; Flax, 1990; Foucault, 1984). As we will elaborate, the limitations of these taken-for-granted notions warrant critique; they produce the world in ways that are often "harmful to women as well as to other groups of people. This is hardly surprising, since patriarchy, racism, homophobia, ageism, etc. are cultural structures, cultural regularities that humanism allows and perpetuates" (St. Pierre, 2000, p. 479).

Recognizing both the positive and potentially detrimental inheritances of humanism, leisure scholars working within post* traditions have already begun to deconstruct aspects of this problematic inheritance (e.g., Berbary, 2015, 2017; Fullagar, 2017; Kumm & Johnson, 2017; Lashua, 2017; Malick, 2017; Sharpe, 2017). Yet, we have not specifically questioned humanism as that which undergirds and supports established qualitative research approaches. And why is that? Why should we consider stepping outside of humanism? Why bother or care?

One reason is to make similar space to reconsider the contextual "why" of our research endeavors. Far from a banal set of protocols or procedural structuring processes for research, methodology is extremely political (Dewsbury, 2010; Law, 2004). Methodology often passes in the guise of technique, but it does so in the heavy garb of convention, tradition, and

---

[1] For broader discussion of humanist social science, please see St. Pierre (2000); Braidotti (2013), and Bennett (2010). Specific to leisure studies, we suggest Kumm and Johnson (2017) and Berbary (2017). Although not necessarily "bad," humanism is necessarily problematic. The most noble humanist projects tend to erect hierarchical, binary divisions, structures with unintended, adverse consequences. Humanism sustains man/woman, adult/child, human/nonhuman power disparities via vertically structured chains of being (ontology), positioning standardized man as apex. These authors go to considerable lengths to demonstrate these problematics, offering insights for developing posthumanist alternatives.

expectation, which often stipulates and regulates what counts as knowledge. Methodology is dis/abling, affording limited im/possibilities and probabilities of knowledges produced, built up, sustained, and/or de/stabilized (Law, 2004). Contrary to merely deriving/constructing knowledge, research methodologies *enact* pre-existing social and material relations that fix its conditions of possibility (Foucault, 1972; Law, 2004). In other words, the methodologies we choose *enact* ways of knowing, always already "appropriate." This limits our abilities to see/do research differently, to produce new, previously unthinkable knowledges. The problem is not that methodology is exclusive, limiting, and restricting (necessarily so), but that methodology is often an unquestionable, brute orthodoxy. We fail to *see* that which frames our *seeing*, reproducing limited "visions" in what research makes *visible* (Richardson & St. Pierre, 2005). Preoccupied with the "how" of research, we blind ourselves to methodological process that preload, preauthorize, and predetermine knowledge production—often to the detriment of those positioned on the poorer end of binary divides and hierarchical structures.

Some qualitative researchers remaining with/in humanism have already leveled this argument against aspects of technique, protocol, and procedure (Denzin & Lincoln, 2005; Tuck & Yang, 2014). But what if we apply this argument to question the humanist underpinnings of qualitative methodologies themselves? What then, if we step outside humanism? How else might we conceive research/methodology? What would research become, when stripped of its *a priori* baggage and conceived more generously as *thinking about our thinking*? What knowledge becomes possible, thinkable? Would knowledge even continue as our principal concern?

At the threshold of the next 40 years, we ask these questions by engaging *postqualitative inquiry* (St. Pierre, 2011), a movement among social science researchers asking similar questions and posing modest responses, fodder for conversations-to-come. As a movement, postqualitative inquiry is emerging as generative criticism, a politics of refusing humanist methodologies. The contention is less specific to any given research approach and more germane to humanism's "hegemonic and dominatory pretentions" (Law, 2004, p. 4) that perpetuate "methodological positivism" through a combination of "empiricist ontology, positivist epistemology, and a scientific version of naturalism" (Steinmetz, 2005, pp. 277–278). Even in many of its most critical forms, humanist, qualitative methodologies retain much of the positivism of that which preceded them. Conventional qualitative research failed to fully break with the onto-epistemologies of quantitative methods, which we fought hard to resist and rework. Postqualitative inquiry attempts to move toward the radical critique and boundless potentials that early qualitative research aspired to, with less fixed, dogmatic, and *a priori* designs. Postqualitative inquiry is *not* about creating a new, better, or more accurate *a priori* methodology; rather, we aim to create space for difference in how we think, feel, and live in the midst of the rapidly changing social and material conditions that enable *and* restrict our research.

Postqualitative inquiry also attempts to keep methodological pace with developments in social theory that enable radically different onto-epistemologies than those of humanism. For example, developments in theories of *affect* (Bennett, 2010; Clough, 2010; Massumi, 2002; Thrift, 2008), *new materialism* (Barad, 2007; Coole & Frost, 2010), *the post-human* (Braidotti, 2010; 2013), and *actor network theory* (Latour, 2005) all emphasize a flattened ontology. Flattened onto-epistemology abandons the vertical, hierarchical, masculine "tree of knowledge," with its root-trunk-branch-twig structure of humanist research. This tree is less a metaphor and more an "image of thought," which can be defined as a spatial "system of coordinates, dynamisms, orientations: what it means to think, and to 'orient oneself in thought'" (Deleuze, 1997, p. 148). It affords humanist research an anchoring, stabilizing, and grounding—an unambiguous thought-orientation. Roots ground, trunks build, on an established, rooted knowledge, and branches spread in different directions, filling the canopy with individual research projects. It is so common that it often goes unnoticed, and our research classes propagate it, uncritically advancing hierarchical, disciplinary structures. This impedes paradigm proliferation through a Classical structure of phallogocentrism—"the proudly erect tree under whose spreading boughs latter-day Platos conduct their class" (Massumi, 1987, p. xii).

Flattened onto-epistemology refuses arborescent structure, relying, instead, on other images of thought. For example, Deleuze and Guattari's (2011) image of the *rhizome*—a subterranean network of tuberous growth that puts up propitious shoots, strangling "the roots of the infamous tree" (Massumi, 1987, p. xiii). Likewise, Bennett's (2010) image of *vibrant matter* counters hierarchical divides and humanist binaries (e.g., man/woman, human/nonhuman, organic/inorganic) because it accounts for how matter, that is, "things," shape human experience. This is important, as Bennett (2010) pointed out, because humanist onto-epistemology "does not have a stellar record of success in preventing human suffering or promoting human well-being" (p. 12). Questioning arborescence, she proposed vibrant matter as a way to "open up space for forms of ethical practice that do not rely upon the image of an intrinsically *hierarchical* order of things" (p. 12).

Flattened ontology removes human beings from the apex of existence, as the arbiter of meaning. This thoroughly breaks from humanism because there is no longer an entirely autonomous, rational, unified agent or subject situated above the non-human. Rather, now the human is on a flattened plane, not above but beside other matterings. Not *apart from*, but *a part of,* matter. Post* theories relying on a flattened, posthumanist ontology situate human being laterally on a continuum of matter, where matter is no longer thought to be dumb, mute, or inert. Instead, matter *matters*, intensely exercising lateral agency, making our lives and knowledges possible (Berlant, 2010, 2011). Postqualitative inquiry attempts a methodological turn commensurate with this flattened ontology, renewing interest in matter, and resisting tendencies to overly privilege the human being.

As we move forward, we argue that this turn is necessary to sustain our collective values. Questioning whether humanism is capable of sustaining our discipline in the next 40 years, we press for conversations-to-come regarding the im/possibilities of (post)inquiry when detached from humanism. We begin by further exploring what is meant by humanist qualitative research, revisiting Berbary and Boles' (2014) proposed scaffolding[2] sous erasure (Derrida, 1974) as a potential departure. We then question how an ontological turn may initiate inquiry outside the "dogmatic, orthodox Cartesian image of thought that drives much of social science research" (St. Pierre, Jackson, & Mazzei, 2016, p 100). Finally, we return to our initial questions of "why?" to briefly discuss some ethical concerns.

Sous erasure: Methodology

Although a great deal of critical qualitative research foregrounds the limits of objectivist and (post)positivist research (Parry, Johnson, & Stewart, 2013), it is common to pose such critiques with/in humanism (Berbary, 2017). In other words, even our most innovative qualitative work locates meaning making, Truth(s), bias/subjectivity, the "self," and representation within humanist onto-epistemologies, with less engagement with the radical ontologies of postinquiry (St. Pierre & Lather, 2013). Even a great deal of our field's most critical, innovative research privileges legacies of the Enlightenment, modernity, interpretivism, and

---

[2] Following Derrida (1974), Berbary and Boles (2014) put "scaffolding" under erasure, or *sous rature*, to "retain the structure of qualitative research methodology—its structuring concepts and categories—because it appears necessary and, at the same time, [to] cross it out because it is inaccurate" or too limiting (St. Pierre, 2011, p. 613).

structuralism (Berbary, 2017). Berbary and Boles's (2014) ~~scaffolding~~ for humanist qualitative inquiry illustrates the prevalence of these legacies over the past 40 years.

With the intention of contributing to already strong qualitative traditions, Berbary and Boles (2014) proposed ~~scaffolding~~ sous erasure (Derrida, 1974), for humanist, qualitative, leisure research to provide students and scholars with an open, yet contingently-structured framework to organize and align onto-epistemological and theoretical allegiances across the complex choices available in humanist research, or what Lather (2013) might characterize as the humanist traditions of Qual 1.0, Qual 2.0, and Qual 3.0 (Berbary & Boles, 2014). Lather (2013) described these traditions as Qual 1.0—"the conventional interpretive inquiry that emerged from the liberal humanism of sociology and cultural anthropology"; Qual 2.0—"the centered, disciplined, regulated, and normalized" inquiry of "qualitative handbooks, textbooks, and journals" that "remains within the humanist enclosure"; and Qual 3.0—inquiry that "begins to use postmodern theories to open up concepts associated with qualitative inquiry" yet still remain within a more structured, humanist, and defensive position (p. 635). With this in mind, Berbary and Boles (2014) proposed their ~~scaffolding~~ for researchers grounded within all three humanist qualitative moments. In particular, the ~~scaffolding~~ considered eight philosophical and practical decision points to construct an aligned yet fluid design that included the following concepts and their potentials, and one need not begin in any order as long as each point is considered:

Although this ~~scaffolding~~ was specifically designed for humanist qualitative inquiry, Berbary and Boles (2014) also showed points of departure, potentials to shift toward post-inquiry, as highlighted in their chart. Shifting from Qual 3.0 into Qual 4.0—an inquiry of "becoming in the Deleuzian sense…that cannot be tidily described in textbooks or handbooks" and has "no methodological instrumentality to be unproblematically learned" (Lather, 2013, p. 635)—begins to undo the organizing structures of humanism, rendering the ~~scaffolding~~ useless, except for departure. Acknowledging this disconnect for Qual 4.0, Berbary and Boles challenged scholars to pick up where they left off, to re-interpret the ~~scaffolding~~ through postinquiry.

We take up that call by engaging a flattened ontology, showing how these concepts/structures must be re/de/organized to be useful in a post-paradigm. Yet shifting into post-inquiry requires more than discussing ontology or including post* theory into existing scaffolds. Playing with more radical ontologies of Qual 4.0 and "methodology-to-come" or "a thousand tiny methodologies" (Lather, 2013, p. 635), requires refusing ~~scaffolding~~ because such "methodological a priori" (Marcus, 2009, p. 5) is itself a principally humanist notion. Post-humanist research requires re-evaluating most qualitative concepts, including the "we" of epistemology, theory as a "lens" above what we "study," data/data collection/analysis, claims of subjectivity, representation, and structured ~~scaffolding~~ with the assumed researching "doer behind the deed" who "outlines the doing before she begins" (Lather & St. Pierre, 2013, p. 630). We cannot call our work post-qualitative simply because we think with post* theories, within a humanist framework. This ignores ontological differences and simply inserts post* thinking "into the recognizable, comfortable structure," or ~~scaffolding~~ of humanist inquiry (St. Pierre, 2014, p. 8). Rather, postinquiry requires re-defining depth/surface representations, restoring balance to material-discursive practices, *and* de-centering the human by challenging the privilege of *presence* in notions of data. We are forced to refuse humanist methodologies, required "to give it up, to try to unlearn it, forget it, get it out of [our] minds" (St. Pierre, 2014, p. 8). We must leave behind what we can of humanist inquiries, such as prescribed methods, unified theories (both of natural and social sciences), objective observations, knowledge through reason, and foundational interpretations. Such a departure inevitably no longer makes humanist methodology thinkable (St. Pierre, 2014).

When leaving humanism and moving toward flattened onto-epistemologies, what becomes of inquiry? How is it thinkable? Doubtless, research becomes less sure of itself—displaced from its root-trunk-branch-twig structure. And the human being, human experience, and human leisure becomes more modest, less contained in "conscious reflection" (e.g., self-reported data), less concrete in objectivity and/or subjectivity. Postinquiry becomes supremely partial; we become part-objects and part-subjects, in processes of becoming; which is to say, in the fluidity, complexity, and material comprising each individual unfolding, of what we call a person, group, experience, etc., becomes within and across a flattened ontological continuum, within and across necessary inter- intra-, and infra-activities between human and nonhuman bodies—in becoming. We must resist the seductive tendency to reduce any "form" to any pre-given, predetermined form of "reality" (e.g., neoliberalism, capitalism, heteronormativity, experience, the individual, the social). The wager of postqualitative inquiry, onto-epistemologically, is that these bodies, however "knowable" in some form, are never entirely stabilized, but always already transmorphing into other, multiple modes of existence via shifting entanglements with other bodies (Bennett, 2010; Massumi, 2002). How we account for experience, thus, becomes much more fluid, complex, and singular, and our approaches to any such accounting, *however incomplete*, requires increasing methodological innovation, which we are attempting to foreground as points to consider for post-qualitative conversations-to-come.

With that said, inquiry is never purely outside structure. Even the institutions where we conduct our work are highly structured, as is our discipline. Berbary and Boles' (2014) ~~scaffolding~~ sous rature is simultaneously a hierarchical structure (~~scaffolding~~) and a practical undoing of that same structure (under erasure). It demonstrates the necessity of provisional structure to proceed intelligently, yet resists overly dogmatic appeals to any presumed orthodoxy or unproblematic prescription. It pragmatically illustrates the irresolvable tensions between structure and its others. The question is not whether or not to adhere to given structures, but why? What would such adherence do? What else could be done? There is space to work within/against structure in Berbary and Boles' model, but does it go far enough? This is too a conversation-to-come.

Making the shift

Some scholars feel humanist qualitative research has become conventional, reductionist, hegemonic, and sometimes oppressive, losing radical potentials "to produce different knowledge and produce knowledge differently" (St. Pierre, 1997, p. 175). In particular, aspects of humanism, such as linear, meta-narratives of progress, the belief or call for transparent language (Lather, 1996), reliance on stable categories of similarity, presence (Derrida, 1974), and preservation of binary structures (even in attempts to equalize them) maintain taken-for-granted structures of thought. These images of thought warrant critique because they have produced the world in ways that are often less than useful, even harmful to individuals, groups, and communities (St. Pierre, 2000, p. 479).

Although we support such critique of humanist work, we simultaneously find productive possibilities of humanist qualitative research intriguing and at times useful, especially when utilized for social change and/or justice. And by encouraging a discussion of post-inquiry, we are not suggesting *all* must make a shift. Our intention is more modest: to generate a "refusal space ... to think within and against," rethinking "humanist ontology," the "categories we have invented to organize and structure humanist qualitative methodology," and question what we have taken for granted (Lather & Pierre, 2013, pp. 629–630). We encourage our field to "ask whether we have become so attached to our invention—qualitative research—that we have come to think it is real. Have we forgotten that we made it up? Could we just leave it behind and do/live something else" (Lather & St. Pierre, 2013, p. 631)?

But what *is* that other and is it meaningful to leisure scholars? Perhaps we cannot summarize what that *other* is fully. Perhaps we can only pose possibilities, movements rather than definitive techniques, because post-inquiry is always "in process and not one thing" (St. Pierre, Jackson, & Mazzei, 2016). There is always much more to read and read carefully because post-qualitative inquiry traces more than a decade-long history.

This history most recently involves groupings of (re)new/ed empiricisms, (re)new/ed materialisms, posthumanisms, and postinquiries, that pull and borrow from multiple theories (e.g., affect, thing, complexity, disorder and disunity, and posthuman). Known for their contributions to this movement are scholars such as Deleuze and Guattari (1980/87) (e.g., assemblage, rhizome, bodies-without-organs), Barad (2007) (e.g., entanglement, agential realism, intra-actions), Bradotti (2013) (e.g., feminist posthumanism, generative capacity, politics of possibility), Clough (2009) (e.g., new empiricism, affect), Coole and Frost (2010) (e.g., new materialisms), Thrift (2008) (e.g., nonrepresentational theories of affect), and Latour (2005) (e.g., actor network theory), and—specifically for postqualitative inquiry—Jackson (2013); Jackson and Mazzei (2013); Lather (2013); St. Pierre (2011), and Ringrose & Coleman (2013). Through these contributions, postqualitative inquiry emerges as an alternative to humanist grids of regularity (Gerrard, Roudolph, & Sriprakash, 2017, p.2) and becomes less about *living up* to a reality representationally, and more about finding new methodological strategies for *living with* reality (Dewsbury, 2010). This often entails performative engagements and generative critiques, affirming different ways of thinking, feeling, and living within a flattened onto-epistemology. Gathering these contributions and various shifts together, we ask if "everything has turned," confronted, as we are, with an "image of thought in which the old categories and distinctions can no longer be thought," and believe this has "turned us towards something very new and very possible (St. Pierre, Jackson, & Mazzei, 2016, p. 100).[3]

---

[3] Postqualitative research is gaining greater visibility in various disciplines; however, much of this work is quite recent. Examples of published research is scarce. An insightful example of postqualitative inquiry within the field of leisure studies is Kumm's (2015) dissertation, *Modest Experiments in Living: Intensities of Life.*

Revising scaffolding for postinquiry?

It is possible to make this turn within leisure scholarship, if we embrace an experimental orientation to new onto-epistemologies. But how might Berbary and Boles (2014) eight points for humanist qualitative inquiry be revised and/or left behind to envision something different, if we turn from that which is no longer thinkable? Can we borrow some things and leave others? We will engage these eight points of humanist qualitative scaffolding to show how and where post-qualitative engagements may experiment with departure.

1. Ontology

Perhaps the most difficult and most important shift—given how deeply entrenched our hierarchical ontological inheritance is (Coole & Froste, 2010)—is toward a flattened ontology within postinquiry. It can be anxiety producing to imagine humans along a continuum of matter without complete agency; however, as Deleuze and Guattari (2011), Barad (2007), Bennett (2010), and others teach us, we have never been fully in control, and the track record of humanist projects to improve collective existence is not particularly stellar. The wager is, as Bennett (2010) suggested, to "raise the status of the materiality of which we are composed" (p. 12), an alternative strategy to improve life, create more humane, if less human-centered, futures. The methodological question is "how." The answer, not so simply, is to devise our projects with close attention to the problems and theories at hand, *inventing* approaches that consider the mattering of the world, the self, etc. (becoming) on an ontological continuum, including within that same continuum the mattering of our very research as intra-active agents and forces in becoming.

2. Epistemology

Epistemology must be informed by this ontology. Not only are the divides between ontology (being) and epistemology (knowing) largely artificial—hence our writing of "onto-epistemologies"—but the concepts of being and knowing also suggest a capturable reality, a stilled, arrested, or static reality. Post-inquiry concerns process, becoming, mattering. As such, we question whether "being" or "knowing" are still terms we need. We must expand our vocabulary to not only describe the "what," "how," and "why" of research, but also to keep the process moving, to resist the seduction of finality: to adopt epistemological modesty.

It is crucial that we account for ontological matterings more explicitly. When feminist scholars speak of embodiment, without attending to actual bodily mattering (Dewsbury, 2010), we must ask how the actual body informs embodiment? When we use a word like "resonance" to describe generally agreeable feelings, understandings of shared experience, but miss the material processes of actual resonation, feeling and sensing in sharing, we must ask how to engage the body properly in its materiality (Massumi, 2002). Bodily mattering is not just to know or be, interpret or construct—all worthy concerns because the body is a contested site—but also to become, actively engaged in processes that are far from final capture.

Theory

Postinquiry rejects theory as a mere *a posteriori* lens or *a priori* staging for research. Although theory is used at each and every stage of research (Dewsbury, 2010), the critical difference is that theory no longer comes above or below other matters (e.g., data, analysis, subjectivity, findings). Theory is an actively performative dimension of research that affects and is affected by the other elements in the mix. Like all other elements, it is not considered immobile, but approached pragmatically to see what it can do, how it might help open vistas onto becoming, not landing but moving again. Against finality, there is modesty but also boldness—insofar as we might leverage critique against the presumed finality regarding what counts as research, thought, knowledge, being, and becoming (Dewsbury, 2010; Thrift, 2008).

3. Methodology

Depending on the research "mix," some may not "sweat the construction of any elaborate step-by-step methodology much at all" (Seigworth & Gregg, 2010, p. 14). Postinquiry presses to get on with the work that is important, without defensive postures against established frameworks (Lather, 2013). This is not to say anything goes. Far from it! Postqualitative researchers take methodology seriously, so much so they refuse repose upon any notion of methodology as a given, a formulaic, as if each new problem can be unproblematically engaged with the same old tools. Methodology fundamentally operates to narrow the research focus, limiting what becomes visible within particular methods. But as Law (2004) critiqued, this can also work to distort complexity into clarity and make a further mess of what is already diffuse. Postinquiry attempts, instead, a practice of "deliberate imprecision" (Law, 2004, p. 3), of expanding rather than narrowing, to "keep the researcher alive to change and chance, to … new twists and turns of direction and focus" (Dewsbury, 2010, p. 324). The call is to creatively reimagine, at every stage, methodological possibilities, to follow inquiry into unfamiliar terrain while reinventing approaches all along the way.

4. Method/data collection

Postinquiry de-centers the human subject, and necessarily does not prescribe or proscribe any form of data/data collection. Rather, we are concerned with how data appears (St. Pierre, 2013b), how something in the research "mix" becomes data—and not other things—and made to be brute, evident, evidential. Postinquiry questions the privileged status of data and what counts as data. If postinquiry works against finality, in becomings, data represent a category held in suspension just enough to avoid brute, evidential arrestment, to allow more to count in the research process (e.g., theory, bodies, things, matter) that are unassimilable to humanist, categorical, understandings of data. A shift to move matterings and becomings along.

5. Analysis/interpretation

According to Dewsbury (2010), we "miss a trick if we solely task ourselves in our research to live up to reality, when it is precisely about finding alternative methodological strategies for living with reality" (p. 139). Postinquiry offers a difficult proposition: research should produce more than an account of lived experiences, more than reportage, and more than analysis. Utilize whatever is at hand, over *analyzing,* to produce, to make differences in how we think, feel, and live in our everyday lives. A tall order, yes! But embracing an experimental, performative, mangling practice (Jackson, 2013), and non-representational orientation to research (MacLure, 2013), post-inquiry attempts to create concepts, strategies, movements, actionable products, interrupting the status quo. Deleuze and Guattari (2011) described this as a cartographic endeavor—a highly experimental and risky enterprise that transforms whatever is at hand into something productive of difference in how we think, feel, and live. Thus, postinquiry often foregoes deep explanation of the work, focusing, instead, upon putting ideas to *work*, making them actionable, challenging the status quo.

6. Representation

Discontent with the show-and-tell politics of conventional, humanist methodology (Thrift, 2008), postinquiry is performative (Dewsbury, 2010). We resist and question tendencies to capture, contain, reflect, signify, or represent (Clough, 2009). Rejecting representational logic—the belief that any "reality" can be captured and transparently reflected or represented in language or any other form—postinquiry is instead concerned with approaching the non-representable. How does one, for example, represent love, death, or friendship? Common experiences that defy representational, reflective capture. We write stories, poetry, or songs, but these are inflections or modulations, not representations. Again, modesty behooves us. Narratives, poems, and songs are pragmatic endeavors to see what we can produce, make, modulate, inflect rather than represent; and this is an ethical issue because we cannot deflect, as in a representation of something else, our burden of authorship.

7. (Non)Conclusions

Postinquiry, as becoming, is often left open-ended or spilling over. As we have tried to articulate, postinquiry works by adding, rather than subtracting; broadening rather than narrowing; and by connections that potentially open, augment, or expand how we think, feel, and live. When it works, inquiry is performative, active, and engaging. But there is no point of saturating, completing, or exhausting the project, even though a researcher may feel herself, particularly exhausted. Instead, one reaches an edge that cannot be breached, one runs out of space or opens space just enough to move on, reaching a plateau and walking away. The guiding question, however, is "does it work" (Massumi, 1987, p. xv)? In other words, what difference does it make? We must ask, "What new thoughts does it make possible to think? What new emotions does it make possible to feel? What new sensations and perceptions does it open in the body?" (Massumi, 1992, p. 8).

In revisiting these eight points, post-inquiry attempts to *enact and perform differences with all the the elements in the research "mix."* Methodology may become less linear, structured, or rigid. The "what" of research and the "how" of methodology must also engage the question "why." We are not advocating abandonment of interviews, participant observation, etc. but modestly asking "why" we should or should not use those strategies. Are they adequate for the problems we confront? We modestly suggest that methodology requires continued interrogation even as we reinvent/redeploy it in new ways. What becomes of data, analysis, thought, and representation with a posthumanist ontology? Our answers are modest (and brief) but we think modesty is necessary to counter the hubris associated with terms like "research." And in making this "turn," other ways of doing research are modestly becoming possible.

Becoming-world

The introduction of this article posed several why questions. Along the way, we asked other questions. Rather than recapitulate or answer all our questions, we wish to devote these remaining pages to a few modest thoughts on ethics. The entire project of postinquiry is, in many ways, complementary to our collective values to improve social life. But sometimes our field can also presume a moralism, as if we always know what to do and how to do it, as if our "why" question was always already answered. Not knowing what, how, or why to do something is the *dilemma* that begs for ethics.

Methodology is complicit in moralism inasmuch as it keeps dilemma at bay. And though we have made significant strides toward paradigm proliferation (albeit within humanism), and more importantly toward social justice, we believe our contemporary social, economic, and political conditions are destabilizing any ability to say with confidence that we know what to do or how to do it. As researchers with strong commitments to social justice, we acknowledge that postinquiry may be troubling, given that many marginalized people and groups are just now gaining visibility and voice in established traditions. But we also feel an urgency to expand that important work into this emerging movement, especially given the uncertainty and ambiguity of our times. It is easy to dread unlearning what has become so familiar to us; it is as easy to dread because of the precariousness that has become palpable in our contemporary moment of uncertainty. Yet as Deleuze (1990/1992) wrote, "there is no need to fear or hope, but only to look for new weapons" (p. 4). And post-inquiry maybe just what we need.

Whether hopeful or fearful, it is necessary to embrace ambiguity and invent new ways of doing research to remain true to our core values. As an ethical project, we not only need to educate institutional review boards, but also care for ourselves as researchers working "without a net." It is crucial to build support networks and partnerships as we navigate the possibilities of post-inquiry.

Post-inquiry removes familiar research landmarks, signposts, making it easy to become engulfed in disorienting despair. Care of the self must not be neglected; it is necessary to retain something familiar to orient our departures. For us, we retain our core values and commitments, as a broad frame of reference, even while on a yet-unknown trajectory of postinquiry. And we are hopeful that this trajectory will generate humane futures, for the next 40 years and beyond, even if those futures are less human.

Reimagining what counts as research and how to contend with the matterings of life, even while uncertain, places us on a threshold of ethics. It is worth questioning humanist underpinnings, even if it makes us unsure. As St. Pierre (2000) described, these underpinnings are everywhere, in "the language we speak, the shape of the homes we live in, … the politics we practice, the map that locates us on the earth, the futures we can imagine, the limits of our pleasures" (p. 478). In uncertainty, ethics manifests to unshackle pleasure, home, politics, and imagination. Where better to begin questioning these humanist shackles than in our own field of leisure?

References

Arai, S. (2011). What will you assume about my difference? A poem. In K. Paisley & D. Dustin (Eds.), *Speaking up and speaking out* (pp. 21–30). Champaign, IL: Sagamore.
Barad, K. (2007). *Meeting the universe halfway: Quantum physics and the entanglement of meaning.* Durham, NC: Duke University Press.
Bennett, J. (2010). *Vibrant matter: A political ecology of things.* Durham, NC: Duke University Press.
Berbary, L. A. (2017). Thinking through poststructuralism in leisure studies: A detour around "proper" humanist knowledges. In K. Spracklen, L. Lashua, E. Sharpe, & S. Swain (Eds.), *Handbook of leisure theory* (pp. 719–742). London, England: Palgrave.
Berbary, L. A. (2015). Creative analytic practices: Onto-epistemological and theoretical attachments, uses, and constructions within humanist qualitative leisure research. *International Leisure Review,* 2(4), 27–55.

Berbary, L. A. (2012). Don't be a whore, that's not ladylike: Discursive discipline and sorority women's gendered subjectivity. *Qualitative Inquiry, 18*(7), 535–554.

Berbary, L. A., & Boles, J. C. (2014). Eight reflection points: Re-visiting scaffolding for improvisational humanist qualitative inquiry. *Leisure Sciences, 36*(5), 401–419.

Berlant, L. (2011). *Cruel optimism*. Durham, NC: Duke University Press.

Berlant, L. (2010). Cruel optimism. In M. Gregg & G. J. Seigworth (Eds.), *The affect theory reader* (pp. 93–117). Durham, NC: Duke University Press.

Braidotti, R. (2013). *The posthuman*. Malden, MA: Polity Press.

Braidotti, R. (2010). The politics of "life itself" and new ways of dying. In D. Coole & S. Frost (Eds.), *New materialisms: Ontology, agency, and politics* (pp. 201–218). Durham, NC: Duke University Press.

Clough, P. T. (2010). The affective turn: Political economy, biomedia, and bodies. In M. Gregg & G. J. Seigworth (Eds.), *The affect theory reader* (pp. 206–225). Durham, NC: Duke University Press.

Clough, P. T. (2009). The new empiricism, affect, and sociological method. *European Journal of Social Theory, 12*(1), 43–61.

Coleman, R., & Ringrose, J. (2013). Introduction: Deleuze and research methodologies. In R. Coleman & J. Ringrose (Eds.), *Deleuze and research methodologies* (pp. 1–22). Edinburgh, Scotland: Edinburgh University Press.

Coole, D., & Frost, S. (2010). Introducing the new materialism. In D. Coole & S. Frost (Eds.), *New materialisms: Ontology, agency, and politics* (pp. 1–43). Durham, NC: Duke University Press.

Deleuze, G. (1992). *Postscript on the societies of control*, October, 59(Winter), 3–7. (Original work published 1990)

Deleuze, G. (1997). *Negotiations* (M. Joughin Trans.). New York, NY: Columbia University Press. (Original work published 1990 by Les Editions de Minuit)

Deleuze, G., & Guattari, F. (2011). *A thousand plateaus: Capitalism and schizophrenia* (B. Massumi, Trans.). Minneapolis, MN: University of Minnesota Press. (Original work published 1980 by Les Editions de Minuit, Paris)

Denzin, N., & Lincoln, Y. (Eds.). (2005). *The Sage handbook of qualitative research* (4th ed.). Thousand Oaks, CA: Sage.

Derrida, J. (1974). *Of grammatology* (G. C. Spivak Trans.). Baltimore: Johns Hopkins Univeristy Press. (Original work published 1967)

Dewsbury, J. D. (2010). Performative, non-representational, and affect-based research: Seven injunctions. In D. DeLyser, S. Herbert, S. Aitken, M. Crang, & L. McDowell (Eds.), *The SAGE handbook of qualitative geography* (pp. 321–334). Thousand Oaks, CA: Sage.

Flax, J. (1990). Postmodernism and gender relations in feminist theory. In L. J. Nicholson (Ed.), *Feminism/postmodernism* (pp. 39–62). New York, NY: Routledge.

Floyd, M. F. (2014). Social justice as an integrating force for leisure research. *Leisure Sciences, 36*(4), 379–387.

Foucault, M. (1972). *The archaeology of knowledge and the discourse on language* (A. M. S. Smith Trans.). New York, NY: Pantheon Books.

Foucault, M. (1984). What is enlightenment? (C. Porter, Trans.). In P. Rabinow (Ed.), *The Foucault reader*. Ne York, NY: Pantheon Books.

Fullagar, S. (2017). Post-qualitative inquiry and the new materialist turn: Implications for sport, health and physical culture research. *Qualitative Research in Sport, Exercise and Health, 9*(2), 247–257.

Gerrard, J., Roudolph, S., & Sriprakash, A. (2017). The politics of post-qualitative inquiry: History and power. *Qualitative Inquiry, 23*(5), 384–394.

Glover, T. D. (2007). Ugly on the diamonds: An examination of white privilege in youth baseball. *Leisure Sciences, 29*(2), 195–208.

Henderson, K. (2011). Postpositivism and the pragmatics of leisure research. *Leisure Sciences, 33*(4), 341–346.

Jackson, A. Y. (2013). Data-as-machine: A Deleuzian becoming. In R. Coleman & J. Ringrose (Eds.), *Deleuze and research methodologies* (pp. 111–124). Edinburgh, Scotland: Edinburgh University Press.

Jackson, A. Y. (2013). Posthumanist data analysis of mangling practices. *International Journal of Qualitative Studies in Education, 26*(6), 741–748.

Jackson, A. Y., & Mazzei, L. A. (2012). *Thinking with theory in qualitative research: Viewing data across multiple perspectives*. New York, NY: Routledge.

Kivel, B. D. (2011). What does society need done and how can we do it? In K. Paisley & D. Dustin (Eds.), *Speaking up and speaking out* (pp. 9–14). Champaign, IL: Sagamore.

Kumm, B. E., & Johnson, C. W. (2017). Subversive imagination: Smoothing space for leisure, identity, and politics. In K. Spracklen, L. Lashua, E. Sharpe, & S. Swain (Eds.), *Handbook of leisure theory* (pp. 891–910). London, England: Palgrave.

Kumm, B. E. (2015). *Modest experiments in living: Intensities of life* (Unpublished doctoral dissertation). The University of Georgia, Athens, GA.

Lashua, B. (2017). "Let's murder the moonlight!" Futurism, anti-humanism, and leisure. In K. Spracklen, L. Lashua, E. Sharpe, & S. Swain (Eds.), *Handbook of leisure theory* (pp. 487–506). London, England: Palgrave.

Lashua, B., & Fox, K. (2007). Defining the grove: From remix to research in the Beat of Boyle Street. *Leisure Sciences, 29*(2), 143–158.

Lather, P. (2013). Methodology-21: What do we do in the afterward? *International Journal of Qualitative Studies in Education, 26*(6), 634–645.

Lather, P. (1996). Troubling clarity: The politics of accessible language. *Harvard Educational Review, 66*(3), 525–545.

Lather, P., & St. Pierre, E. A. (2013). Post-qualitative research. *International Journal of Qualitative Studies in Education (QSE), 26*(6), 629–633.

Latour, B. (2005). *Reassembling the social: An introduction to actor-network theory*. Oxford, England: Oxford University Press.

Law, J. (2004). *After method: Mess is social science research*. New York, NY: Routledge.

Lewis, S., & Johnson, C. W. (2011). But it's not that easy: Negotiating trans leisure space. *Leisure/Loisir, 35*(2), 115–132.

MacLure, M. (2013). Researching without representation? Language and materiality in post-qualitative methodology. *International Journal of Qualitative Studies in Education, 26*(6), 658–667.

Mair, H. (2011). What about the "rest of the story?" Recreation on the backs of others. In K. Paisley & D. Dustin (Eds.), *Speaking up and speaking out* (pp. 117–124). Champaign, IL: Sagamore.

Malick, M. (2017). Postmodernism and leisure. In K. Spracklen, B. Lashua, E. Sharpe, & S. Swain (Eds.), *Palgrave Handbook of leisure theory* (pp. 689–704). London, UK: Palgrave.

Marcus, G. (2009). Notes toward an ethnographic memoir of supervising graduate research through anthropology's decades of transformation. In J. Faubion & G. Marcus (Eds.), *Fieldwork is not what it used to be: Learning anthropology's method in a time of transition* (pp. 1–34). Ithaca, NY: Cornell University Press.

Massumi, B. (2002). *Parables for the virtual: Movement, affect, sensation*. Durham, NC: Duke University Press.

Massumi, B. (1987). Translator's foreword: Pleasures of philosophy. In G. Deleuze & F. Guattari (Eds.), *A thousand plateaus: Capitalism and schizophrenia* (pp. ix–xv). Minneapolis, MN: University of Minnesota Press.

Massumi, B. (1992). *A user's guide to capitalism and schizophrenia*. Cambridge, MA: MIT Press.

Mowatt, R. A. (2012). Lynching as leisure: Broadening notions of a field. *American Behavioral Scientist, 56*(10), 1361–1387.

Neville, R. D. (2013). The pragmatics of leisure revisited. *Leisure Sciences, 35*(4), 399–404.

Parry, D. C. (2007). There is life after breast cancer: Nine vignettes exploring dragon boat racing for breast cancer survivors. *Leisure Sciences, 29*(1), 53–69.

Parry, D. C., & Johnson, C. W. (2007). Contextualizing leisure research to encompass complexity in lived leisure experience: The need for creative analytic practice. *Leisure Sciences, 29*(2), 119–130.

Parry, D., Johnson, C., & Stewart, W. (2013). Leisure research for social justice: A response to Henderson. *Leisure Sciences, 35*(1), 81–87.

Richardson, L., & St. Pierre, E. A. (2005). Writing: A method of inquiry. In N. K. Denzin & Y. S. Lincoln (Eds.), *The Sage handbook of qualitative research* (3rd ed., pp. 959–978). Thousand Oaks, CA: Sage.

Ringrose, J., & Coleman, R. (2013). Looking and desiring machines: A feminist Deleuzian mapping of bodies and affects. In R. Coleman & J. Ringrose (Eds.), *Deleuze and research methodologies* (pp. 125–144). Edinburgh, Scotland: Edinburgh University Press.

Samdahl, D. (2011).What can "American beach" teach us? In K. Paisley & D. Dustin (Eds.), *Speaking up and speaking out* (pp. 83–94). Champaign, IL: Sagamore.

Seigworth, G. J., & Gregg, M. (2010). An inventory of shimmers. In M. Gregg & G. J. Seigworth (Eds.), *The affect theory reader* (pp. 1–25). Durham, NC: Duke University Press.

Sharpe, E. (2017). Against limits: A post-structural theorizing of resistance in leisure. In K. Spracklen, B. Lashua, E. Sharpe, & S. Swain (Eds.), *Palgrave Handbook of leisure theory* (pp. 911–926). London, UK: Palgrave.

Shaw, S. M. (2001). Conceptualizing resistance: Women's leisure as political practice. *Journal of Leisure Research, 33*(2), 186–201.

St. Pierre, E. A. (2014). A brief and personal history of post qualitative research: Toward "post inquiry." *Journal of Curriculum Theorizing, 30*(2), 2–19.

St. Pierre, E. A. (2013). The appearance of data. *Cultural Studies-Critical Methodologies, 13*(4), 223–227.

St. Pierre, E. A. (2011). Post qualitative research: The critique and the coming after. In N. K. Denzin & Y. S. Lincoln (Eds.), *Sage handbook of qualitative inquiry* (4th ed.) (pp. 611–635). Los Angeles, CA: Sage.

St. Pierre, E. A. (1997). Methodology in the fold and the irruption of transgressive data. *International Journal of Qualitative Studies in Education, 10*(2), 175–189.

St. Pierre, E. A. (2000). Post-structural feminism in education: An overview. *International Journal of Qualitative Studies in Education, 13*(5), 477–515.

St. Pierre, E. A., Jackson, A. Y., & Mazzei, L. A. (2016). New empiricism and new materialism: Conditions for new inquiry. *Cultural Studies ←→ Critical Methodologies, 16*(2), 99–110.

Steinmetz, G. (2005). The epistemological unconsciousness of U.S. sociology and the transition to post-Fordism: The case of historical sociology. In J. Adams, E. S. Clemens, & A. S. Orloff (Eds.), *Remaking modernity: Politics, history, and sociology* (pp. 109–159). Durham, NC: Duke University Press.

Stewart, W. (2014). Leisure research to enhance social justice. *Leisure Sciences, 36*(4), 325–339.

Thrift, N. (2008). Intensities of feeling: Towards a spatial politics of affect. *Geografiska Annaler Series B: Human Geography, 86*(1), 57–78.

Tuck, E., & Yang, W. K. (2014). Unbecoming claims: Pedagogies of refusal in qualitative research. *Qualitative Inquiry, 20*(6), 811–818.

The Time Machine: Leisure Science (Fiction) and Futurology

Brett D. Lashua

ABSTRACT
There is a long, underlying presence of futurology—attempts to predict the future based on current or past events—throughout much of the leisure literature. On the occasion of the 40th anniversary of *Leisure Sciences*, I build on the work of futures scholars (e.g., Adam, 2008; Harrison, 2015) to explore how past ideas about the future have shaped the present. I revisit H. G. Wells's (1895) classic science fiction novel *The Time Machine* in view of recent trends and recurring debates (e.g., cybernation, (un)employment, the "leisure society," and Universal Basic Income) that are (or were) forecast to shape the future. Throughout, I argue that the ways that leisure scholars envision the future have significant impact on the actions of the field and its practitioners today.

Introduction

At the end of 2016, a number of news reports about the future of work and leisure caught my attention (e.g., Brooks, 2017; Finley, 2016; Otlermann, 2016; Overly, 2016; Sodha, 2016; Stewart, 2016). Debates about leisure only occasionally enter into mainstream media (Rojek, 2010; Shaw, 2007), and these high-profile reports (e.g., *BBC News, The Guardian, The Washington Post*, and *Wired*) asked: what will happen in the future when (if) millions of people lose their jobs to automation, artificial intelligence and robots? Will there be a new crisis of (un)employment? Will those educated and skilled in science and technology become an employed elite, while the vast majority of unemployed are idle, supported by some form of Universal Basic Income (UBI)? In the absence of work, what would people do? While these are familiar questions for leisure scholars, philosophers, sociologists, political scientists, and economists (e.g., Clarke & Critcher, 1985; de Grazia, 1962; Dumazidier, 1967; Parker, 1971; Rifkin, 1995; Rojek, 2002), I was certain that I had read this story elsewhere before. In this essay I (re)turn to science fiction.

In H.G. Well's (1895) *The Time Machine*, the protagonist travels to the year AD 802701 and encounters two posthuman societies: Eloi are naïve inhabitants of an undemanding leisure utopia, while crude Morlocks toil with machinery underground, providing for the Eloi. The first science fiction novel written for an adult audience, *The Time Machine* is cautionary futurology—an attempt to predict possible futures based on the present and the past. Roughly contemporary with Marshall's (1890) and Veblen's (1899) foundational texts on wealth and leisure, *The Time Machine* called critical attention to leisure and class inequities. It is as much an indictment of the industrial revolution and capitalism as it is a work of fiction. While widely read, like most fiction (and especially sci-fi) Wells's tale has received less academic attention than its contemporaries (Scott, 2010; Veal, 2009). While Scott (2010) expressed surprise at the absence of Veblen's work in analyses of current leisure, in this essay I offer that *The Time Machine* is also insightful and instructive in considerations of leisure, work and social class. More importantly, I offer that texts like *The Time Machine* alert us to the social construction of the future (Adam, 2008; Harrison, 2015); the ways that leisure scholars envision the future have significant impact on the actions of the field and its practitioners today.

Across its quadragenarian run, little scholarship in *Leisure Sciences* specifically addresses the future. It does find particular form, as futurology, in wider leisure debates, such as the "leisure society" (Bramham, 2006; Rojek, 2010; Veal, 2011) or an "age of leisure" (Sessoms, 1972). Unlike Wells's Eloi, the leisure society foreseen by leisure scholars included arts, self-actualization, learning, and other "noble" pursuits when people are freed from work. In the 1970s, when *Leisure Sciences* launched, this ideal had been in circulation for decades due to perceived shorter working hours and labor-saving technologies (Parker, 1971; Sessoms, 1972). For (Sessoms, 1972, p. 312), an "age of leisure" had already arrived:

> There is much evidence to support the view that we are entering the leisure age. Our advances in technology have freed many from the drudgery of routine work. We are moving from a hard industry-based economy to a service-based one. For the most part we no longer hold work to be the central interest of life […] In fact we are rediscovering the concept of homo ludens […].

Automation could free people from work to pursue the leisure society – but what kinds of leisure, what kind of society?

By the millennium, the leisure society thesis was generally viewed as naïve and undertheorized, and the concept had largely disappeared (Aitchison, 2010; Gilchrist & Wheaton, 2008). It endured in Rojek's (2001, p. 115) "postwork thesis" that reasserted "society is moving into a condition in which the cybernation of labor dramatically reduces the working week and the concomitant notion of the work career." Although the lines between work and leisure have blurred (Lashua, 2014), the cybernation of society is increasingly viewed as creating new and interconnected crises of leisure, (un)employment, and education. To think through these crises, I first turn to "futures studies", in particular, the work of time and futures scholar Barbara Adam. Following this, through the work of Veal (2011) and others (Bramham, 2006; Rojek, 2002) I revisit "the leisure society" concept as a kind of futurology—what kind of a future of leisure does this notion allow us to construct? What are the impacts of this potential future in our lives today? Finally I return to debates about Universal Basic Income and a world without work, before drawing some conclusions about the kinds of possible futures that *Leisure Sciences* might envision and enact.

Futurology, and the history of leisure futures

Leisure scholarship often trades in futurology (Parker, 1998). Futurology (or futures studies) involves systematic attempts to forecast possible, probable and preferable futures, based on historical trends and current contexts. That is, given what we know now, and what has happened in the past, what is likely to happen in the future? Because such perspectives are shaped by the production of particular sets of ideas, or knowledge(s), it is important to understand the future as a social construct (Adam, 2008, 2010).

For Adam (2010) the social sciences have been too focused on the construction of the present and past (e.g., historiography), and inattentive to the future. We should particularly focus on how ideas of the future have been conceived historically, of how scholars used to envision what the future would be like:

social scientists [should] engage with the fine-grained knowledge provided by historical study of past futures. On the basis of this history of the future, they can begin to identify larger patterns which form the foundation for social science analyses of social future-making and future-taking. (Adam, 2010, pp. 362–363)

Shifting away from commonsense or taken-for-granted views of the future, Adam (2008, 2010); see also Adam and Groves (2007) offer two views of the history of the future: the future as fate or God(s)' gift, versus the future as a commodity. Both views assert that the origins of the future are historically contingent (e.g., how we think of the future has changed over time), ideas about the future are shaped by particular methods of knowledge production (e.g., mythologies or cosmologies of time, versus scientific or industrial 'clock' time), and both views are constructed by different experts or "owners" of the future. For example, in "a future that belongs to gods and ancestors" (Adam, 2008, p. 112):

[the future] is conceived as a pre-existing realm because it has been predetermined by its owners. Here, knowledge of that future does not empower experts to change the predetermined fate, not enable them to alter it. Rather, the expertise grounded in knowledge is intended to help people prepare for their fate. Thus, for example, Greek and Nordic mythologies abound in stories of predestined futures and unsuccessful attempts to avert fates that had been foretold.

Such a view contrasts starkly with today's secular societies driven by clock time. In these the future is a commodity and it is assumed that we "own the future. The future, we say, is ours to take and shape. We treat it as a resource for our use in the present. [...] we plan, forge and transform the future to our will and desire" (Adam, 2008, p. 112).

The idea of future-as-commodity is one of both risk and potential. While we are freed to shape and alter the future, Adam cautions against a commodified future that "can be traded, exchanged and discounted without restrictions or limits. [...] Imagined as an abstract, empty territory it is amenable to colonization and control, plunder and pillage" (2010, p. 366). However, with historical, contextual knowledge and planning, the future-as-commodity holds vast potential, where the future "is a realm destined to be filled with our desire, to be formed and occupied according to rational blueprints, holding out the promise that it can be what we want it to be" (Adam, 2010, p. 366). By foreseeing the future as malleable and changeable, we become not only future-takers but also future-makers:

Every deliberate future-making inevitably involves future-taking: it prefigures and shapes successors' future present [...] the assumption of the future as free resource for present use, upon which much of western and westernized societies' affluence and global dominance has been created, becomes today difficult to uphold as past empty futures begin to impose themselves on the present, restricting choices and options. Amidst debates about climate change, environmental degradation and pollution, we are beginning to recognize that our own present is our predecessors' empty and open future: their dreams, desires and discoveries, their imaginations, innovations and impositions, their creations. [...] Our present was their uncertain future, where all that was solid melted into air, their discounted future, exploited commercially for the exclusive benefit of their present. (Adam, 2010, pp. 368–369).

In other words, how we think or construct knowledge about the future affects how we act in the present. Desirable futures are part of the construction of present behaviors and actions, where "the future loses its determined quality and emerges as a domain of possibility, as a realm of pure potential, which we influence, co-produce and realize in and for the present" (Adam, 2008, p. 113). If our present was once someone's future, how has leisure scholarship, and particularly *Leisure Sciences*, constructed and shaped this *future present*? Based on recent debates about the coming crisis of cybernation and UBI, I explore a handful of examples of futurology in leisure scholarship related to the idea of the "leisure society" and the current perceived crisis of leisure in higher education.

A crisis of possible futures?

In times of various perceived crises, leisure's past has been deployed to examine the future of the field (Bramham, 2006; Henderson, 2010; Roberts, 2015; Spracklen, 2017). For example, Flecther, Carniceli, Lawrence, and Snape (2016) recently responded to the perceived crisis of the future of leisure studies in UK Higher Education in neoliberal times. Set against diminished support for social sciences, arts and humanities, and increasing support for STEM subjects (science, technology, engineering and mathematics), the word "leisure" has nearly disappeared from the titles of UK Higher Education courses. Fletcher et al. (2016) quote (Carrington 2015, p. 393), who warned:

> In our neo-liberal age of public sector austerity and instrumental learning, wherein grant-driven scientization and the biomedicalization of research dominates the corporate university, trying to convince undergrads (let alone Deans) to appreciate the relevance of Antonio Gramsci's writings to the sports they love seems nostalgically utopian.

That is, the current state-of-play in the social sciences of leisure and sport, and higher education more broadly (at least in the United Kingdom), is worryingly shortsighted and (ironically) lacking "utopian" visions of preferred futures. Aitchison (2006) and Rojek (2014) also noted a shift in university degree programs away from leisure studies toward instrumentally vocational "events management" types of courses. Such shifts, most of these scholars appear to agree, are attempts to apply current trends to (near) future employment opportunities for students. In this, predictions about the soon-to-be future (projections for employment) are shaping, if limiting, present possibilities for leisure courses and curricula. Flecther et al. (2016) proposed that in order to reclaim the "L word" (leisure), we need to engage in interdisciplinary "ideational 'border crossings' to advance thinking on leisure in the social sciences" (p. 1). For Fletcher et al., the current crisis of leisure is one of representation rather than a "crisis of relevance" (p. 1). Such a crisis of representation is evident in my opening examples of popular press items concerned with future work and unemployment but not particularly attuned to leisure.

Amidst the fragmentation of leisure studies in neo-liberal higher education that "thirst[s] for vocational courses with a priority for employability, rather than academic rigor" (p. 9) Fletcher et al. foresee the challenge before us as one of "determining the core mission, place and value of leisure studies and communicating these to other subject fields and wider society" (2016, p. 10). A decade ago Shaw (2007, p. 59) voiced similar concerns: "Despite several decades of academic research and growing numbers of books and journal article publications, the field of leisure studies has received relatively little recognition or attention outside its own disciplinary borders." While scholars (Parker, 1971; Veal, 2011) have discussed a range of future-oriented projects, Rojek (2010) noted the "leisure society thesis" was one possible future that had received wide recognition:

> Nothing before or since has been as successful in capturing the public imagination. For students of leisure, the results of the gradual submergence of the thesis in public life have been serious. The discipline has suffered a relative decline. […] leisure studies is left with an identity crisis of major proportions: it is embarrassed about where it has come from (the promise of a shorter working week, early retirement, and well-funded activities for all), and it has not generated a new idea, one big enough to put leisure back on the agenda of public debate and make student enrolments in the subject expand. (p. 277)

In addition to the leisure society thesis, other responses to the crises of leisure futures have been considered (Henderson, 2010; Veal, 2012). Writing in *Leisure Sciences*, Henderson (2010) used the fable of "Chicken Little" to draw attention to instances when the field of leisure studies has been perceived as worryingly near, or approaching, a crisis (e.g., "the sky is falling"), and "offer[ed] suggestions for how researchers and educators might move forward in the near future" (2010, p. 392). Learned societies have invited leisure scholars to ponder the future too, such as the *Future of Leisure Studies Seminar* held by the Australia New Zealand Association for Leisure Studies (ANZALS) in 2009. Other anniversaries also have inspired moments of futurology. In his commentary on the 50th anniversary of de Grazia's (1962) *Of Time, Work, and Leisure*, Sylvester (2013, p. 253) noted de Grazia's "treatment of technology and consumerism foresees the future"; however, this view is lost on contemporary readers: "even if *Of Time, Work, and Leisure* were to regain an audience, my concern is that de Grazia's message and challenge would resonate very little in leisure studies, and the inattention would just continue." In this, Sylvester hints that not only ideas about leisure but also *the future of leisure* have changed.

Ten years ago, in a moment of "retro-futurism"—examining predictions of the future as envisioned by people in the past, or "historical (past) futures" (Adam, 2010, p. 362)—the 2007 Leisure Studies Association (LSA) conference theme asked "What ever happened to the leisure society?" The conference invited papers to draw from "Critical and Multidisciplinary [Retro]spectives" of over 30 years of leisure scholarship to better understand work-leisure shifts in contemporary society. From this invitation, Veal (2009, revised 2011 in *World Leisure Journal*) provided an extensive review of academic trajectories, within and without the field of leisure studies, of how a future "leisure society" (or "age of leisure") was envisioned. Veal's (2009) superb review of nearly 70 texts was driven by two lines of enquiry: first it sought to discern if, in its origins, leisure scholarship was "preoccupied with the concept of a predicted future idyllic leisure society" (p. 84), and second, to link these debates with predictions of reduced working hours and increased leisure time. I will take up this second point again in relation to increasing automation and "Universal Basic Income" later in this essay. Regarding the first point, Veal concludes that the leisure society concept is complex, problematic and elusive—even something of a myth or "exaggeration"—in the literature. First appearing in the 1920s, the leisure society concept builds on ideas in Marshall (1890), Veblen (1899), (and, I would argue, Wells (1895), and asserts that increasing automation and decreasing work will eventually deliver human society to a leisure utopia of some sort. Veal traces the presence of this idea through a broad swath of academic literature, for example, from (Haywood, Kew, & Bramham, 1989, p. 254) "For many writers the future is seen as 'the leisure society'"; to Gratton (1996, p. 1), "we do not have to go back very far to find many commentators [who] predicted that by the end of the twentieth century (i.e., now!) we would be moving towards a 'leisure age'"; to Brown and Rowe (1998, p. 89), "in the 1970s many social commentators predicted a 'leisure revolution' driven by automation and new technologies in industry and in the home." Referred to as "the leisure revolution," "age of leisure" (Sessoms, 1972), or "leisure society" (Rojek, 2002), Veal comments that, although invariably noted, few scholars offer much detail and often use such terms in passing. In this, ideas such as the leisure society take on mythic capacities.

Myths are more than fables or falsehoods; they involve the social construction of shared social realities and meanings (Barthes, 1972). A myth can be considered "a story by which a culture explains or understands some aspect of reality or nature" (Fiske, 1990, p. 88). The stories that we tell ourselves about possible futures are thus important myths. Myths serve "to organize shared (coded) ways of conceptualizing often under-theorized cultural practices" (Manan & Smith, 2014, p. 207). At this level of myth, a crucial question that resonates throughout the literature relates to what kinds of leisure will dominate in any so-called leisure society. This echoes from Marshall:

> [...] human nature improves slowly, and in nothing more slowly than the hard task of learning to use leisure well. In every age, in every nation, and in every rank of society, those who have known how to work well, have been far more numerous than those who have known how to use leisure well. But on the other hand it is only through freedom to use leisure as they will, that people can learn to use leisure well: and no class of manual workers, who are devoid of leisure, can have much self-respect and become full citizens. Some time free from the fatigue of work that tires without educating, is a necessary condition of a high standard of life. (1890, p. 720)

The (in)ability to use leisure well echoes in the work of Sessoms, who raised similar questions about the limits of the age of leisure:

> For those who are unprepared for this adventure, it is frightening and overpowering. Consequently, we demean the importance of recreation and fill our free time with busy work, neurotic phobias, and narcotic consumption. [...] Unfortunately, they are not always sure how to achieve it, so like lemmings, they scurry to the countryside seeking fulfilment. (Sessoms, 1972, pp. 312–313)

Sessoms's (1972) admonishment that many people do not use leisure well echoes Marshall (1890) and others (Parr & Lashua, 2004; Sylvester, 2013). Furthermore, predictions about the role of leisure and education in shaping identity and citizenship are readily linked to more recent debates about leisure, social class, and social capital (Glover & Hemingway, 2005).

Social capital is well-considered terrain in leisure studies, particularly in *Leisure Sciences* (see Glover, 2004; Devine & Parr, 2008; Van Ingen & Van Eijck, 2009). Dorling (2014) also reminds us that for most people social class is no longer about occupation (and perhaps never was). Rather, social class is a construct (like the future) that is ever changing, given the prevailing trends and technologies that shape the present:

> The current classes we recognize are classes of the machine age, of cities, of the age we think of as modern. We call these 'social classes' as if they were cast in stone, as if they were akin to taxa of species, but they are only a very recent rank ordering and they will soon be replaced in their turn. The older social classes that predated our current occupational hierarchy we now call castes. It did not take long after the start of industrialization to recognize that it was the machines which made current class systems so different from the agricultural class systems before them: 'The soil grows castes; the machine makes classes'. (Dorling, 2014, p. 455)

In an era of computers, networks, and information (Castells, 1996), we might ask: if soil made castes, and industrialization made classes, what does technology make us now? If we have indeed reached an "age of leisure" or nascent "leisure society," are we already more like Morlocks and Eloi than we realize?

Back to the future? Leisure and universal basic income

Following recent socioeconomic crises and critiques of neoliberalism (Roberts, 2015), the leisure society concept has reemerged, particularly in debates over UBI. A response to increasing class inequalities and the (continuing) crisis of automation, UBI involves a flat government payment to all citizens whether or not they are in work. UBI infers people freed from work would be creative, take entrepreneurial risks, and pursue their dreams (Stewart, 2016). Switzerland held a 2016 national referendum on UBI, asking voters "what would you do if your income were taken care of?" (The measure was overwhelmingly defeated.) In 2016, U.S. Democratic presidential candidate Bernie Sanders championed UBI. The UK Green Party has UBI within its platform, and Finland and the Netherlands are trialing UBI programs in 2017 (Otlermann, 2016); Scotland plans to trial UBI in two counties in 2017 (Brooks, 2017). The future leisure society is *now*.

British commentators dismissed UBI as "the right to be lazy" (Sodha, 2016), claiming it encourages idleness, hyper-consumerism and State dependence. This is perhaps, echoed again in Wells's *The Time Machine* where the time traveler can see no machinery, no evidence of industry of any kind, and the Eloi:

> displayed no vestige of a creative tendency. There were no shops, no workshops, no sign of importations among them. They spent all of their time playing gently, in bathing in the river, in making love in a half-playful fashion, in eating fruit and sleeping. I could not see how things were kept going. (1964 [1890], p. 60)

Wells presents a dim view of this leisure utopia, and by extension, such idle views of leisure offer a scant better prospect for UBI: someone, somewhere is exploited. For Wells it was Morlocks toiling underground with infernal machines—an analogue for Victorian Britain's industrial working-classes; in (post)neoliberal times, it is often the unskilled laborers of global capitalism locked into an uncertain "gig economy" who are exploited. Someone, or something, has to "keep things going." In recent news, the focus has been, rather futuristically, on robots.

In the popular press, the twinning of UBI and automation has been treated with both skepticism and mild alarm. An article in the technology magazine *Wired* titled "The White House's Fix for Robots Stealing Jobs? Education" (Finley, 2016) opened:

> the White House warns that millions of jobs could be automated out of existence in coming years. But it cautions against one much discussed solution: giving away free money.

The emphasis on education, unfortunately, refers not to education about what to do with increased time for leisure, but rather education for employment in science and technology-related jobs. The concept of leisure remains out of the frame. Writing a decade ago, Shaw (2007) recalled similar instances where leisure has received wider, if similarly oblique, attention:

> One such moment goes back to the 1950s and 60s when there were many predictions about the coming 'Age of Leisure' (e.g., Dumazedier, 1967; Larrabee & Meyersohn, 1958), based on the assumption that rapid technological progress would reduce the need for labour and thus for paid employment. When it became obvious that these predictions were not going to be realized, the issue was dropped as a topic of debate, with a surprising lack of interest about why the predictions were so inaccurate and/or why work continued to dominate people's lives despite technological progress and efficiency. What is noteworthy here is that the interest in this debate focused less on an interest in leisure *per se*, and more on concerns about unemployment, underemployment, and the resultant social unrest that might occur. (p. 60)

This final point is the nub of the matter since it reduces leisure to questions of idle masses and measures of social control. An article in the *Washington Post* (Overly, 2016) worried that "growing popularity of artificial intelligence technology will likely lead to millions of lost jobs, especially among less-educated workers" yet celebrated the potential for "higher average wages and fewer work hours" for those educated and working in "technical fields." Like many of the press items I've read about these debates, the article seems unconcerned with the vast social divide such a position would create:

> To reconcile the benefits of the technology with its expected toll […] the federal government should expand access to education in technical fields and increase the scope of unemployment benefits. Those policy recommendations, which the Obama administration has made in the past, could head off some of those job losses and support those who find themselves out of work due to the coming economic shift. (Overly, 2016)

As Spracklen (2017, p. 3) noted in his review of Parker's (1971) classic *The Future of Leisure and Work*, "if we are to be replaced by robots, we need to invest resources into planning how we find meaning and purpose when we no longer have our work." The stark division of social classes along lines of skilled technology workers and universally supported unemployed reminds me very much of Wells' (1895) predictions of Morlocks and Eloi in *The Time Machine*. In other words, current policy and visions of leisure futures drive us precisely towards the kind of world that Wells envisioned, with educated (if only technically so) Morlocks in work, and uneducated Eloi who blithely enjoy a form of UBI.

Conclusion: Leisure future-makers

Leisure scholars often, and rightly, read the past. In this article, I have argued that we can also read the future, both in terms of futurology and science fiction. In his essay on the legacy of de Grazia's (1962) *Of Time, Work, and Leisure*, Sylvester (2013) repeats de Grazia's warning that "conceptions of leisure 'live in two different worlds'" (p. 8). Whether looking back at classical Greek and Roman concepts of leisure like Sylvester, or looking forward through Wells's early science fiction, both attempt to use the past to foresee some kind of possible future(s). As argued by Harrison (2015, p. 24, original emphasis), different practices "enact *different*realities and hence work to assemble *different futures*."

So what of the future of leisure and *Leisure Sciences*? Arguably, the journal presents a kind of time machine itself: looking back, it offers a space to read issues and trends that demand greater attention, to explore the ways that both the history and future of leisure research have been written. Similar to science fiction literature, it too provides a space to explore the kinds of future(s) that have been envisioned for leisure. Here the journal is increasingly a space for critique of unjust and discriminatory leisure, and in this *Leisure Sciences* points toward better future-making. Recent emphases on social justice (Johnson, 2009, 2014; Parry, Johnson, & Stewart, 2013) offer hopeful examples. In this sense I find Adam's (2010) ideas about desirable futures exciting and useful: if we place leisure at the center of broader movements for social justice and other struggles for creating "different worlds" (e.g., environmental justice, fostering a more democratic society; addressing class inequities) then these futures become more possible too. In this, instead of hoping for wider recognition to come to the field, we also can take the field to wider debates in the popular imagination. In doing so, leisure scholar-practitioners become better future-makers. Science fiction can help to alert us to these possible future(s)—or at the very least, such as in Wells's *The Time Machine*—the futures we would prefer not to make.

References

Adam, B. (2008). Future matters: Futures known, created and minded. *Twenty-First Century Society*, *3*(2), 111–116.
Adam, B. (2010). History of the future: Paradoxes and challenges. *Rethinking History*, *14*(3), 361–378.
Adam, B., & Groves, C. (2007). *Future matters: Action, knowledge, ethics*. Boston, MA: Brill.
Aitchison, C. (2006). The critical and the cultural: Explaining the divergent paths of leisure studies and tourism studies. *Leisure Studies*, *25*, 417–422.
Aitchison, C. (2010). Labouring the leisure society thesis: A commentary on Rojek's 'Leisure and emotional intelligence.' *World Leisure Journal*, *52*(4), 265–269.
Barthes, R. (1972). *Mythologies* (Annette Lavers, Trans.). New York, NY: Hill and Wang.
Bramham, P. (2006). Hard and disappearing work: Making sense of the leisure project. *Leisure Studies*, *25*, 257–273.

Brooks, L. (2017, January 1). Universal basic income trials being considered in Scotland. *The Guardian* [Online]. Retrieved from https://www.theguardian.com/politics/2017/jan/01/universal-basic-income-trials-being-considered-in-scotland

Brown, P., & Rowe, D. (1998). The coming of the leisure society? Leisure time use in contemporary Australia. In D. Rowe, & G. Lawrence (Eds.), *Tourism, leisure, sport: Critical perspectives* (pp. 89–99). Sydney, Australia: Hodder Education.

Carrington, B. (2015). Assessing the sociology of sport: On race and diaspora. *International Review for the Sociology of Sport, 50*, 391–396.

Castells, M. (1996). *The network society*. Oxford, England: Blackwell.

Clarke, J., & Critcher, C. (1985). *The devil makes work: Leisure in capitalist Britain*. London, England: Macmillan.

De Grazia, S. (1962). *Of time, work, and leisure*. New York, NY: Twentieth Century Fund.

Devine, M. A., & Parr, M. G. (2008). "Come on in, but not too far:" Social capital in an inclusive leisure setting. *Leisure Sciences, 30*(5), 391–408.

Dorling, D. (2014). Thinking about class. *Sociology, 48*(3), 452–462.

Dumazedier, J. (1967). *Toward a society of leisure*. New York, NY: Free Press.

Finley, K. (2016, December 21). The White House's fix for robots stealing jobs? Education. *Wired* [Online]. Retrieved from https://www.wired.com/2016/12/white-houses-fix-robots-stealing-jobs-education/

Fiske, J. (1990). Ethnosemiotics: Some personal and theoretical reflections. *Cultural Studies, 4*(1), 85–99.

Fletcher, T., Carnicelli, S., Lawrence, S., & Snape, R. (2016). Reclaiming the 'L' word: Leisure Studies and UK Higher Education in neoliberal times. *Leisure Studies, 36*(2), 293–304.

Gilchrist, P., & Wheaton, B. (2008). Eds. *Whatever happened to the leisure society? Theory, debate and policy*. Eastbourne, England: Leisure Studies Association.

Glover, T. D. (2004). Social capital in the lived experiences of community gardeners. *Leisure Sciences, 26*(2), 143–162.

Glover, T. D., & Hemingway, J. L. (2005). Locating leisure in the social capital literature. *Journal of Leisure Research, 37*(4), 387–401.

Gratton, C. (1996). Introduction: Whatever happened to the 'leisure age'? In C. Gratton (Ed.), *Work, leisure and the quality of life: A global perspective* (pp. 1–5). Sheffield, England: Leisure Industries Research Centre, Sheffield Hallam University.

Harrison, R. (2015). Beyond "natural" and "cultural" heritage: Toward an ontological politics of heritage in the age of Anthropocene. *Heritage & Society, 8*(1), 24–42.

Haywood, L., Kew, F., & Bramham, P. (1989). *Understanding leisure*. Cheltenham, England: Stanley Thornes.

Henderson, K. A. (2010). Leisure studies in the 21st century: The sky is falling? *Leisure Sciences, 32*(4), 391–400.

Johnson, C. W. (2009). Writing ourselves at risk: Using self-narrative in working for social justice. *Leisure Sciences, 31*(5), 483–489.

Johnson, C. W. (2014). "All you need is love": Considerations for a social justice inquiry in leisure studies. *Leisure Sciences, 36*(4), 388–399.

Lashua, B. D. (2014). DWYL? YOLO. *Annals of Leisure Research, 17*(2), 121–126.

Manan, M. S. A., & Smith, C. L. (2014). Skateboarding with Roland Barthes: Architecture, myth and evidence. *Journal for Cultural Research, 18*(3), 203–215.

Marshall, A. (1890). *Principles of economics*. London, England: Macmillan.

Oltermann, P. (2016, June 2). State handouts for all? Europe set to pilot universal basic incomes. *The Guardian* [Online]. Retrieved from https://www.theguardian.com/world/2016/jun/02/state-handouts-for-all-europe-set-to-pilot-universal-basic-incomes.

Overly, S. (2016, December 20). Artificial intelligence could cost millions of jobs. The White House says we need more of it. *Washington Post* [Online]. Retrieved from https://www.washingtonpost.com/news/innovations/wp/2016/12/20/ai-could-cost-millions-of-jobs-the-white-house-says-we-need-more-of-it/?hpid=hp_hp-more-top-stories_ai-0910pm%3Ahomepage%2Fstory&utm_term=.0e51153ebf21

Parker, S. (1998). The future of leisure: Making leisure work: A rejoinder. *Leisure Studies, 17*(1), 53–55.

Parker, S. (1971). *The future of work and leisure*. London, England: MacGibbon and Kee.

Parr, M. G., & Lashua, B. D. (2004). What is leisure? The perceptions of recreation practitioners and others. *Leisure Sciences, 26*(1), 1–17.

Parry, D. C., Johnson, C. W., & Stewart, W. (2013). Leisure research for social justice: A response to Henderson. *Leisure Sciences, 35*(1), 81–87.

Rifkin, J. (1995). *The end of work: The decline of the global labor force and the dawn of the post-market era*. New York, NY: Putnam.

Roberts, K. (2015). Social class and leisure during recent recessions in Britain. *Leisure Studies, 34*(2), 131–149.

Rojek, C. (2001). Leisure and life politics. *Leisure Sciences, 23*(2), 115–125.

Rojek, C. (2002). Civil labour, leisure and post work society. *Loisir et Société/Society And Leisure, 25*(1), 21–35.

Rojek, C. (2010). Leisure and emotional intelligence: A response to my commentators. *World Leisure Journal, 52*(4), 274–278.

Rojek, C. (2014). Global event management: A critique. *Leisure Studies, 33*(1), 32–47.

Sessoms, H. D. (1972). Recreation. In M. N., & C. R. Hormachea (Eds.), *Recreation in modern society* (pp. 311–320). Boston, MA: Holbrook Press.

Scott, D. (2010). What would Veblen say? *Leisure Sciences, 32*(3), 288–294.

Shaw, S. M. (2007). Re-framing questions: Assessing the significance of leisure. *World Leisure Journal, 49*(2), 59–68.

Sodha, S. (2016, July 15). Is the left's big new idea a 'right to be lazy'? *BBC News* [Online], Retrieved from http://www.bbc.co.uk/news/uk-politics-36782832.

Spracklen, K. (2017). Review of the book: The future of work and leisure, (Ed.) S. Parker, 1971. *Annals of Leisure Research, 20*(3), 394–396.

Stewart, H. (2016, June 5) John McDonnell: Labour taking a close look at universal basic income. *The Guardian* [Online]. Retrieved from http://www.theguardian.com/politics/2016/jun/05/john-mcdonnell-labour-universal-basic-income-welfare-benefits-compass-report.

Sylvester, C. (2013). Fiftieth anniversary: Of time, work, and leisure. *Journal of Leisure Research, 45*(2), 253–259.

Van Ingen, E., & Van Eijck, K. (2009). Leisure and social capital: An analysis of types of company and activities. *Leisure Sciences, 31*(2), 192–206.

Veal, A. J. (1987). *Leisure and the future*. London, England: Allen and Unwin.

Veal, A. J. (2009). *The elusive leisure society: School of leisure, sport and tourism*. Working Paper 9. Sydney, Australia: University of Technology.

Veal, A. J. (2011). The leisure society: Myths and misconceptions, 1960–1979. *World Leisure Journal, 53*(3), 206–227.

Veblen, T. (1899). *The theory of the leisure class*. London, England: Allen and Unwin.

Wells, H. G. (1964[(1895)]). *The time machine*. New York, NY: Airmont Publishing.

Index

Note: **Boldface** page numbers refer to tables and *italic* page numbers refer to figures. Page numbers followed by "n" denote footnotes.

Aboriginal women's healing 93–4
Adam, B. 122, 123, 128
age of leisure 122, 125, 126
Aitchison, C. 3, 124
Allison, M. T. 63, 67
anti-immigration sentiments 65, 66
ANZLAS *see* Australia New Zealand Association for Leisure Studies
Arai, S. 38
Aristotelian notion of leisure 20, 23
Aronowitz, S. 44
art in research 90–1
Australia New Zealand Association for Leisure Studies (ANZALS) 125

Barad, K. 114
BDSM culture *see* Bondage and Discipline, Sadism and Masochism culture
Bennett, J. 110, 114
Berbary, L. A. 6, 111, 114
Berdychevsky, Liza 5
Between the World and Me (Coates) 80
Black-on-Black crime 81
Black people: advocating for change 84–5; campers of color 83; quality of life 81–2; racial threat 75–6; silence and relevance of leisure research 76–8, 86; structural nature of racism 79–81; *see also* death by racism
Blackshaw, T. 38, 43, 44
Blalock, H. M. 75–6
Bocarro, J. N. 63–5
body-mapping 94, 94n4, 99
Boles, J. C. 111, 114
Bondage and Discipline, Sadism and Masochism (BDSM) culture 13
bonding, social capital 28
Bonilla-Silva, Eduardo 64, 66
Brashears, M. E. 26

Breeze, M. 38, 44
bridging, social capital 28
Bronowski, J. 55, 56, 60
Brown, C. A. 41, 45
Brown, P. 125
Bryan, H. 39
Buckle, J. L. 92
Burton, T. L. 57
Butler-Kisber, L. 95, 96

Cacioppo, J. T. 31
campers of color, Valley Swim Club 83
Canada: Aboriginal women in 93; colonial dynamic in 97; Statistics Canada 93
CAP *see* creative analytic practice
casual leisure 40–2
casual leisure-serious leisure (CL-SL) continuum 46–8
Caton, K. 59
"Chicken Little" fable 124–5
Clarke, C. 22
class inequities, leisure and 121
CL-SL continuum *see* casual leisure-serious leisure continuum
Coalter, F. 2
Coates, Ta-Nehisi 80
Colby, S. L. 67, 68
Colistra, C., 28–9
collective action, social capital and 29
color-blind racial ideology 85; color-evasion 79; evasiveness in 79; power-evasion 79; structural nature of racism 79–81
"color-blind racism" 66
commercial sex work 11
complementary theory 39, 43, 49
"consensual hallucination" 78
Corbyn Dwyer, S. 92
Crabbe, T. 44
Craig Ranch pool party 83
creative analytic practice (CAP) 91, 102
crime 81, 82; fear of 80
Critcher, J. 22
Cure Violence 13

INDEX

D'Amours, M. 56
Dancer, A. 103
"dark tourism" 13
data poems 95
Davidson, P. 42
death by racism: Garner, Eric 83–4; Lennon Lacy, hanging "suicide" of 82, 82–3; 2015 Texas pool party incident 83; *see also* Tamir Rice, death of
DeGraaf, John 23
De Grazia, S. 56, 125, 128
Deleuze, G. 110, 114, 115, 117
Denzin, N. 92
Derrida, J. 110n2
deviant leisure 9, 10, 12–14
"Devil Makes Work" (Clarke & Critcher) 22
Dewsbury, J. D. 115
"dharma punx" 20
DiFazio, W. 44
Dilley, R. E. 38
Dorling, D. 126
Dupuis, S. L. 2, 3
Durham, A. 77, 77, 78, 81
Dustin, D. 22, 56

economic threat 75
Ellis, C. 95
empirical testing 42
empiricism, over-reliance on 56–7
epistemology, postqualitative inquiry 114–15
"established theory" process 37, 38
Establishment Clause, violation of 66
ethical crafting 93
ethical practice: and aesthetic considerations 93; in research 92–3; researchers' emotions in 93; in Sandy's poetic representation process 96–100
ethnicity, leisure research on *see* race, ethnicity, immigration, and leisure
Europe, leisure research in 3
expressive action 29

family violence 93
Faulkner, S. L. 91n1, 96
Fine, M. 93
flattened onto-epistemology 109–10
Floyd, M. F. 63–5, 85
forensic leisure 4
Foundations of Behavioral Research (Kerlinger) 55
found poetry 91 *see also* poetic representation
future-as-commodity 123
Future of Leisure and Work, The (Parker) 128
Future of Leisure Studies Seminar 125
futurology 122–3; crisis of possible futures 124–6; *Time Machine, The* (Wells) 121, 122

Gallant, K. 38
Galvin, K. 98
García, R. 82
Garner, Eric 83–4

"gig" economy 22
Gillespie, D. L. 38
Glesne, C. 95, 96
global humanitarian crisis 65
Glover, T. D. 6, 27–31
Golden, L. 21
Goodale, T. L. 56, 58
Goodale, Tom 55
Graham, T. 29
Gratton, C. 125
"grounded theory" process 37, 38, 41
Groves, C. 123
Guattari, F. 110, 114, 115

Hallowell, E. M. 25
Halpern, D. 30
Hamilton-Smith, E. 38, 42, 44
Harrison, R. 128
HealthWise South Africa 12
Heintzman, Paul 6
Hemingway, J. L. 3, 56
Henderson, K. A. 124–5
Henson, W. 31, 32
Hiemstra, N. A. 64
Homans, G. C. 41
humanism, notion of 108, 108n1
humanist qualitative inquiry 110–12
humanities 55; in *Leisure Sciences* 57–8; leisure studies education 59
Hunnicutt, Benjamin 21
Hutchinson, S. L. 27, 43

Idea of a University, The (Newman) 55
"identity crisis" 3
Illinois Caucus for Adolescent Health 12
"image of thought" 109
immigration patterns 65–6 *see also* race, ethnicity, immigration, and leisure
instrumental action, social capital and 29
"intergroup harmony", recreational sport participation 66
intrinsic theory 40–3
Ioannou, S. 95
Iwasaki, Y. 27

Jackson, E. L. 57
Johnson, A. J. 27
Johnson, C. W. 91
Jones, I. 38, 41
Journal of Leisure Research 2, 20, 56–8
Journal of Recreation and Park Administration 20
journals, leisure 57
Journey Women project 93–4

Katerberg, L. 21
Kelly, J. J. 2
Kerlinger, F. N. 55
Kivel, B. Dana 5

INDEX

Kleiber, D. A. 27, 43
Klinenberg, E. 27
Kovach, M. 97
Kuentzel, W. F. 44
Kumm, Brian 6

labor movement 21
Lashua, Brett 5
Lather, P. 111
Law, J. 115
Leech, T. G. J. 84
Lefler, A. 38
leisure activity-experience 48; draft checklist of **49**
"leisure experience perspective" 50
"leisure lifestyle", concept of 43
leisure research 3, 5; black lives in 82; discussion and implications 58–9; on ethnicity and race 64; in Europe 3; future of 4–5; insularity of 3; leisure practice and 3; nature of 57; and recreation programming 80; silence from 75, 86; *see also* "risky" leisure research
"Leisure Research and the Humanities" 56–9
Leisure Research Symposium 59, 60
leisure scholars 6–7
Leisure Sciences 1, 4, 20, 26, 32, 55, 57, 128; 40th anniversary of 1; history of 2; humanities in 6, 57–8; scholarship in 122; scientific inquiries 56; special issues of 2
leisure society: concept 125; thesis 122, 124–5
leisure studies: education 59; future of 124; in neo-liberal higher education 124
Leisure Studies 57–9
Leisure Studies Association (LSA) 125
Lennon Lacy, hanging "suicide" of 82, 82–3
Lerner, E. 38
Lin, N. 29
"Listening for a Leisure Remix" 58
loneliness, social isolation and 26–7
Long, J. 57–9
LSA *see* Leisure Studies Association

Macnaughton, J. 28
Maffesoli, M. 40
Managing Leisure 57
Mannell, R. C. 27, 43, 50
marginality thesis 69
Marshall, A. 121, 125
Marszalek, B. 21
McKinney pool party 83
McPherson, M. 26
mephitic leisure 12
"methodological positivism" 109
methodology, postqualitative inquiry 108–9, 115, 117
minority populations, leisure research on *see* race, ethnicity, immigration, and leisure
Mommaas, H. 3
Montreal, homeless immigrant women in 91

moralism 117
Mowatt, Rasul 6
Mulcahy, C. M. 31
"multiparadigmatic rivalry" 48
myths and misconceptions 125

National Recreation and Parks Association (NRPA) 5
needs-based research 39
negative life events, leisure in 27–8
New Life Centers of Chicagoland 13
non-Hispanic Whites 68
NRPA Leisure Research Symposium 56

objective social isolation 27
obstructive actions 29–30
O'Dell, I. 45
Of Time, Work, and Leisure (de Grazia) 56, 125, 128
ontology, postqualitative inquiry 114
optimal leisure lifestyle 41–3
ORRRC studies *see* Outdoor Recreation Resources Review Commission studies
Ortman, J. M. 67, 68
Outdoor Recreation Resources Review Commission (ORRRC) studies 62

Parigi, P. 31, 32
Parker, S. 42, 128
Parr, M. G. W. 3
Parry, D. C. 27–31, 91
passive leisure 30
Patrick, W. 31
Patterson, M. E. 2
Patton, Stacey 81, 86
Pendleton, M. 81–2, 84
phallogocentrism 110
"Philosophical and Historical Aspects of Leisure" 59
"Philosophical, Historical and Cultural Aspects of Leisure Behavior" 59
phronesis 56
Pinckney, Harrison 77–8, *78*
"pockets of peace" 84–5
poetic inquiry 91
poetic representation: academic sources 92; advantages of 102; aesthetics of poet 91; creative analytic practice and 91; ethical crafting 93; ethical practice 92–3; issues of 91–2; new research paths with poetry 102–3; poetic knowing and 91; researcher location and subjectivity 92; *see also* Sandy's poetic representation process
political threat 75
pool party incident (2015) 83
postqualitative inquiry 107, 116; analysis/interpretation 115–16; *a priori* methodology 109; data collection 115; "deliberate

INDEX

imprecision" 115; embodiment 114; epistemology 114–15; flattened onto-epistemology 109–10; as generative criticism 109; humanism, notion of 108, 108n1; humanist qualitative inquiry 110–12; implications 116–17; legacy of diverse investigations 108; methodology 108–9, 115, 117; onto-epistemologies and theories 108; ontology 114; qualitative methodologies 109; representation 116; social theory, developments in 109; sous erasure 110–12; theory 114–15; "tree of knowledge" 108–10
Prendergast, M. 93
profit hypothesis 41
project-based leisure 40–2, 45, 47
Pronovost, G. 56
provocative theory 64
public trust doctrine 85
Putnam, R. D. 30, 31

qualitative research 90
quality of life 81–2

race, ethnicity, immigration, and leisure 62; anti-immigration sentiments 65, 66; "black-white" color line 64; continued significance of race and racism 66–7; demographic predictions 68; Executive Orders 13769 & 13780 66; existing research on 62–3, 65–6; global humanitarian crisis 65; interdisciplinary approaches 69; journals related to 63; "majority minority" status 68; migration trends 67; minority children and teenagers 65; national/global crisis 64; non-Hispanic Whites 68; Outdoor Recreation Resources Review Commission studies 62; PEW report analysis 68; provocative theory 64; quantity and qualitative content of studies 63; recreational sport participation 66; shifts in immigration patterns 65–6; shortcomings of 64; social justice paradigm 63, 67; study implications 69–70; suggestions for future research 63–5; systematic review of research 64; theoretical developments 69; three-tier racial structure 64; Washburne's marginality thesis 69
racial hierarchy 64, 67
racial ideology 76, 78 *see also* color-blind racial ideology
racial threat theory 75–6
racism: dangers of 79; media and 75; race and 66–7; structural nature of 79–81; *see also* death by racism
"Radical Leisure" (Swidler) 21, 23
recreational sport participation 66
Recreation Research Review 57
regular exercise activity 43
Reid, D. G. 21
representation, postqualitative inquiry 116

researcher reflexivity 100–1
"retro-futurism" 125
Richardson, L. 91
Rifkin, J. 44
"risky" leisure research 9–10, 15–16; impediments to 14–15; sexual leisure 10–12; violent and deviant leisure 12–14
Rojek, C. 30, 43, 44, 48, 122, 124
Ronai, C. R. 92
Rose, J. 22, 56
Rowe, D. 125

Samdahl, D. M. 2
Sanders, Bernie 126
Sandy's poetic representation process 92, 92n2, 95; accurate representation 100; auditory and performance dimension 96; back-and-forth process 102; bodymapping exercise 94, 94n4, 99; conscious and deliberate reflexivity 101; critical reflections 96; data poems 95; embodied interpretation 98; emotions 96, 98, 100–1; evocative poems 98; "experimentation with words" 96; holistic approaches 98; Indigenous methodology 97; intuition and embodied reactions 101; *Journey Women* project 93–4; listening process 98; reflexive process 100–2; researcher-poet 96; social position, recognition of 96–7; sound quality 95; telephone interviews, analysis of 95; tensions and discomfort 98–9, 101, 102; white Canadian, position as 96–7; witnessing 94
Schmalz, D. 28–9
Schor, Juliet 21
Schwab, K. 56
Science and Human Values (Bronowski) 55, 56, 60
Scott, D. 46, 122
Scraton, S. J. 38
serious leisure-casual leisure (SL-CL) dichotomy 48, 50
Serious Leisure Inventory and Measure (SLIM) scale 47
serious leisure perspective (SLP) 36, *37*; complementary theory 39, 43; credentials of 37; "established theory" process 37, 38; feature of 36; goal 41; "grounded theory" process 37, 38; identification with the activity 40–1; intrinsic theory 43; motivation to participate 41–3; pursuit of 44; serious leisure theory 38; social worlds/tribes 40; subcategories of 40; theory deficit 43–4; as typology 44–8
serious leisure theory 38
Sessoms, H. D. 126
sex tourism 10–11
sexual enhancement programs 12
sexual leisure 9–10; erotic and pornographic materials 11; HealthWise South Africa 12; Illinois Caucus for Adolescent Health 12; impediments to 14–15; leisure–sexuality

INDEX

relationship 11–12; nightclubs, women's experiences in 11; prostitution cases 11; psycho-socio-cultural perspective 11; sexual enhancement programs 12; in tourism 10–11
"sexual scrutinizers" 11
Shafer, C. S. 46
Shaw, S. M. 124, 127
Shen, X. S. 38, 41, 45, 47, 50
Shinew, K. J. 63
Siegenthaler, K. L. 45
"significant theoretical development" 38
SLIM scale *see* Serious Leisure Inventory and Measure scale
Smale, B. 38
Smith-Lovin, L. 26
social capital 28, 126; collective action 29; erosion of 30; expressive action 29; instrumental action 29; linking 28; relationship building and 28–9
social change 44
social class 126
social contact, benefits of 25
social isolation 6, 25–6; by-product of modernity 31; combating 29; detrimental consequences of 26; leisure as antidote 27–8; loneliness and 26–7; pitfalls of leisure on 32–3; risk factors of 26–7; as sociological construct 31; topical areas in 26
social justice 63, 67
social media, loss of community in 31–2
social media/networking (SM/N) platforms, 31, 32
social network researchers 27
social sciences 122
social skills 27
social theory, developments in 109
social worlds/tribes 40
Society of Park and Recreation Educators (SPRE) 22
soft enforcement policies 84
Solomon, J. 94
Spracklen, K. 128
SPRE *see* Society of Park and Recreation Educators
Stebbins, Robert 36, 38–45
Stewards of Access/Custodians of Choice 56
Stewart, W. 67
"stocks of knowledge" 75
Stodolska, M. 6, 63–5
St. Pierre, E. A. 117
Strauss, A. L. 95
structural model of serious leisure 41, 47
subjective social isolation 27
Sullivan, A. 95, 96
Swidler, E. 21
Sylvester, C. 3, 56, 58, 59, 125, 128
symbolic threat 75, 76, 85; of Black youth 81
Szreter, S. 28

"Take Back Your Time" organization 23
TALS *see* The Academy of Leisure Sciences
Tamir Rice, death of 73–5, 85; color-blind racial ideology 79–81; Durham's social media posting 77, *77*, 78; Facebook posts 76, 77; Pinckney's social media posting 77–8, *78*; racial ideology 76, 78; racial threat, notion of 75–6; silence and relevance of leisure research 76–8, 86; structural nature of racism 79–81
The Academy of Leisure Sciences (TALS) 22, 60
theory, postqualitative inquiry 114–15
Thompson, T. D. 63–5
three-tier racial structure, in United States 64
Thrift, N. 101
Time Machine, The (Wells): Eloi 121, 122, 128; futurology, notion of 121, 122; Morlocks 121, 126, 128
Todres, L. 98
tourism: "dark tourism" 13; sexual behavior in 10–11
"tree of knowledge" 108–10
Truth and Reconciliation Commission of Canada 93
Tuhiwai Smith, L. 94
12-year-old boy, case of *see* Tamir Rice, death of

UBI *see* universal basic income
United Kingdom: Green Party 126; Higher Education courses 124
United Nations High Commissioner for Refugees (UNHCR) 65
United Nations Refugee Agency 65
United States: Establishment Clause, violation of 66; Executive Orders 13769 & 13780 66; leisure in 22; racial and ethnic minorities 68; racial ideology in 78; three-tier racial structure 64
universal basic income (UBI) 5, 121, 126–7

Valley Swim Club, campers of color 83
vampires 13
Veal, A. J. 122, 125
Veblen, T. 121, 122, 125
Victoria Dreams program 28
violence as leisure 12; BDSM culture 13; Cure Violence 13; impediments to 14–15; leisure and correctional recreation 14; mephitic leisure 12; tourism 13; vampires 13; victim 13

Walker, G. J. 63–5
Washburne, R. F. 69
Washington Post 127
Washington, R. D. 96
Weis, L. 93
Wells, H. G. 121, 122, 125, 127, 128
Weseen, S. 93
Western scientific thought 90
White dominance, in leisure research 84

INDEX

"White House's Fix for Robots Stealing Jobs? Education, The" 127
Williams, D. J. 4
Williams, R. 27
Wilson, S. 97
witness, in art therapy 94
Woman Abuse Awareness Month 94

Wong, L. 93
Woolcock, M. 28
work, leisure and 22
Worthington, B. 38

Yarnal, C. 38, 41, 45, 47, 50
Yuen, F. 27, 29